ISBN 978-1-332-33089-8
PIBN 10315053

English
Français
Deutsche
Italiano
Español
Português

www.forgottenbooks.com

Mythology Photography **Fiction**
Fishing Christianity **Art** Cooking
Essays Buddhism Freemasonry
Medicine **Biology** Music **Ancient**
Egypt Evolution Carpentry Physics
Dance Geology **Mathematics** Fitness
Shakespeare **Folklore** Yoga Marketing
Confidence Immortality Biographies
Poetry **Psychology** Witchcraft
Electronics Chemistry History **Law**
Accounting **Philosophy** Anthropology
Alchemy Drama Quantum Mechanics
Atheism Sexual Health **Ancient History**
Entrepreneurship Languages Sport
Paleontology Needlework Islam
Metaphysics Investment Archaeology
Parenting Statistics Criminology
Motivational

THREE

FIFTEENTH-CENTURY CHRONICLES,

WITH

HISTORICAL MEMORANDA BY JOHN STOWE,

THE ANTIQUARY,

AND CONTEMPORARY NOTES OF OCCURRENCES

WRITTEN BY HIM IN THE REIGN OF QUEEN ELIZABETH.

EDITED BY JAMES GAIRDNER.

PRINTED FOR THE CAMDEN SOCIETY.

M.DCCC.LXXX.

1843

WESTMINSTER:
PRINTED BY J. B. NICHOLS AND SONS,
25, PARLIAMENT STREET.

37/4/

[NEW SERIES XXVIII.]

COUNCIL OF THE CAMDEN SOCIETY

FOR THE YEAR 1880-1

President,

THE RIGHT HON. THE EARL OF VERULAM, F.R.G.S.

WILLIAM CHAPPELL, ESQ., F.S.A., *Treasurer.*

HENRY CHARLES COOTE, ESQ., F.S.A.

F. W. COSENS, ESQ., F.S.A.

JAMES E. DOYDE, ESQ.

JAMES GAIRDNER, ESQ.

SAMUEL RAWSON GARDINER, ESQ., *Director.*

WILLIAM OXENHAM HEWLETT, ESQ., F.S.A

ALFRED KINGSTON, ESQ., *Secretary.*

CHARLES A. J. MASON, ESQ.

STUART A. MOORE, ESQ., F.S.A.

FREDERIC OUVRY, ESQ., V.P.S.A.

THE EARL OF POWIS, LL.D.

EVELYN PHILIP SHIRLEY, ESQ., M.A., F.S.A.

REV. W. SPARROW SIMPSON, D.D. F.S.A.

JAMES SPEDDING. ESQ.

PREFACE.

SOME years ago, while engaged on my edition of the *Paston Letters*, I was anxious to examine as far as possible every original source of information for the reigns of Henry VI. and Edward IV.; and, having found some unedited matter relating to those reigns in two MSS. in the Lambeth Library, I recommended them to the Council of the Camden Society for publication. My proposal was at once agreed to; but in the meantime, a more interesting MS. having presented itself relating to the same period, the work was kept back to make way for *The Historical Collections of a Citizen of London*, which appeared in 1876. I have, however, steadily kept in view the fulfilment of my original promise to the Society; and the result is that I have been led to do somewhat more than I originally contemplated. For it will be seen that the present volume, besides containing contributions from the two Lambeth MSS. above referred to, includes an unpublished chronicle of the same period, from a MS. in the College of Arms. Moreover, I had scarcely begun to examine the work seriously, when I found that it was quite impossible to omit the bulk of John Stowe's Memoranda in the Lambeth MS. 306; and, although they extend to a much later period, these also have been inserted.

But I must now speak of this MS. more particularly, as it furnishes the greater part of the materials of this work.

MS. 306 in the Lambeth Library is a stout folio volume in an ancient ornamental binding, now very much worm-eaten. The

back has been renewed; but the two wooden boards covered with
stamped leather preserve their original appearance. The clasps,
however, which once held them together, are gone, the brass nails
alone remaining in the one cover, and part of the ornamental fittings
on which they clasped still existing in the other. The design on
each cover consists of lozenge-shaped compartments filled with foliated
ornaments and a framework parallel with the edges, in which the
Beaufort portcullis, a branch of oak with acorns, a crowned lion
and a dragon, are discernible. It is quite evidently a Tudor
binding.

The contents of the volumes are various in character. The
handwritings are partly of the fifteenth and partly of the sixteenth
century. The short Chronicle printed in this volume stands at the
beginning. It was probably penned in the reign of Edward IV.
not long after the date to which it comes down. Marginal notes,
however, have been added to the text in a hand of Henry VIII.'s
time, and the text itself is occasionally corrected with additions
and insertions in the same hand. Where these corrections are
important they will be found noted in footnotes in this volume.
The same writing also can be traced in a number of other articles
throughout the volume, chiefly of the nature of medical receipts,
and in some notes on the inside of the cover, which refer to the
dates of events as late as the middle of the reign of Henry VIII.
It must have been during the time of this penman that the MS.
was bound; for several of his marginal notes in the chronicle are
mutilated, owing to the edges of the paper having been cut by the
binder; yet it is clear that he wrote the memoranda inside the cover
after the book was bound.

The Short Chronicle, though it looks like one, is really three
short chronicles written or transcribed consecutively by the same
pen. The first is a very brief abridgment of the well-known

Chronicle of the Brute, beginning the history of Albion with the fabled Albina, and ending in the first year of Henry IV. This composition, it is almost needless to say, is absolutely destitute of historical value; but as "the Brute" itself has never yet been edited, and is consequently inaccessible to all but students of black letter and readers of mediæval MSS., this epitome of what was once the most popular history of England may not be without interest. One point which may strike the reader as curious, and which might even be worth a little investigation, if any one could afford to spend some time in the comparison of various MSS., is the considerable addition here made, through transcribers' errors and otherwise, to the list of mythical kings in Geoffrey of Monmouth. Thus we have "Gynder" instead of "Guiderus," "Grandobodian" instead of "Gorbonian," "Hesydere" for "Elidurus," "Higamus" for "Vigenius," and a number of other *aliases* which are certainly quite as legitimate names as their prototypes for utterly unreal personages. The most curious transformation perhaps is that of Aurelius Ambrosius into Aurylambos.

Immediately following the abridged "Brute" we have a copy of Lydgate's verses on the Kings of England, showing some slight variations from the text printed in the "Collections of a London Citizen."

After which comes one of the regular city chronicles, beginning with the keepers and bailiffs of London in the time of Richard I., and a register of mayors and sheriffs from the first institution of the mayoralty in the time of King John. It is in this composition, and of course in the latter part of it only, that the real historical value of the work consists; for down to the reign of Henry V. the record of each mayor's year is a very bald one, and contains nothing that is not found elsewhere. The catalogue of civic officers itself however may possibly be of some slight value; for

amid the many corruptions of names given more correctly elsewhere appear to be some genuiue *aliases*, such as the name of
Richard Soperlane, sheriff in the 27th year of Edward I., who is
commonly known as Richard de Refham.

Opposite the name of each mayor are given in the margin, as
shown during the reign of King John at pages 32 and 33, the year
of our Lord corresponding to his year of office, and a Roman
numeral in the case of mayors who had served more than once,
indicating whether it was for the first, second, third, or what later
time he was then mayor; but, as these numbers are added by
a different hand, and are moreover practically useless and often
very inaccurate, I have not thought it necessary to give more than
a specimen of them at the beginning.

It does not appear that this chronicle has ever been referred to
as a source of historical information. Yet the MS. seems at one
time to have belonged to Stowe the Chronicler, who has made
copious memoranda on the blank leaves of the volume. There
are also pencilled notes in some places in a hand of the time of
James I. or Charles I., showing that it had attracted the attention
of at least one antiquary in that age of historical research. But
beyond this we have no evidence that it has been consulted by
any one, and even Stowe has not made such use of it in his
Chronicle that we can distinctly say he derived his information
on any point from this one particular source. In fact it seems
rather as if he had found little in it that he could make use of save
what was common to this and other chronicles, and therefore
neglected to refer to it.

Such might very well have been the impression even of a great
historical collector in those days, whose aim was rather to obtain a
complete outline of English history than to fill in details and
illustrative matter. Nevertheless the latter part of this chronicle

has all the value of an original and independent authority for the
reigns of Henry VI. and Edward IV., at least from the time of
Jack Cade's rebellion to the year of Edward's marriage with Elizabeth Woodville, in which it comes to an end. And on careful
examination it will be found that this chronicle contains facts of
some importance that have been passed over by other writers, to
some of which I have already called attention in other publications.
For one thing, this chronicle states positively as a fact a thing
which is not set forth in any of our histories, and which I myself
maintained several years ago only as a matter of inference, viz. that
Cade's pardon was invalidated in consequence of the discovery that
his real name was not Mortimer;[a] so that it would seem his
pretence of high birth was generally believed in till after the
insurrection in London had been appeased. There is certainly
something marvellous in the fact that he was able to maintain false
pretensions so long—especially when we consider the formidable
dimensions of the movement in which he took the lead. It was
not only that all the gentry of Kent followed his standard, but even
the King's own followers told him plainly, that, unless execution
were done upon the traitors who were so unpopular, they too would
desert to the captain.[b] The misgovernment that provoked the
insurrection was, in fact, generally felt to justify pretty strong
measures by way of remonstrance. But, this being so, the wonder
is all the greater that the remonstrants should have put themselves
under the leadership of a man whose true character was so ill

[a] *Fortnightly Review*, New Series, xlvi. 448. I was able, however, afterwards to
cite the positive testimony of this chronicle in the Introduction to the first volume
of the Paston Letters, p. lv.

[b] "And the Kinge came to the Blacke Hethe with his lordys. They hirynge of
this jorney anone the lordis meyne went togeder and said, but the kynge wolde do
excussyon on suche traytors as were named, else they wolde turne to the capteyn of
Kent." (p. 67.)

known to them. That there must have been collusion on the part
of some of the Kentish gentry seems past a doubt. By setting up
a pretender they avoided incurring the highest responsibility themselves.

Little need be said about minute details, such as the disputed
question whether Cardinal Kemp went along with Bishop Wayn-
flete to the interview with Cade at Southwark after the battle on
London Bridge. This is the statement in Hall's Chronicle, but as
Fabyan, an earlier authority, states that the cardinal, being then
Lord Chancellor, *sent* pardons under the great seal to Cade and
his followers, it seemed doubtful whether Hall was not here in error.
Our chronicle, however, confirms Hall's statement.

" And forthe withe went the Chaunseler to the capteyne and sessed him and yave
him a chartur and his men another, and so [they] withdrowe hem homward."

It has also been a point of controversy among local antiquaries
whether Cade was captured in Sussex or in Kent. Of course Iden's
jurisdiction as Sheriff of Kent did not extend into Sussex; and this
fact may have led to a general impression that he was taken in
Kent. Thus in the text of our chronicle it was originally
written:—

" And so the xiij day of Jule John Cade was take in Kentt."

But the Tudor corrector had certainly obtained more perfect
information on the subject, and altered the passage thus :—

" And so one Alexandre Iden, a squyre of Kent, toke hym in a garden yn Sowthsex, the xiij day of Jule."

In fact there seems little doubt that even if Iden was at this time
really Sheriff of Kent (which is scarcely probable, all things con-
sidered, within a fortnight after the murder of Sheriff Crowmer[a])

---

[a] William Wyrcestre, after mentioning the retreat of the rebels to Rochester, says
only, " Et super hoc *postea eodem anno* Alexander Iden factus est in officio vice-
comitis."

he pursued the traitor a considerable distance into the neighbouring county.

The English Chronicle, edited for the Camden Society by Mr. Davies, says distinctly that Cade was pursued into "the wood country beside Lewes;" and Gregory states that he was captured in the Weald of Sussex.[a] But without going quite so far south as Lewes local traditions and other evidences seem to show that he was apprehended in a garden at Heathfield, in the very middle of the county.[b]

It is important to observe that the alteration in the text here made by the Tudor corrector is in exact agreement with Fabyan's Chronicle, and very likely Fabyan was the authority he relied on. Nevertheless the exact date of Cade's capture, which Fabyan did not know, is supplied even by the original text of our chronicle, and is preserved by the corrector.

In the 33rd year of Henry VI. we meet with the following piece of information:—

"And this yere the Kynge of Scottys with the rede face layde sege to Berwyke bothe by water and londe. But he was dryve thensse, and all his ordenaunce and vitayle that was on the watir syde lefte behynde them."

King James II. of Scotland, as we are informed by Lesley, "was called James withe the firye face, be ressoun of ane bread reid spott quhilk he had upon ane of his cheikis." [c] But I find no mention of this siege of Berwick in any other old chronicle, except this Lambeth MS. It is however confirmed by some minutes in the Privy Council Proceedings.[d]

[a] *Collections of a London Citizen*, 194.

[b] The question whether the capture took place in Kent or Sussex is very fully discussed in Furley's *History of the Weald of Kent*, ii. 386-390; where the author, notwithstanding his original prepossession in favour of Kent, decides that it must have been in Sussex.

[c] Lesley's *Hist. of Scotland*, 11.

[d] Nicolas's *Privy Council Proceedings*, vi. 248-9.

In the 34th year also we meet with a new fact, viz. the arrest of an alderman and mercer of London named Cauntelowe, who was summoned before the King's Council and imprisoned, as an accessory in the attack on the houses of the Italian merchants. This is, doubtless, the William Cantelowe who afterwards captured Henry VI. in a wood, and brought him to King Edward.[a] He is mentioned in various accounts before this date as having dealings with the Crown, at one time as conveying money over sea for bringing Queen Margaret to England, at another time for supplying the Castle of Cherbourg with gunpowder when it was in the hands of the English.[b]

The outrage in which Cantelowe was accused of taking part was one of those occasional outbursts of jealousy and dislike towards foreigners which are met with at intervals in the early annals of London. The circumstances of the case are related by Fabyan, and the execution of two of the rioters is alluded to in the *Paston Letters*.[c] But some addition has recently been made to our knowledge of the matter by the publication of *Gregory's Chronicle*[d] and the *Calendar of Venetian State Papers*.[e] The formidable character of the outbreak may be judged from the fact that the Italian merchants were compelled to quit London, and take up their abode at Winchester and Southampton. Their withdrawal in all probability produced a sensible effect upon the commerce of the city; for they made a bye-law among themselves, that no individual merchant of Northern Italy should henceforth go to London and trade there. This ordinance the signory of Venice ratified by a decree of the Senate, and prohibited, under a heavy fine, all Venetian vessels

[a] Hearne's *Fragment at the end of Sprott*, 292. Fabyan, 654.
[b] Stevenson's *Wars of the English in France*, i. 446, 502.
[c] Vol. i. p. 387 (new ed.)   [d] *Collections of a London Citizen*, 199.
[e] Vol. i. Nos. 331, 339.

from visiting the port of London. Nevertheless, if our chronicle
be right, some of the Lombards, at least, must have returned to the
city; for next year another affray between them and the mercers is
recorded, which led to the arrest of eight and twenty mercers' men,
who were first committed to Windsor Castle, and afterwards brought
to the King's presence. But it may perhaps be doubted whether
this is is not a misdated account of the same riot copied from some
other source.

After this, in the 37th year, we have " A great fray between the
city of London and men of court, which were driven with the
archers of the city from the Standard in Fleet Street to their Inns,
the 13th day of April." This is another addition to our knowledge
of the times. There were plenty of "frays" going on elsewhere
from time to time, and even the city chroniclers forgot to tell us of
this one. It is remarkable that Alderman Tayllour was summoned
to Windsor to answer for it, along with some others who were
implicated, and that they remained in prison till Hewlyn was
mayor, when they were released at his intercession. The mayoralty
of Hewlyn began in 1459, about the same time as the parliament
of Coventry, in which the Yorkists were attainted. But, after a
sweeping Act against great political opponents, the Court could
well afford to relax its severity against a handful of citizens, whom
it had already detained long in prison.

It is impossible to dwell on minute points of information supplied
by this chronicle, the significance of which could only be made
apparent in an elaborate history of the period. But, taken along
with the other contents of this volume, it certainly adds somewhat
to the meagre outline of events given by William of Worcester and
Fabyan, especially in the first four years of Edward IV.—a period
in which all the three MSS. here edited are more or less important.
And though this chronicle, perhaps, of all the three contains the

least amount of positively new matter, it may be sufficient to refer to what it says of the arrest of Henry VI. by the Earl of Warwick at Islington, to show its value as an independent authority.

A few words, perhaps, may suffice as to the other historical matter printed from the same MS. as the chronicle. Articles ranging in date from the siege of Calais by Edward III. to the middle of the reign of Queen Elizabeth certainly seem a little out of place in a volume intended mainly to illustrate fifteenth-century history. But the account of the retinues at the siege of Calais appeared not to have been printed before, and, as Stowe's memoranda and transcripts were important even for the period to which I had proposed to limit this publication, it would have been unpardonable to suppress those relating to his own time, which are the most interesting of them all.

It is quite unnecessary to expatiate on the value of these materials. The first, which is styled a proclamation made by Jack Cade, but which seems rather the declaration put forth by his followers of the causes of their revolt, is a thing of which the importance is sufficiently obvious. Yet it has never been printed at full length even by Stowe himself, though he has cited in his Chronicle another version, or perhaps another manifesto, in which some of the articles are nearly the same. The satirical dirge which follows upon Jack Napes (or the Duke of Suffolk) is also better known in another and shorter version. The account of the christening of Prince Arthur has not, I think, been published before, though another description of the same ceremony is printed in Leland's Collectanea.

These and other matters had the laborious historian carefully transcribed from older MSS. But in addition to this he has added in his own hand memoranda of occurrences which happened in his own time and mostly within his own experience. Of these a good number are recorded in his Chronicle or Book of Annals nearly in the same words; but with them are mixed up many other matters, which, either as being of less public importance or perhaps in some cases not altogether safe to comment upon, he did not think fit to print. Thus in 1562 we have an account of a certain Lady Cary (a relation of Queen Elizabeth herself, though who she was precisely I have not been able to discover) being imprisoned along with other ladies in the Fleet for allowing a priest to say mass at her house in Fetter Lane.[a] This was evidently a matter on which it would not have been politic to comment, and nothing about it is found in the printed Annals. An equal silence is preserved about the attempt of the Margrave of Baden and his wife to escape in disguise from their creditors.[b] No wonder, when the host of unpaid tradesmen, the butcher, baker, tailor, and such like, who endeavoured to prevent their escape, were ordered to the Fleet and the Marshalsea for their pains, that John Stowe did not see it to be his duty to record the circumstance in print!

On the religious condition of the times these memoranda of Stowe reflect very considerable light, and cannot fail to be read with interest in connection with the controversies of our own day. The accession of Queen Elizabeth, while it relieved the Protestants from the fear of Smithfield fires, undoubtedly gave a strong stimulus to that party whose object was to break entirely with the past, and destroy as far as possible the jurisdiction, rites, ceremonies, vestments, and every other external means by which reverence for the Church and faith in her doctrines had hitherto been maintained. Archdeacon Cole, preaching before the Lord Mayor, aldermen, sheriffs, and crafts of the city, could not congratulate the citizens on the cessation of the plague without attributing the infliction to the superstitious religion of Rome, which he said was so much in favour. He denounced it as a false religion, worse, he said, than

---

[a] pp. 121-2.   [b] p. 136.

that of the Turk, and even than that of the Devil. At another
time he gracefully likened priests to apes, as being both bald alike,
only the priests were bald before, and the apes behind.[a] When
such flowers of rhetoric as these, which Stowe with quiet satire
records under the title " Points of Divinity," could proceed from
a dignitary of the Church, who can wonder that the feeling of the
common people found still more forcible expression? Clergy and
laity were alike rabid with party spirit. In vain had the Queen
herself issued injunctions for the decent observance of divine
worship. Her orders were very generally disregarded. The
London clergy were accordingly summoned to a conference at
Lambeth on Tuesday, the 26th March, 1566, where they were
admonished to obey, on pain of suspension from their cures; and
more complete instruction was given them as to their duties by the
publication of the Archbishop's celebrated " Advertisements " in
the following week; but even this had very little effect. Several of
the clergy flatly disobeyed both injunctions and advertisements.
In the greater number of parishes parochial duty was left to the
sextons; but in others the clergy themselves did service in the for-
bidden gowns and cloaks, and preached violently against the order
taken by the Queen in Council, not forbearing to censure the
bishops for yielding their consent to it. The vicar of St. Giles's,
Cripplegate, went so far as to stop a funeral entering his church,
because six clergymen accompanied it wearing the legal surplices.
The Queen, he said, had given him the benefice for life, and he
would not suffer any Romish superstitions to enter. At the risk of
a considerable tumult he carried his point, the surpliced clergy
wisely giving way and remaining outside.[b]

One of the principal agitators among the clergy was a Scotchman
who was accustomed to preach twice a day at St. Magnus', and

[a] pp. 128, 133.   [b] pp. 135, 136.

who ministered the sacrament in a gown or cloak. On Palm
Sunday he preached a violent sermon at All Hallows the Less in
Thames Street, where the incumbent, who had complied with the
injunctions, sat listening to him with a sarcastic smile quite visible
upon his features. The result was, that, after the sermon, some of
the congregation addressed a remonstrance to the incumbent, which
began in argument and ended in a scuffle between the opposite
sides. The general excitement on these subjects was increased by
a host of pamphlets which were scattered freely about the streets,
and many of which were, according to the ideas of that age, nothing
less than seditious libels. Between Easter and Whitsuntide, however, the Scotchman seems to have been converted—by what
influences we are not told. On Whit Monday he found his conscience
allowed him to do duty in a surplice at St. Margaret Pattens in
Rood Lane. But, unfortunately for him, his audience liked his
former preaching better than his later practice, and his appearance
caused a regular riot inside the church, especially among the women,
who threw stones at him, and pulled him out of the pulpit, tearing
his surplice and scratching his face in their violence.[a]

Two others of the London clergy, who were prominent in their
opposition to the injunctions, were Philpot and Gough, each holding
a plurality of cures, some of which appear to have been within the
diocese of Winchester. Robert Horne, Bishop of that see, summoned them to a conference at Winchester, in which the subject
was to be discussed for one-and-twenty days. As they passed over
London Bridge into Southwark, they were accompanied by two or
three hundred women, laden with bags and bottles " to banquet at
their departing." Whether this was an open-air entertainment the
author does not say ; but it was not the only form in which the
crowd displayed their enthusiastic liberality. Presents of gold,

[a] pp. 138-9.

silver, spice, sugar, and other things were made in abundance, and the travellers were everywhere exhorted to stand fast in the doctrine they had taught, touching the important subject of caps and surplices.[a]

On the other hand, the Bishop of London himself, on coming to St. Margaret's church in Old Fish Street, was hooted at by the congregation, and especially by the women, because he wore the cornered cap belonging to his dignity. A cry of " Ware horns! " rose up, with other opprobrious language. The episcopal dignity had certainly fallen into strange disrepute, at all events in the city of London, when such a scene was possible. Nor was it easy to inflict appropriate punishment on the offenders. One woman indeed was taken on the following Saturday and placed upon two ladders " like a cucking stool," for the space of a whole hour; but, like Defoe in a later age, she only rejoiced in her punishment, and was encouraged by the spectators to glory in having been thought worthy to suffer persecution for the sake, as they declared, of righteousness and truth in protesting against superstition.[a]

I leave the reader to examine for himself the notice of the original Puritans and Brownists, which completes the religious picture of the times,[b] the minute accounts of the mortality from the plague,[c] the description of the tournament at the marriage of Lord Ambrose Dudley,[d] the meeting between the Queen and Leicester in 1566,[e] the proclamation for the sale of the houses on the site destined for Sir Thomas Gresham's Exchange,[f] and other matters of the like character; all of which possess much interest for the historical reader.

The reader has now before him everything that is of a distinctly historical character in the Lambeth Volume No. 306. That

[a] p. 140.   [b] p. 143.   [c] pp. 123-5, 144-7.
[d] p. 134.   [e] p. 137.   [f] pp. 134-5.

volume, however, also contains, as will be seen by the catalogue, a quantity of poetry, medical receipts, and scraps of various kinds, which do not, generally speaking, greatly repay perusal. I have, however, printed two little scraps at the end of this preface (Note A) which are not altogether uninteresting as curiosities.

The "Brief Notes," which form the second portion of this volume, are derived from a MS. (No. 448 in the Lambeth Library) which seems to have been penned within the monastery of Ely. It is a small quarto volume, containing 153 leaves, of which the greater part are parchment; but the last 37 and some in the middle are of paper. The earlier portion is the history of the monastery and of the bishops of Ely printed by Wharton in his *Anglia Sacra*, pp. 593—674. It extends from the days of the founder, Queen Etheldreda the Virgin, to the episcopate of Morton, afterwards Archbishop of Canterbury and Cardinal, who succeeded to this see in the year 1478. This history is written on parchment as far as folio 77, and is continued for 22 pages further upon paper, the continuation being evidently a portion of the draft from which the whole was copied. This is shown by the fact that on the top line of folio 78 the first four words of a sentence are cancelled, being contained in the last line of the vellum leaf immediately preceding. The handwriting on the paper leaves is different from that of the portion written on vellum, but both are evidently of the same period, the close of the fifteenth century. The work, however, is continued by a sixteenth-century pen, from the episcopate of Alcock, Morton's successor, to that of Thirlby.

After this follow 25 leaves of parchment, filled with matter relating to the statutes and benefactors of the monastery, all in fifteenth-century handwriting, and containing much that is of considerable interest to the student of monastic usages. In the

middle of this portion, however, are a few leaves which had been
left blank, and which have been filled up by a later scribe with the
genealogy of Robert Steward, the last Prior and first Dean of Ely,
who died in 1557. This genealogy has also been printed by
Wharton, pp. 686-8.

From folio 117 to the end is again paper, filled with writing of
the fifteenth century; and it is from this portion alone that our
extracts are taken. The contents, however, are very miscellaneous,
being partly jottings and extracts from various sources, in which
the only point of real interest is an account of the great fire at Bury
St. Edmund's in 1140, and partly an exceedingly rough and careless,
but still contemporary, register of current events. The entries here
have not even been written in consecutively as the events occurred,
but later occurrences precede earlier ones, although the date of the
year is invariably given at the head of the paragraph. Evidently
this part of the volume was a mere memorandum book, filled up
irregularly at intervals, and intended merely to aid in the com-
pilation of some more polished chronicle. Even the dates given
prior to the year 1450 are very inaccurate; indeed a good number
of the occurrences in that year are referred to the year 1449. But
in point of fact these brief notes are, with one exception, of little
or no consequence before the year 1459, and most of the preceding
entries are probably derived from some other source. An exception,
however, ought certainly to be made as to the paragraph relating
to the Parliament at Bury in 1446-7, and the suspected murder of
the Duke of Gloucester. The strong impression produced by that
event is shown by all the historical evidences of the period; and it
is all the more interesting to read what appears to have been a *first*
impression produced when the news was fresh, in a monastery not
thirty miles distant from the scene of its occurrence.

This paragraph moreover contains circumstantial information not found elsewhere. Whatever the facts may have been, Suffolk professed to apprehend danger to the King from the machinations of his uncle, and caused him to be protected by a very strong guard (about 60,000 men and villeins, says our MS.) at every town in which he stopped on his way to the Parliament. The writer however altogether discredits the danger, and tells us that Duke Humphrey came up from Wales in obedience to the King's command without a thought or suspicion of evil in his mind, merely hoping to obtain the King's favour for Dame Eleanor his wife, who had been for some time imprisoned. The writer's incredulity as to the conspiracy was doubtless shared by the majority of the people, as it is by most of the writers of this period; but it seems strange that, such being the case, the strong bodyguard is not even noticed by any other writer.

Great confusion exists in some parts of the narrative; in one place the writer actually speaks of Pomfret Castle being near Southwark (p. 154). The battle of Northampton is dated 1459, instead of 1460 (p. 153), and in the account of the circumstances which led to it the name of Northampton seems to be introduced prematurely where Ludlow was the place that is really referred to.[a] These and a variety of other errors show the carelessness with which these notes of occurrences were drawn up.[b]

[a] "Anno Domini MCCCC.lix° (1460), et anno Regis Henrici vj^{ti}xxviij°, mense Julii venerunt comes de Warwyk, comes de March, et comes de Salisbery ; quia cum prius venissent ad *Northampton* (*Ludlow*), et audito quod Rex erat præsens clam fugierunt ad mare," &c.

[b] Carelessness, however, is contagious, and I take this opportunity both to confess and to explain a curious slip of my own occasioned by the slovenly character of the MS. At page 159, in the account of the sieges in Northumberland in 1462, occurs the sentence:—"At the seege of Hem sunt comes de Wyceter, comes de Arundel, dominus de Ogyl, et dominus de Muntegew cum x. M^l." I could not but suppose when I transcribed the MS. that "Hem" was a place, though I was unacquainted with it. I find, however, the word should have been spelt with a small *h*, "hem" being here a personal pronoun referring to the Duke of Somerset and others,

But, while inaccuracies such as these might seem to detract from
the value of the record, its importance as an original source of information on many points cannot be overlooked. The news of the
battle of Hedgley Moor has evidently been taken down when it
was quite fresh, prefaced by the words, " These tidings hath my
lord of Lincoln, and the same be come to Stamford " (p. 156).
Again, the exploits of Earl Douglas in 1462, of which no other
account has been preserved to us, are introduced in like manner,
with the words, " These been the tidings sent out of Scotland "
(p. 159). It may be added that the sieges in Northumberland in
1462 (p. 159) are described in the present tense, as if they were
still going on, and the account of them is concluded by the statement, " Rex tenet Natale suum apud Dorham " (the King *is keeping*
his Christmas at Durham). Even the errors as to matters of fact
in some cases are such as could only have been made at the time;
as, for example, in the list of those killed at Towton (p. 160), which
includes not only Queen Margaret and her son, but at least seven
noblemen besides,[a] who certainly survived that day, and some of
whom lived after it for twenty years or more.

who were keeping Bamborough Castle for Henry VI., as mentioned in the preceding sentence! Of all writings in the world illiterate writings are certainly the
easiest to misinterpret.

    [a] The Dukes of Exeter and Somerset, the Earls of Cumberland and Shrewsbury,
Lords Scales, Willoughby, and Roos. " Dominus Henricus de Bokyngham " is
probably an eighth; for I imagine the person intended was the Duke of Buckingham,
afterwards beheaded by Richard III., whose succession to the title was not yet
acknowledged, his grandfather from whom he inherited it having been slain at
Northampton in the preceding year. In the list of *knights* slain also we meet with
" Dominus R. de Percy," probably Sir Ralph Percy who was killed three years
later at Hedgley Moor, and Sir Ralph Gray who also survived for three years and
was beheaded for treason in 1464. The error in the case of Sir Ralph Gray was
however discovered and the name is accordingly erased. At page 161 again we
have another list of those slain in this battle, including, as the former one did, the
Earl of Devonshire. Yet the Earl of Devonshire is stated on the same page to have
been beheaded after the battle, which of course is more accurate.

Inaccuracies of this kind are instructive, for in the present case they testify to the exaggerated impression produced by a great victory. Even what may be called the official report, written just after the battle by King Edward himself, wrongly enumerated among the slain Lords Willoughby and Scales, while it spoke with rather less certainty of the death of Northumberland, who certainly was one of them; and mentioned truly that King Henry and Margaret with their son, the Dukes of Somerset and Exeter, and Lord Roos, had escaped to Scotland.[a] But the report which first reached the monastery of Ely confounded those who had fled with those who had fallen in battle, and added two more noblemen besides to the appalling list. Almost anything must have seemed credible as to the fatal results of a conflict after which it was positively stated that 28,000 corpses had been numbered upon the field by heralds.[b]

There can be no doubt, therefore, whether its statements be accurate or the reverse, that this MS. contains the first intelligence of a number of occurrences as they were reported in the monastery of Ely in the beginning of Edward the Fourth's reign. And after the fullest allowance made for error these brief notes certainly make a considerable addition to what was already known of that obscure and turbulent period. Here we have not only the account of several actions fought and sieges laid, but of Lancastrian conspiracies detected, and of the foreign alliances by which it was believed the defeated party would be enabled to invade England at several points at once (p. 158). The account of the discovery of the conspiracy of the Earl of Oxford in 1461-2 (pp. 162-3) is also new and not altogether unimportant. Nor must we pass by in silence the long

---

[a] See *Paston Letters* (new edition), ii. 5.

[b] *Paston Letters*, ii. 6. Here in this Ely MS. we are told with beautiful precision that the number of the slain "was reckoned at 35,091, as it was reported" *(per æsti-mationem* xxxvᴹ.iiijˣˣ *et* xj, *ut dicebatur)*, and a little lower that it was 33,000 and more *(quasi* xxxiij *milia et plures)*.

catalogue at p. 157 of the noblemen and knights who accompanied
King Edward to the borders of Scotland in December 1462. But
on these things, as on the minute fragments of information in the
Short English Chronicle, it is quite impossible to enlarge in a
Preface like this, and we must be content with having thus briefly
indicated the sort of material which this MS. contains.

Before finally taking leave of it, however, it may be interesting
to give here an extract from the earlier part of the volume relative
to an earthquake in the year 1488. On the back of folio 116 occurs
the following note:—

Anno Domini M°cccc°lxxx^{mo}viij°, in festo Sancti Thome Martiris erat terre
motus magnus per quarternium unius hore ante horam duodecimam in nocte, ex quo
plures audientes et sensientes erant exterriti ; qui duravit per spacium unius^a *Ave
Maria*.

The third source from which the contents of this volume are
derived is the MS. numbered 5 in the Arundel Collection in the
College of Arms. It is a great parchment folio still preserved in
the old wooden covers, and, as mentioned in the catalogue, " on
the right hand one is a curious horn tablet, covering a piece of
parchment, with the titles of the contents written by the original
scribe." Nothing seems to be known of the history of this volume
beyond the fact that it once belonged to Fox the Martyrologist and
afterwards became the property of Lord William Howard of
Naworth—a collector whose historical and religious views being
totally opposed to those of his predecessor, he has left a note in one
place accusing Fox, but it must be said most untruly, of interpolating
a passage in the text concerning the death of King John.

The contents are, first, what is called a *Scala Mundi*, or tabular
chronology of universal history, with dates extending down to the
year 1619, the events however being only filled in to the year 1469.

─────────

^a The word *dimidii* here followed, but is erased.

Second, a double history of Popes and Emperors on opposite pages, the former carried down as far as the year 1334, and the latter to the period of the Guelph and Ghibelline factions. And third, a "Compilacio de Gestis Britonum et Anglorum," continued to the year 1471. It is the concluding portion of this last work that alone has any value for the historian, because there is no doubt that for the reign of Edward IV. at least it is a strictly contemporary record. As such it has been already cited by Mr. Halliwell Phillipps, who quoted some extracts from it in his Appendix to Warkworth's Chronicle—the first work ever published by this Society.ᵃ But the whole narrative for the reign of Edward IV. is full of interest, and, as it is difficult to say at what point the work begins to be an original composition, I have given a complete transcript from the beginning of Henry VI.'s reign.

Whoever the compiler was, he certainly lived in the days of Henry VI. and Edward IV. Yet for the most part, if not the whole, of Henry VI.'s reign his narrative is of very little value. So slender is his record of events that the first battle of St. Alban's is altogether omitted, though there is a retrospective allusion to it in connection with the pacification of 1457-8 (p. 168). The disgrace of Bishop Pecock in the same year is related with a good deal of the usual theological bitterness (pp. 167-8). But there is really nothing in this Chronicle that cannot be found elsewhere before the year 1460, and little even in that year, though the circumstances connected with the battle of Northampton and the Duke of York's claim to the crown are recorded somewhat more fully than previous events. An abstract of the Duke of York's claim in parliament is quoted in English (p. 170), and it is clear the writer has much sympathy both with him and with his son.

Just after Edward the Fourth was proclaimed King in London, we find that his title was set forth in a sermon at Paul's Cross by

ᵃ *Warkworth's Chronicle*, pp. 39, 40, 43, 44, 45, 46.

George Nevill, Bishop of Exeter, the Earl of Warwick's brother. When the sermon was finished, King Edward rode through the streets to Westminster in a great procession of lords spiritual and temporal, and sat down in the royal seat (*sedes regalis*) in Westminster Hall, as if taking formal possession of the throne.[a] This intelligence is very remarkable, and suggests at once the question how far Richard III. intended to use the case as a precedent when Dr. Shaw preached in behalf of *his* title from the same pulpit. That Richard hoped to be made King (or make himself so) by acclamation like his brother is the belief that has always been accepted ; and it is remarkable that, though Dr. Shaw's sermon was a failure, and Richard took no steps *that* day to secure possession of the throne, he actually did on the day of his accession, which was only four days later, take his seat in the marble chair in Westminster Hall, the *sedes regalis* mentioned by our chronicler.

This *sedes regalis*, or marble chair of royalty, was apparently the King's Bench, from which the court derives its name;[b] and it is interesting to find, a little further on (p. 175), that it was not a mere antiquated tradition in Edward the Fourth's days that kings might administer justice in person; for we are told that Edward himself in 1462, sitting in the King's Bench (*in bancho suo regali*) at Westminster, heard a particular cause tried before him, his Chancellor and Justices assisting him with their advice.

---

[a] Page 173.

[b] I had written this without referring to any other work upon the subject, but I find the same opinion put forward in a note in Smith's *Antiquities of Westminster,* p. 258; and it appears from a reference there to Bailey's *Antiquities of London and Westminster,* p. 240 (ed. 1734), that this marble chair was believed to be still in existence at the beginning of the last century, though it was then hidden from view, being built over by the two Courts of Chancery and the King's Bench. What has become of it ? My friend Mr. Henry Brewer, who has always taken much interest in the architectural history of Westminster Hall, believes that Bailey was labouring under a mistake, and that the chair had been destroyed before his time. See note B at the end of this Preface.

Of the military and naval movements at the commencement of
Edward IV.'s reign this is perhaps the clearest contemporary account
that we possess; Worcester's narrative, though rather more minute,
being defective in some places, and particularly in the year 1463,
where a leaf of the original MS. is lost.ᵃ From what we read in
the present Chronicle that does not appear to have been a very
eventful year; but the tone of the writer's comments upon it is
noteworthy. He takes note of the assembly and prorogation of
parliament, and observes that he is not aware that it had redressed any evils or initiated any reforms during its seven weeks'
sitting. He makes no mention of what was apparently the only
business transacted—the vote of 37,000*l.* for the defence of the
kingdom.ᵇ But this was a matter that only affected the laity, and
evidently the writer was a churchman. The taxation of the laity
was a mere trifle to what was extorted at the same time from the
clergy, and on this subject our author writes feelingly. The Con
vocation of Canterbury granted the king the sum of one mark, or
thirteen shillings and four pence, on every ten marks clerical income;
" at which," he says, " many were aggrieved and complained, both
because they were poor and because moneys so extorted from the
clergy rarely or never lead to any good result, but rather to the
confusion and disgrace of those who use them. For after the feast
of the Nativity of the Blessed Virgin Mary King Edward mustered
a great army and prepared to subdue his adversaries by land and
sea. I know not, however, what good he did in that expedition.
And the Earl of Worcester with his ship and sailors, lurking as it
were by the shores and havens of the sea and consuming their pro-
visions, returned empty without doing anything. O unhappy result,
shame and confusion!"

The King's necessities about the same time, or shortly afterwards,

ᵃ W. Wyr. 497.   ᵇ *Rolls of Parliament,* v. 497.

led him to enhance the value of the coinage and seize upon the revenues of the two Colleges founded by his predecessor at Cambridge and Eton, the latter of which he had some thought of suppressing altogether by the aid of a papal bull. Happily he was persuaded to abandon this intention; but the endowments of both Colleges were reduced and a large portion went to meet the King's requirements.[a]

It is evident that the cause of Henry VI. was at this time by no means desperate, and might even have triumphed without the unexpected aid which it afterwards received from the Earl of Warwick. For the civil war was by no means so intermittent and spasmodic an affair as the meagre contemporary notices might well lead us to imagine. Through the early part of King Edward's reign it was quite continuous, and we now learn for the first time that in 1464 the Lancastrians obtained possession of the castles of Norham and Skipton in Craven. The news took Edward by surprise while he was feasting with his lords in London, and presently he proceeded to the North to resist the enemy. But his going seemed to produce very little result, and after a good deal of time had been wasted Edward's Chancellor, George Nevill Bishop of Exeter, the brother of Warwick and Lord Montague, took his journey also to the North for the relief of the latter lord, who had to sustain the brunt of the conflict. But on the 2nd May, we are told, a decisive battle was fought by Montague, in which the Lancastrian party were defeated, the Duke of Somerset and others put to flight, and Sir Ralph Percy slain.[b]

So the facts are related, but I am bound to state that the narrative in this place does not seem quite so accurate as elsewhere. From the dates of King Edward's privy seals it appears that he remained in or near London till the end of April. He was at the Tower on

[a] Page 177.   [b] Page 178.

the 26th of that month, and this must have been about the time when the news came of the capture of Norham and Skipton Castles. On the 29th April we find him at St. Alban's, and by the 2nd May he had reached Northampton, so that by that date, when the decisive battle above alluded to is said to have been fought, the King certainly had not lost much time. He contrived to waste a little, as we know quite well, the day before, when he secretly stole away from Stony Stratford and got married to Elizabeth Woodville at Grafton. But as he rejoined his company the same day, and no one knew of the affair for some months after, it cannot be said that even this was a great delay, so far. It was after the decisive battle had been fought, and no doubt because it had been fought and won, that Edward manifestly slackened speed on his progress northwards. He stayed at Leicester from the 8th to the 13th May, was at Nottingham on the 15th, had reached Pomfret by the 14th June, and Doncaster by the 23rd, and seems to have advanced no further. In July we find him again at Leicester, and in August we trace his movements southwards by Stamford and Fotheringay to Woodstock, which he reached on the 24th. The only material waste of time therefore, that we can detect on the King's part, was after the danger was practically at an end.

Again, the decisive battle in which Sir Ralph Percy was slain was, it is well known, the battle of Hedgley Moor; but it appears by the concurrent evidence of Gregory's Chronicle and the Rolls of Parliament to have been fought, not on the 2nd May, but on St. Mark's Day, the 25th April,[a] so here seems to be another inaccuracy. These however are exceptions. The account of the executions after the battle of Hexham corresponds with that in Gregory's Chronicle (*Coll. of a London Citizen*, 224-6), and must have been derived from a common source, but the Latin text seems to be the more accurate.

---

[a] *Coll. of a Lond. Citizen*, 224. Rolls of Parl. v. 511.

From the year 1464 to the close of this Chronicle in 1471 there is comparatively little recorded that is not to be found elsewhere; but the narrative, slender as it is, ought certainly not to be overlooked by any one who proposes to study the history of the period from original sources.

NOTES.

A.—*See page* xv.

At folio 203 of the Lambeth MS. 306, occur the two following scraps, which seem worth preservation as curiosities:—

I.

Who so wyll be ware of purchassyng,
Consydre theese poyntes folowyng:—

1. Fyrst se that the lande be cleere,
2. And the tytle of the sellere,
3. That it stonde in no dawngeer
   Of no womans doweere,
4. And whethir the lande be bonde or free,
5. And the leese or releese of the feoffe,
6. Se that the seller be of age,
7. And whethir it be in any morgage.
8. Looke if ther of a tayle be fownde,
9. And whethir it stonde in any statute bownde.
10. Consydre what servyce longyth ther to
11. And the quyte rent that there of owte shall goo.
12. And yf thou may in any wyse
    Make thy chartyr on warantyse,
    To thyn heyres and assygnes all so.
    Thys shall a wyse purchasser doo;
    And in tenne yere if ye wyse be.
    Ye shall a geyne youre sylver see.

II.

The longitude of men folowyng:—

Moyses, xiij fote & viij ynches & di.

Cryste, vj fote & iij ynches.

Our Lady, vj fote & viij ynches.

Crystoferus, xvij fote & viij ynches.

Kyng Alysaunder, iiij fote & v ynches.

Colbronde, xvij fote & ij ynches & di.

Syr Gy, x fote iij ynches & di.

Seynt Thomas of Caunterbery, vij fote save a ynche.

Long Mores, a man of Yrelonde borne, and servaunt to Kyng Edward the iiijth, vj fote & x ynches & di.

B.—*The Marble Chair; see page* xxii.

I am favoured with the following observations by Mr. Henry Brewer:—

In Smith's *Westminster*, p. 258, is inserted a letter from one John Cranch quoting the following passage from Bailey (the passage which, I suppose, you refer to in your letter to me):

"At the upper end of Westminster Hall is a marble ' *stone* ' (*sic*) [perhaps table or bench], of nineteen feet in length and three feet in breadth, and a marble chair, where the Kings of England formerly sat at their coronation dinners: and at other solemn times the Lord Chancellors, but now not to be seen, being built over by the *Courts of King's Bench* and Chancery" (p. 240). "It is to be wished that when the purposed alterations of these places shall commence, every lover of our monarchical antiquities will interest himself in the preservation of these venerable relics, since the same barbarous insensibility that buried them alive will scruple as little to profane or destroy them when disclosed.

"JOHN CRANCH."

Appended to this letter is the following most valuable note:

"When this communication was delivered in writing by Mr. Smith to Mr. Groves, Clerk of the Works of the Old Palace of Westminster, that gentleman gave immediate orders for an investigation of the fact.   But it appears that the search was made *close* to the southern wall, and that he was completely disappointed. It is highly probable that the chair and *table* [he has here, I fancy, fallen into the mistake of confusing the architectural expression a ' *basement table*,' *which really means a stone bench attached to a wall*, with the ordinary idea of a table!] were placed at a distance from the wall . . . . . so that had the examination taken place at about 15 feet from the wall these relics might have been discovered.   Is not the title of *Court of ' King's Bench '* derived from this identical *marble bench?* because it is well known that our early kings sat in parliament in Westminster Hall."

This is very interesting, but to my mind it proves most distinctly that the throne and bench had been destroyed before Mr. Groves made his search.   I think that the two facts taken together—1. That this feature is sometimes called a " bench," and sometimes a "table," and 2ndly, that we always find these thrones and benches in combination attached to the wall—go a very long way to prove that " the marble seat and bench in Westminster Hall were attached to the south wall of the building."   That they must have been destroyed before Mr. Groves made his search is, I think, certain, because had they existed they must have been discovered when the interior of the hall was restored by Sir Robert Smirke for George the Fourth's coronation; but Brayley, who relates most exactly the discoveries in St. Stephen's Chapel, says nothing whatever about them, and I have no doubt, myself, that they were destroyed in 1680, when a doorway was cut through the south end of the Hall; in fact, if, as I suppose, the throne was attached to the wall, this doorway would have exactly occupied its place.

A SHORT ENGLISH CHRONICLE,

From Lambeth MS. 306.

Cronycullys of Englonde.

In the noble londe of Surrye[a] was some tyme a greate kynge and
a myghty that was named Dioclesyan, and he was the moste
worthiest kynge than levinge on erthe, as the story seythe. And
this brevelye to procede, he hade by dyverse wiffes xxxiij[ti] doughteres,
the whiche were geven in to maryage to xxxiij[ti] kynges of dyverse
contres. And all the kynges were under Dioclesyan, and obedient
unto hym. And after it be fell so that thes wiffes wexen so proude
and sterne toward ther husbondes by one assent compleyned upon
hem to Dioclesyan the grete kynge ; and so ther fader were gretly
amevid of ther governaunce; and so he gave his daughtres a grete
rebuke in presens of all her husbondes. And so the nexte nyght
folowynge for male talent and greate ire that they were so foule
blamed of ther fader through grete complaynte of ther husbondes,
they toke their counselle togeder, and thought to be avenged.
And so the nexte nyght by one assent thei cut her husbondis
throtes, and violensely they were slayne alle. And tho were all
the xxxiij[ti] false women that were quenes of diverse londis exiled
oute of all the londe of Surrye, and put into a shippe withouten
helpe of any man. And toke hem vitaile for halfe a yere or more,
and be toke hem to Mahonde and Appolyne to kepe. And so thei
were in the see longe and mony a daye. Till at the last thei were
drevyn in to this londe, that tho was all disserte and wildernesse
and full of wilde bestis. And than they come alande wher they
fonde no creature þerin. Tho saide Albyne, the eldest sister, I se

[a] Syria.

well by reyson that we ben the fyrst creatures that ever came here; wherefor I will have this lond called after my name, Albyon londe. Tho levid they here in this londe as bestis by erbis and rotis, and ete rawe flesshe and dranke wilde bestis blode, and so they wex coragious and ranke, and desired gretely the feleshippe of men. And tho came sprytes of the ayre and wonderly delid with hem, and so they brought forthe giantes as the story reherseth, as Gogge, Ma gogge and other; and so levid forthe the geauntes un till the cominge of Brute.

Fro the begynnynge of the worlde unto the distruccion of the grete cyte of[a] Troye was iiij$\mathrm{M^l}$iiij^{xx} and iiij yere. That is for to sey, afor the Carnacion of Crist $\mathrm{M^l}$cxv yere. [Fro þe begynnynge of the worlde unto the destruccion of the grete cite of Troye was $\mathrm{M^l}$iiij^{xx} and iiij yere.][b] And fro that tyme in to the comynge of Brute fyrst into this londe was lxxiiij yere. And that was by for the Incarnacion $\mathrm{M^l}$xlj yere, &c.

e was a Trojane. The fyrst kynge that ever was in this londe was Brutus, the whiche was come of the gentill blode of Troye, as the storye telleth. And he began first London, and named hit at that tyme Newe Troye, because he was com of the lynage of the Troye. And also he lette call this lande Brutayne after his name, and the people that he brought with hym he named Brutones, and he yave his men grete yeftis, and gaffe hem londe to lyve upon, and they bilded howses and bilded many townes through helpe of ther kynge Brute. And when Brute had regned xxv yere than he dyed, and lieth at Newe Troye that nowe is called London. And ther he was worthely entered, and he was xxx^{ti} yere of age or he was crowned kynge of Brutayne. The some of his age or he dyed was lv yere, and that was be for the Incarnacion of Criste $\mathrm{M^l}$xvj yere.

ne. Afftyr kynge Brutus regned his sonne Locryne, a gode knyght and a myghty, and he regned but vj yere.

---

[a] *the grete cyte of.* These words are interlined by a second hand, by which most of the side-notes have been supplied.

[b] Erased in the MS.

Aftir kynge Locryne regned his wiffe Guendolyn, the whiche Guendolyne. that hade a sonne that hight Madahan, þat was kynge Locrynes' Madahan. sonne. And the queue kepte him in hir governaunce till that he was xx^{ti} wynter olde. And than he was made kynge, and so the quene regned xvj yere after Locryn dyed. And so regned Madahan, that was Locrynes sonne, xxxij yere, and lythe at Newe Troye.

After him regned his sonne Memprice xxviij yere.   Mempryce.

After hym regned his sonne Eboranke,[a] the which was a gode Eborank.[a] knyght and a myghty, for he conquered all the londe of Fraunce, and gate grete umbre of gode. That whane he come home a yene he lete make a fayre cite and lete called after his name Eborawyke,[a] that nowe men clepeth Yorke. And he hade by dyverse women xx^{ti} sonnes and xxiij^{ti} doughtres; and his sonnes were grete lordys, and conqured many contres. And this kynge Eboranke[a] regned lxj yere; he dyed and lieth at Yorke.

After hym regned his sonne Brute Greneshyld, the whiche was a Brute Grenesh[y] gode knyght and a worthy, and whan that he had regned xxxij yere he died, and lithe at Yorke. After regned his sonne Lyell; Lyell. he made the towne of Carlyll, he regned the full of xxiij yere, and lyeth at Karleyll; and that time regned Kynge Salamonde in Jerusalem. After that regned Lud Ludebras, Lyell is sonne, ix yere. Lud Ludibras. After hym regned Bladud, his sonne, the whiche was a grete negre- Bladud. mancer, and he made the hote bathe be his sotill crafte of nigromancye; he regned xxij yere.

After him regned Kynge Leyre, a gode kynge and a worthie, Leyre. and he made the towne of Leyseter; he regned xliiij yere.

Than regned Cordell, that was Leyres doughter, þ^e whiche was Cordel. Quene of Fraunce; she regned v yere.

After that regned Cordell sonne, that right Morgane and his Morgan. brother Conadage; thei departed the londe be twene hem, and regned bothe to geder in pese xij yere. And after that fell a dis-

---

[a] In the names Eborank and Eborawyke, the "o" is inserted between b and r by the second hand, both in the text and in the margin.

taunce, and Conadage slough Morgan.   And after that Conadage regned in rest and pece full xxx yere.

After hym regned his sonne Regnolde, a gode knyght and an hardye, and in his tyme hit reyned blode durynge iij dayes; and he regnid xxij yere, and lithe at Yorke.

After hym regned Corbodian in rest and pese xvij yere.   Than stode this londe dissolate withowten kynge xvj yere.   Than was ther an erle in Gornewale that hight Gloton; and he hade a sonne

that heght Doneband, and he was right eyre of this lande.   And he

was the fyrst kynge Þat ever wered crowne of golde in this londe; and he hade ij sonnes, Beleyn and Bren; he regned durynge xlj yere.

Aftir hym regned Kynge Beleyn, and he made Beleynges gate, with a castell and a fayre towre, upon Temmesside; he was a noble knyght, for he conquerd Romayn and Lombardye; and whan he had regned xij yere he dyed, and lieth at Newe Troye.

After hym regned his sonne Cornebatrus, a gode knyʒt and a worthye; and he regned xxvj yere, and lieth at Newe Troye.

Aftyr hym regned his sonne Gwentholyn xxvj yere.

After him regned his sonne that heght Kynnore,[a] and he regned xix yere.

After hym regned his sonne Howayne Þe fers xj yere.

After him regned his sonne Morwyth Þe wekkyd ix yere.

After hym regned his sonne Seysell xvj yere.

After him regned his sonne Grandobodian, and he made the toure of Grantam and Cambryge; and he had iiij sonnes, Artogayll, Hesydere, Hygamus, and Petiture, and whan Grandobodyan had regnyd xij yere he dyed, and lithe at Newe Troye.

After him regned his eldeste sonne Arthogayle v yere, and for his wekidnes the Bretons pute him downe and made his brother Hesydere kynge, and he regned v yere; and than Artogale put downe Hesydere, and so he regned a yene vj yere, and than he died, and lieth at Grantham.

---

[a] The " o " in this name is altered by another hand into " a."

After that Higamus and Petiture departed the londe by twene Higamus and Pe
hem both, and so they regnyd togeder **vij** yere; tho dyed Higamus, byparty ted the le
and a none after died Petiture at the **vij** yere ende.

And after that the Bretons crownyde Hesydere kynge a yene, Hesydere.
and tho he regued here in pees **xvij** yere, and lieth at Newe Troye
Some of the regne of thes **xxiiij** kynges **vjc** and **ix** yere.

After that regned **xxxiij** kynges in rest and pese everyche after
other, as the story telleth, and how long tyme they regned.

Fyrst regned Grandabodian Rouse **xiij** yere and a halfe; item,
Morgan regned **vij** yere; item, Eyghanas regned **vj** yere; item,
Edwalyn regned **viij** yere; item, Rohngo Regina **xj** yere and di.;
item, Voghem regned **xiij** yere; item, Katyll regned **xv** yere; item,
Porrex regnid **vj** yere; item, Cheryne regnid **xvij** yere; item, Coysell
regnide **xij** yere; item, Surgeus regned **xiij** yere; item, Andragie
regnid **xviij** yere; item, Uryan regnid **vj** yere; item, Elyaud regnid
vij yere; item, Eldaux regnid **v** yere; item, Cornegund regnid **vij**
vere; item, Caphe regnid **ij** yere and di.; item, Morthan regnid **vj**
yere; item, Bladagh regnid **vj** yere; item, Geen regnid **vj** yere; item,
Seysell blod regnid **xxj** yere; item, Grabreth regned **xxij** yere; item,
Archynall regnid **xiiij** yere; item, Errok regnid **xxx** yere; item,
Rodyngum regnid **xxxj** yere; item, Hertyer regnid **vj** yere; item,
Hamprey regnid **vj** yere; item, Carpoire regned **vj** yere; item,
Dyngneyld regnid **vij** yere; item, Ragaa regned **xxij** yere; item,
Samoell regnid **xxiiij** yere; item, Rede regned **vj** yere; item, Kynge
Elye reind but halfe a yere. Summa of the regnie of **xxxiij** kynges, Hely.
ccclxxix yere. And this was a for the Incarnacion of Crist.

Fro the begynnyng of the worlde un to the regne of Kynge Lud.
Lud **vm'cxlvij**, &c.

After the dethe of Kynge Ely regnid his sone Lud the whiche
turned the name of newe Troye to London, and he lete make a
fayre gate and called hit Ludgate after his name; he regned in pees
xj yere and lithe in Ludgate.

After him regnid his brother Cassibalaun, and in his tyme came Cassibalaun.
Julyus Cesar into the londe and werred upon him longe tyme Julius Cesar

durynge vj yere, and after they were accorded. And Julyus Cesar made the towre of London.

After that regnid Cassibalaun in pees xvij yere. After him regned his brothers sonne Anddroughenne, whiche was Erle of Cornewayle vij yere, and lieth at London.

After him regnid his sonne Kynge Kymbelyne, the whiche was a gode man and right wele belovyde of the comon people, and in the vj yere of his regne was our lord Jhesu Crist borne of the Virgyn Marye. And he regnid after that xvj yere, and he had ij sonnes Gynder and Armyger, and whan he had regned full xxvj yere than he dyed, and lithe at London, &c.

After hym regnid his sonne Gyndere, a gode man and a trewe to alle the comone people, and his tyme came the Emperour Glaudius in to this londe and made greate werre for a trewage the whiche he chalanged of this londe. And the forsaide Kynge Gynder was slayne in his place by tresoun of Hamond, the Emperour styward; he regned xij yere.

After hym regned Armynger, Gyngere broþer, and he made his pese with Glaudyus, and he made the towne of Glowseter. And after that Glaudyus went to Rome ayene. And then regned Armyger in rest and pese all his lyfe tyme; and in the vj yere of his regne, as the story telleth, our lorde Jhesu Crist suffred dethe for redempcioun of manes soule; and whan he hade regned xxvj yere he dyed at London.

After hym regnid his sonne Westmere, a gode knyght and an hardy, and bilded in the northe partye of Brettayne, and called all that contre after his name, Westmerland; and he regned xxvij yere, and lith at Karlhill. After hym regnid his sonne Coyle, a gode man and welbelovyd a monge all the people of Bretayne, and well governed the londe in pese, and he regnid xxj yere. After hym regned Goran the grete, in trouble and debate with his people durynge xxij yere.

After hym regned his sonne Lucye, that was a gode kynge and a trewe, and welbelovyd with all the comyne peple of the londe,

and he sent to Rome to Pope Eleuthie and desired to be a Cristen- _{Anno Domini}
man; and so the pope was joyfull therof and sentt heder ij leggates _{c[l]xiij" erat prim[us] Christi}
that highte Pagan and Olybane for to baptice Kynge Lucye and his _{simus Re[x] A}
peple, and so he was the first cristen kynge þat ever was in this _{nomine Lucium.}
londe.   And fro Brute unto Lucye is M^lclxv yere.   Tho was
Kynge Lucye crowned and regned kynge xxiij yere or he was
cristened aftyr that he regned liiij yere.   Summa of his regne lxxvij
yere; than he dyed and lithe enterred att London.

The yere of oure Lorde Jhesu Crist ccj, A°——

After the dethe of Lucye this londe stode dissolate with outen
kynge and governour in grete werre amonges hem selfe for defaute
of a kynge and governour durynge lxij yere.

The yere of our Lord cclxiij.

And that tyme were the Romayns governers of this londe, and
they chase amonge hem a kynge þat hight Asclepades, the whiche
regned in grete trouble vj yere.

After him regned Coyll, the whiche made the towne of Colchester _{Coyl.}
and the castell of Dover.   And in his tyme come a noble prince
from Rome that hight Constance, and he chalanged the trewage
that the kynge oughte to pay to Rome.   And Kynge Coyll grawnte
him for to paye all that he ought to done of right.   And so they
were acorded that this noble prince spowsed Kynge Coyll is _{Seynt Elyn.}
doughter that high Elyn, the whiche was right eyre to the londe,
and she was a gode holy woman and a grete clerke.   And whan
Kynge Coyle had regned xiiij yere he dyed, and lieth at Colchester.

After him regned Constaunce of Rome, for he had spoused Eleyn _{Constaunce.}
that was Coylls doughter, and by hir he had a son that hight Constantyne that was Seint Eleyns sonne, and this gode Kynge Constance regned xv yere and lieth at Yorke.

ᵃ *Lucium.* So in MS. This marginal note is mutilated, the edge of the paper
having been cut by the binder, so that it is uncertain what the date assigned to
the conversion of Lucius was. But it was most probably 163 (CLXIII), the L being
now lost.

After that regnid his sonne Constantyne[a] that was Seint Elyns ——
sonne, and in the ij yere of his regne come tidingis to the kynge
that a wode tyrawnte Maxence was come to Rome for to distroye
the cite, and he distroyed all the Cristen folke that he myght come
by; and that same tyme was Seint Kateryne martered, the yere of our
Lorde cccx. And when Costantyne herde tell ther of, he gedered
a grete nombre of peple, and toke his moder with him, and wente to
Rome, and gate the cite, and slowe the Sarsynes, and distroycd all
that were in mys beleve, and after he was Emperour of Rome and
kynge of the londe. Tho was Octavyan, Erle of Cornwayle, warden
of the londe and keper under the emperour and kynge, and the x
yere of his regne he died at Rome the yere of our Lorde cccxvij[e].

After that was Octavyan, wardeyn of this londe, crownyd kynge,
and he regned durynge xvij yere.

After him regnid Maximean, that was Costantinges cosyne, and
he wedded Octavians doughter; and he went over the see in to the
londe of Morycon[b] and conquerd the londe and called hit Litell
Brettayn; and tho he made Canon Meredok kyng of that londe.
And aftir this was done Maximian went to Rome and was made
emperour the xj yere of his regne. And the same yere Seint Ursula,
the Erles doughter of Cornwale, was sent over the see with xj m[l]
maydenes in to Lytell Bretayne, and tho þei were drevyn with
tempest in to Holonde; and ther was a Saresyn kynge of that londe
that hight Gawhan, and he brought all the forsaide maydenes to
Coleyne, and ther they were martered the yere of our Lord cccxlvj.

A none after came Gawhan into this londe and warred upon Cristen
peple many a yere; and the lordis of this londe were at grete de bate
within hem selfe, and þerfore were the Saresynes myche the more
the bolder, and at that tyme was no kynge ne governor in this
londe, wher for the Brutis made grete mone and sorowe. And at
that tyme was Seint Albone marterd, the yere of our Lorde

<hr/>

[a] Over the name "Constantyne" in the text is written by the annotator
"Emperowre."   [b] Armorica.

ccclxxviij. Tho sent the Bretones to Rome for socoure and helpe
for to dryve oute the Sarsynes of this londe and to save the Cristen
people. After that came a worthi prince from Rome that was
called Grayne, and brought with him xxiiij thousande of fyghting Grayne.
men, and came in to this londe, and chasid oute the Sarsynes, and
Gowhan fled home into his owne contre. And this trouble dured in
this londe xlj yere. And than Gracyan was crownyd kynge of this Gracyan.
londe. After he wax so stoute and stere a yens the Bretens that thei
lovid him nought, and the thred yere of his regine he was slayne,
the yere of our Lorde lxxxx^c

After that came Gouhan ayene in to this londe and werred and Gouhan.
distroyed the Cristen peple all that ever he myght durynge vij
yere.

Than came a worthi knyght oute of Litell Bretayne that hight
Constantyne, the which was the kynges cosyne, and he came with
a grete oste and yave the Sarseyns a batayle, and ther was the
tirawnte slayne and all the Saresynes discomfited.

And tho came Costantyne, of London, and ther he was crowned
kynge of Grawnte Brettayne, and after he regnid well and worthely
xxvj ye., the yere of our Lord ccccxxiij^e yere. And he hade iij
sonnes; the eldest heght Custance, and he was made a monke at Constance, Auril
Wynchester by his faders leve. And Aurylambos and Uter were but bos, Uter, iij fili
yonge children when her fader dyed, and none of them bothe were Constantini.
not of age to ber the crowne, for ther was so grete wer and stryffe
in this londe. Tho was Urtager, Erle of Esex, he consayled
Counstance that was a monke for to forsake his abitt and to ber the
crowne, and Urtager to be governour of the londe, so under that
forme he myght be made kynge, for Constaunce was innocent and
cowthe no skyll of wer. And so Constaunce was crowned kynge, Constance.
and he made Urtager his governour of his londe, and whan he had
regned iij yere he was slayne. Anone after that was Urtager made Urtager.
kynge, and the Bishop of London, hight Coslyn, and he, sent the ij
brethren Aurylambros and Uter into Litell Brettayne to norysshe
and fede till they came of age. Sone after came Engest of Saxonye, Engest Rex Can

of the londe of Germayn, with a grete noumbre of people whiche were fayre folke, but they were not cristned; and at the last they encresid so faste in this londe that they over come the Bretones, for they slewe in one daye with treyson xxxm¹.lxij of gode knightes and chevaleres of the best that were in this londe. And tho Engest seysed all this londe in to his honde and hade Urtager in prison; and than he changed the name of this londe of Brettayne in to Englonde and called the peple Englishe men, and the peple of the londe that were Bretones fled into Wales and into Cornwayle. And

a divisa in octo a. ion tunc erat annorum.

Engest devided this londe in viij parties, ande made him sylfe kynge of Kente and lord of londe; and at that tyme was Merlyon xiiij yere of age. And this werre duryd in this londe xxij yere, the yer of of our Lorde ccccxlviij. And whan Engest had departid the londe aftir his owne device in viij kyngdomes, that is to sey, Kent,ᵃ Esex, Mydangle, Westsex, Estangle, Morchelond, Derham, and Ebrusam that nowe is called Yorkeshire. And this Engest was kynge aboven hem all, and he regened xij yere.

lambos.

Tho came Aurylambos and Uter his brother oute of Litell Brettayne with a grete noumbre of peple, and all the Brettones that were in Cornwayle and in oþer parties of this londe that durst not be seyne for drede of Engest, they came to Aurylambros and his broþere to helpe hem dryve oute the Saxons. Fyrst he went in to Walis, and there he slowe Urtager, and after Engest and his peple were overe come and discomfid all the paynymes. And the Saresynes sawe the people þat were converted to God; and than Aurylambros had regnid viij yere; and he was enpoysoned with a drynke and died slepynge, the yere of our Lord cccclxviij.

ʳ Pendragon.

After him regned his brother Uter Pendragon, þe whiche was a gode knyght and a worthi; and he weddid a faire lady the whiche was called Ingrene, that was the Erlys wife of Cornewayle, and she came of the lynage of Cornebyus of Troye; and at that tyme was a grete abbicion for the londis name. Some did call hit Brettayne, and some called hit Engelonde; and for the love that Uter had to

---

ᵃ The names of the eight kingdoms are repeated in a marginal note.

his wyfe, and for the gentill blode that she came of, he named this londe after hir name Ingerne, Englond; and upon hir he gate the doughty Kynge Arthure. And whan Uter hade regned wele worthely xlvij yere, the yere of our Lorde vcxvj^e.

After that regned the gode Kynge Arthur, the worthy con- Arthure querour that conquered many a region. Fyrst he began at Irlande, Skotlond, Norwey and Denmarke, Fraunce, Burgoyne, Gascoyne, Gyan, Lombardy, and Almayne, and Romayne; and after he came home ayene into Englonde and regned well and worthely xxvj yere, the yere of our Lorde vcxlij^e; but where he is beryed the story make no mencion.

After the dethe of Brute unto the regne of Kynge Arthur regnid in Englande diverse kynges, that is for to sey an c, of the whiche was xvj Cristen.

After Arthur regned Constantyne, Erle of Cornwayle, in peese Constantyne. viij yere; and after fell grete stryfe a monge the lordes of the londe, that every lord werred upon oþer in dyverse partyes of Englond duryng vj yere, the yere of our Lorde vclvj^e.

Aftir him regned Kyng Cordyff, and in his tyme fell so grete wer Cordyff. and stryfe with in this londe sylffe thatt this londe was all moste loste throwe werre, &c. And than came the Saxsones in to this londe that called hem selfe Englisshemen for the name of the name of the Engest, for to conquer the londe, and werred sore upon the Bretons and drove hem oute of this londe in to Walis and Cornwayle, and some in to Litell Brettayne; and þat tyme fell the grete myschefe in this londe, that Cristendome was distroyed through the Saxsones that were paynymes and hethen folke, for they keste downe houses and chirches of religeoun, and quelled all the Cristen folke that they myght come by; and whan the Saxsones had conquered the londe of the Bretones tho they departed tho lond a monge hem like as it was in Egestes tyme; and this grete trowble and sorowe dured in this londe xiij yere, the yere of our Lord vclxx.

And at that tyme regned Athelbryght, Kynge of Kent, and he Athylbryght, Ky was a gode man and loved well rest and pece; and he had a cosyne Kent.

that was called Sygeberde,[a] that was Kynge of Westsex, and a noþer cosyne, that hight Elfride, the whiche was Kynge of Northe homberlond; and thes thre kynges loved wele peese; mo other kynges ther were, but they were noþinge of theire condicion; and Athilbryght was chefe kynge a bouen hem all. And in the xxv yere of his regne Seint Augustyne came in to Engelonde for to cristen the Englisshe men that were come of the Saxones. And therfor Seint Austyne is called postill of England, for he brought fyrst Cristendome to Englisshe folke. But the Bretons that were dwellinge in this londe were Cristen peple many yeres afore. And whan Athilbright was cristen and all his people, sone after he lete make in the honour of God and Seynte Poule the churche of Poules at London.

acio ecclesie
i Pauli, A° Do[t]

Anno of our Lorde vc.iiij[xx]xviij was the fondacion of the chirche of Poules by Altherbryght. And when this gode Kynge Altherbryght had regnyd after that he was cristened xxj yere, and so he regnyd in all xlvj yere, and than dyed, the yere of our Lord

)ert, Kyng of
;ex.

vjc.xvj. And in Athilbryghtes tyme Sygebert[a] was Kyng of Westsex, and he was founder of Westminstre, anno of our Lorde vjc.xv.

ne, Kynge of
ehumberlond.

After that regned Kynge Edwyne of Northehomberlond above all the kynges of Engelond, and he regnid xj yere, the yere of our Lorde vjc.xxvij[e].

lde, Kyng [of]
ehumberlond.

After him regened Seint Oswalde, Kynge of Northchomberlonde, and he regned above all the kynges of Engelond; and in the ix yere of his regne he was martred, the yere of oure Lord vjc.xxxvj[e].

ne.

Aftir hym regned Oswyne, his brother, Kynge of Northehumber londe, and whan he hade regned xviij yere he dyed, and lythe at Tynmothe, the yere of our Lorde vjc.liiij[e].

lader.

After hym regnid Cadwaladere of Leyceter for chefe Kynge of Englonde, and he was a Breton; and when he hade regned xij yere ther fell grete stryfe in this londe be twene the Bretones and the

---

[a] The "ge" in this name, in both these places, alike in the text and in the margin, is an interlineation by another hand.

Englisshemen, that every kynge werred upon oþer. And the same
tyme fell so grete derthe of skarssyte that men myght neþer gete
mete nor drynke to by for no money, for almaner cornes and frutes
fayled; and all maner of bestis, bothe wilde and tame, both foules
and fysshes, dyed in all maner partes of Engelonde, that men myght
no vitayle gett, so grete skarssete ther was; and at that tyme fell
the grete mortalite of pestilence, that peple dyed sodeynly goynge
in the stretes, with gronyng, fuesynge, and coughynge, slepynge
and wakynge, and in all maner weyes peple dyed. Than Kyng
Cadwaladre, seynge this grete vengeaunce, he toke a serteyne meyne
with him and went him to shippe and forsoke his owne kyngdome,
and went in to Lytell Brettayne to his cosyne, Kynge Aleyne, Alanus Rex.
and after went to Rome and þere dyed, the yere of our Lorde
vjc.lxxvj.

After that Cadwaladre had forsake his owne londe and was in
Litell Brettayne, came the noble Quene Sexburga, with a grete Sexburga.
nombre of people oute of Saxony, and they toke up all the londe
of Northehomberlande to West Walis; and at that tyme were many
kyngis in this londe in dyverse parties, and thei werred everyche
upon other, and the strengest parti be nome the feblest partyes
loudes; and so this wer endured many yerys be twene the Bretons
and the Englissh. And so, at the laste, Kynge Offa regnid as for Offa.
cheffe Kynge of Englonde; and he lete make the Abbaye of Seint [Ki]ng Offa fou
Albonys, and he regnid xxvij yere, the yere of our Lord vijc of Seynt [Al]bo
and iije.

After him regned his broþer sonne, Kynge Alffryde, a gode man Alfryde.
and a welbelovyd of all his people, and he regnid xxvj yere.

After him regnid Kynge Osbryght of Northhomberlond, the Osbryght
whiche was slayne in playne bataile; he regned xxvj yere.

After him regnid Kynge Godeyne of Denmarke, and he made Godeyne.
werr in this londe durynge many yers, and he regnid xxvij yere.

After him regnid Kynge Albryght of Laycester, the whiche was Albryght.
a gode man and a trewe, and loved well peese, and in the viij yere
of his regne he was martred, and lith at Hertforde.

After him regnid Kynge Elle of Northehomberlonde, in grete weire and stryffe, durynge xxx yere.

Aftir hym regned Kynge Kenelme, a gode man and an holy, and loved well God and Holy Chirche, and in the v^e yere of his regne he was martred, and lithe at Wynchecombe, the yere of our Lord viijc.xxv yere.

Anone after came Danys in to Engelonde for to conquer the londe, and made grete werr, and distroyed Cristen peple, and gate all the contrey off Northehomberlonde and Estangle. This wer duryd in this londe xxx yere, by the kynge him selffe and his successores, the yere of our Lorde viijc.lv.

After him regned Edmond, Kynge of Northefolke, and of all the contre of Southefolke; and tho came the Danys off Northehomber-londe and werred upon Englissh men many yeris. After that Hubla and Hungar, that were princes of the Danes, came to Bury, and ther the gode Kynge Edmonde was take, and they bounde him to a tre and shotte him with brode arowes, and after smote of his hede; and so was Seint Edmond, the gode kynge, martred, the xv yere of his regne, the yere of our Lord viijc.lxxj^e. After that regned

Kynge Aluerde of Southesex, and he werred upon the Danys, and at the last discomfied them and toke the kynge prisoner, and brought him to London; and than he besought the kynge of grace, and seyde he wolde become Cristen for his love, and never to make were a yenes him; and ther Kynge Alurede brought him to West-minster, and ther he was baptysed and called Athelstone. And than were all the Danys cristened that were in Engelonde; and for grete joye that Kynge Alured had for the Danys were converted to God he lete make a grete feste and after levid in pees; and Kynge Adel-ston went home in to Denmarke ayen. And whan Kynge Alurede had regned al most xxx yere he dyed, and lieth worthely enterred at Wynchester, the yere of our Lord ixc primo. After him regnid

his sonne that was called the first Edward; he was a gode man and a trewe, and lovyd well pees. And whan he had regned xxiiij yere he dyed, and lithe at London. And the seyde Kynge Edwarde hade

iiij sonnes, Athelston, Edmond, Eldred, and Edwyn.   And that
tyme regned the gode knyght Gy of Warwyke, &c.

After Edwarde regned his eldest sonne Athelstone.   And in his Adelstone.
tyme was Seint Donstone borne; he regned xvj yere, and lieth at
Malmesburye.   ᵃAftyr hym reyned hys brother Edmonde, and he Edmonde.
reyned vj yere, and lyeth at Glastynbery.

After him renge his broþer Eddrede; he regned ix yere, and lythe Eddrede.
at Wynchestre.

After him regned his broþer Edwyn, crowned at Kyngeston; Edwyne.
and whan he hade regned iiij yere he died, and lieth at Wynchester,
the yere of our Lorde ixc.lxj.

After Edwyne regnid his sonne Edgare, and crowned at Kynge- Edgare.
ston, the wheehe was a gode kynge and a worthi; and in his tyme
regned the doughti knyght Beves of Hampton.   And whan this
gode kyng had regned xvj yere he dyed, and lieth at Glastonburye.

After Edgar regnid his sonne Edward the Secounde, a gode Edwardus ijᵘˢ an
kynge and an holy; and in the iiij yere of his regne his step Conquestum.
                                                           Iste erat martira
moder lete him be marterd, and lieth at Shaftisberye, the yere of (sic).
our Lord ixc.iiijˣˣ primo.

After hym regned his broþer Etheldrede, crowned at Kyngeston, Etheldrede.
and he had a sonne that hight Edmonde Irenside.   And in his
tyme come Kynge Sweyne of Denmarke in to þe londe for to
conquer this londe.   And Kynge Etheldred fled into Normandye,
and ther he wedded the Dukes doughter, and begate on hir ij
sonnes, Alured and Edwarde, and after came a yene in to Engelonde This Edward is ᵗ
with his iij sonnes and conquered the lond a yene of the Danes, holy Kyng and
                                                                Confessour.
and afterward levid in pees; and so he regned al most xxxv yere,
and lith at London at Poules.

Aftir him regned his sonne Edmond Irensyde, the therd Edmond Edmond Irensyd
of Engelonde, and he regned after his fader all moste ij yere.   And iijᵘˢ Edmundus
                                                                    Anglie.
after that he was slayne, sone after that his fader was dede, through
a false Dane that hight Edryght of Stratton; and than he was
heryed at Glastonburye, the yere of our Lorde Mˡxvijᵉ.

ᵃ This sentence is added in by the hand of the marginal annotator.

te Edmond
ydes sones.

After hym regned Kynge Knotte, the whiche was a Dane, and he sent over the see to Denmarke þe twoo brothers Edward and Edwyne, the whiche were right eyres of Engelonde ther to be distroyed. And Edward went him in to Hungerye, and ther he wedded the kynges doughter; and for he was exiled oute of Englonde, he was called Edward the Outelawe. And whan that Kynge Knought had regned xix yere he dyed, and lithe at Wynchester.

The yere of our Lorde M¹ quatragesimo secundo tunc erat a Nativitate Jesu Christi usque ad regnum Sancti Edwardi regis et confessoris.

Fluxerunt divisum[a] in Anglia centum et septaginta[a] quinque reges, de quibus Oswynus, Oswaldus, Ethelbristes,[a] Kenelmus, Edmundus, Edwardus, martinizati;[a] Constans, Edwaldus, Sebertus, Wynfridus, Etheldredus, Edbertus, Offa and[a] Kynredus in monachatum sepulti, anno M¹xl.

tus Edwardus et
essor fuit primus
ıs rex in
'lia], et fuit iijᵘˢ
Edwardus ante
[u]estum. Tamen
Alver[edus]
ınctus ante h[ac]
ıapam Leonem
' in Roma.

After the dethe of Kynge Knoght the Englisshe men wolde not suffre the Danes no more to regne in Engelonde, but drove hem oute of this londe. And than was the gode holy man Seint Edward the Confessoure crowned Kynge of Engelonde; and in the ij yere of his regne he was crowned at Wynchester, the yere of our Lord M¹xlijᵉ. And he was the fyrst anoynted kynge that ever was in Engelande, and he regned well and worthely; and he did make many gode statutes and lawes, the whiche ben used yette in this londe; and he wedded a wyfe and levyde in clennes and virginite all his lyffe, and so he dyed, and lith at Westmester shryned. The forsaide gode Kynge Edwarde regned here xxv yere, the yere of Lorde M¹lxvᵉ.

Haraldus.

After the dethe of Seint Edward, Harolde, Duke of Westsex, that was Godewynes sonne, a Dane, had sesed al Englonde in to his honde a yene the right. And therfor he regned but a while for his untrouthe, for he was sworne upon a boke that he shulde have wedded Duke Williams bastard doughter of Normandye, and

ᵃ Sic in MS.

Harolde shulde have kepte the realme of Engelond to Duke Williams be hove, but Harolde seised alle in his owne hondis, and therfor Duke William conquered the londe of him and slowe him in bataille in the seconde yere of his regne in a felde beside Tonbrygge. And Kynge Haroll lithe buryed in the abbaye of Waltham, the yere of our Lord M'lxij. And the bataill was done upon Seynt Kalixtes daye, &[c]

After him regned William Bastarde that was Duke of Normandy, the whiche conquered all Engelond, and discomfide all the Danes, and drove hem oute of England, and after conquered all Scotland, and made the Kynge of Scottis his liege man. And he was crowned at Westminster on Cristmas day; and whan he had regned xvij yere, þo he made William Rouse his secunde sonne Kynge of Engelond,[a] and him selfe went in to Normandye and levid there iiij yere after; and tho he fell seke and dyed, and lithe beryed at Cane in Normandye.

Willelmus Conquestor.

William Rowse i filius, dyed w'ow yssue.

Aftir him regned his sonne William the Rous, the whiche was crowned at Westmester by his faders lyve, the yere of our Lorde M'lxxxvj[e]; whiche kynge was a contraryous man bothe to God and to Holy Chirche, for he distroyed and kest downe xxvj townes and lij chirches and houses of religion for to make the Newe Forest; and after he was slayne with an arowe in the same forest, the xxiij yere of his regne, and lieth at Wynchester.

The iij[de] sone of Wylliam Conqu(was callyd Rych whiche decesyd.

After him regned his brother Henry Bewclek, the iiij sonne of William Conquerour, the whiche is called the first kynge Henry of Engelonde, and he was crowned at Westmester the v day of August, the yere of our Lord M'.C. Anone after he spoused Dame Maude, Kynge Matelyns[b] doughter, of Scotlond, and upon hir he begate ij sonnes, William and Richarde, and a doughter, the whiche was maryed to the Emperour of Almayne. And after the kynges ij

Henricus Primu: iiij[us] filius.

---

[a] In the margin occurs the following note by another hand: "Robert Curthos primogenitus cui Willelmus Conquestor in sua morte reliquit sibi totam Normaniam, ut habetur in alia cronica."

[b] Malcolm.

sonnes were drevyn over the see in a tempest of weder. And when
Kynge Henry the First had regned almoste xxxv yere he dyed and
lithe heryed at the abbaye of Redynge, wherof he was founder, the
yere of M¹.C.

After him regned his nevewe Stephen, the which was kynge
Herryes sister sonne, an erlis sonne of Boleyn, and he was crowned
at Westmester anone after that his uncle Kynge Henry was dede;
and that was no right; for Henry the empres sonne shulde have be
kynge after the right rule and lyne, and therfor was grete stryfe be-
tw[e]ne hem; and whan Kynge Stephen had regned all moste xix
yere he died and lieth at Feversain. After Kynge Stephen regnyd

Henry the Secunde, that was the Empresse sonne, and he was
crowned at Westmester on the day of Conception of Our Lady by
for Cristmas the yere of our Lorde M¹.C.liiij. And in the xvj yere of

his regne was Seynt Thomas, at that tyme Archebisshope of Caunterbery, marterd for the right and feythe of Holy Chirche, the yere
of our Lor M¹clxxj^e. This Henry helde a paramour besyde the
quene, the whiche was called Rosamoundes Bowre. And by the
quene he had ij sonnes, Richard was the first, and John was the
secunde. And when he had regned xxxv yere he dyed in Fraunce,
and lieth at Fownte Everrard, the yere of our Lorde M¹ciiij^xxix^e.

After him regned his sonne Richarde the Fyrst, the whiche was
called Richard the Conquerour, and he was crowned at Westmester
sone after his faders disses, and after he wente into the Holy Londe
with a grete oste of peple, and ther he werred upon the hethen
folke and gate ayene all that Cristen men had lost a for tyme; and
as this worthi conquerour came homwarde he mett with his enmyse
at the Castell Gaylarde, for ther he was shott with a quarell and
died in the x yere of his regne, and he was buryed at Fownte
Everarde be side his fader, the yere of oure Lorde M¹.C.iiij^xxxix, and
died withoute yssewe.

Aftir Kynge Richarde the Fyrst regnid his brother John, that
ever was a contraryous man to God and to Holy Chirche and to all
the comyn peple, and therfor all Englond was enterdited for vij

yere; and in his tyme Seint Hewe of Lyncole diede. And in his tyme was lost myche londe of Gascoyne, Brettayne, and Normandy. And in his tyme was grete derthe, for a peny lofe was worthe xij^d; and for his wekid rede a monke of the Abbay of Swyneshede yave him poyson to drynke, and so he died in the xviij yere of his regne, and lieth at Worcester, the yere of our Lord M^lCCxvj^e.

The yere of our Lord M^lc[c]iiij^{xx}xviij was the fundacioun of the Fre[re] Prechores.

The yere of our Lorde M^lCCvj was the fundacioun of the order off the Frere Menures.

After the dethe of Kynge John was crowned his son Kyng Henry the Therde, at Glowceter, on Seint Symons day and Jude, of a legct of Rome that hight Swalowe,^a that come into Englond to make peece be twene Lowes of Fraunce and Kynge Henrye; and in the iiij yere of his regne he was crowned at Westmester, of the Erehebisshope of Caunterbery, by the comen assent of all the lordes of Englonde; and in the same yere was Seint Thomas of Caunterberye translated; and in the yere of grace M^lCCxx^e, and in the xlviij yere of his regne, began the werre betwene Kynge Herry and his lordes of the realme for diverse causes for the comyne wele of England, and therfor was the batayle at Lewes on Seint Pancras daye in May; and ther Sir Symonde Momford, Erle of Leycester, had the victorye; and in that battaylle the kinge him selfe was taken, and Sir Edwarde his sonne; and Syr Richarde, Earle of Cornwayle, that was the kynges brother, and many other lordis were in warde of the forsaide Sir Symonde. And the nexte yere after thatt^b and the next yere after that^b aboute the myddis of August was the batayll of Evessham be twene Kynge Henry and the barones of this londe, and ther was slayne Sir Symond Moundford and his sonne and many other lordis, and in the lvij yere of his reg[n]e he died, and lieth at Westmester, on Seynt Edmondis day M^lCCxiij.

Aftir Kynge Henry regned his sone Edwarde the First with

[margin:] Translacio Sancti Thome Martiris, Anno Domini 1½

[margin:] Batyl of Ewssh[

[margin:] Edwardus Primr post Conquestum

---

^a Gualo.　　　　　　^b So in MS., repeated.

the longe
:ys.

longe shankes, the whiche was crowned at Westmestre sone after his
faders death in the yere of grace м¹cclxxiiij.

This Kynge Edwarde was a gracious man, for wher so ever he
came in any londe he had the victorye of his enemyes ; and he toke
homage of Kynge Elysaundre of Scotlonde, and discomfyde Newlyn
Preince of Walis, and conquered all the londe, and toke Irlonde in to
his honde.   And by his first wyfe he hade a sonne that was called
Edwarde of Carnervan ; after that died the quene.   And tho he
spowsed Quene Margerett, Kynge Phelippes sister of Fraunce ; and
upon hir he begatte ij sonnes, Thomas Bretherton, Erle Marchall,
and Emond of Wodstoke his broþer.   And when he had regned well
and worthely all moste xxxv yere he died, and lithe at Westmester
м¹cccvijᵉ.

Anno Domini м¹cccvj, Invencio nove solempnitatis Corporis
Christi.

rdus ijᵘˢ post
uestum.

After him regnid his sonne Edward of Carnarvan, and he was
crowned at Westmester the xx daie of Feverell in the yere of
our Lorde м¹cccvijᵉ.   And in the same yere he spoused Isabell,
Kyng Phelippes doughter of Fraunce, in the chirche of Bolayne,
and he broȝt hir in to Englond.   And in the same yere folowinge

uccio Templari-

were the Templers dist[r]oied thorowe all Cristendome for hir
mysbeleve and untrowith that they used.

Anone after Robert le Bruse, Kynge of Scotland, came oute of
Northe Wales with a grete pussaunce of peple and werred sore in
Northehomberlonde and distroyed all the contrey.   And than Kynge
Edward was scomfide and put to flight and many of his lordis
slayne, for ther was so grete nombre of Scottis, x men ayenest one
Englisshe man.   The batayll was upon Seint Johns daye Baptist, in
the yere of our Lord м¹cccxijᵉ yere, and in the vᵉ yere of his

rdus Tertius

regne.   And in the same yere was borne at Wyndesore Edward the
Thred, upon Seint Brieis daye.   And in the xv yere of his regne fell
grete debate be twene the kynge and the gode lordis of this lond
for thei helden with the comyne wele of þe lond.   Wherfor Sir

us Thomas
Lancastrie
atus.

Thomas, the gode Erle of Lancaster, was be heded at Pomfrett, and
many oþer barons and knyghtes for the same cause, and all

through the false counsell of the Spencers, the fader and the
sonne, the whiche were the robbers of this londe. And in the
same yere fell a grete derthe in this londe, for a quarter of whete ^{Quarterium frum}
was solde for xls., the yere of our Lord M^lCCCxxj^e. After that, ^{xl s.}
by false counsaill off the Spencers, Kynge Edward exiled Quene
Isabelle his wiffe, and Sir Edwarde his eldest sonne, oute of
Englond, and went in to Fraunce; and after that thei came a yene
in to Englond with a grete strenthe of people. And Sir John
Hennawde, the erles brother of Hennawde, come with hem with
all the power that he myght to strenthe hem in right; and thei
londed fast by Herwiche in Southefolke; tho all the contre fell
to them and held with hem to distroye the venym of London.
And anone thei toke the kynges counsellours, that is to sey, the
fader and sonne called the Spencers and Maister Robert Baldok, a
fals peled clerke, that was chaunceler of Englond. And Maister
Water Stapilton, that was þo Bysshoppe of Exceter and Tresourere
of Engelond, and þe Erle of Arondell, and many oþer that was
consent to them, thei were done to dethe in sondrye wise, some
hanged and quarterd and some beheded. And so by counsayll of
all the lordis of Englond, Kynge Edwarde of Carnarvan was
deposed and put downe of his kyngdome, in the yere of our Lorde
M^lCCCxxvj^e, in the xix yere of his regne.

And anone after that was Kyng Edward the Thred of Wyndsore ^{Edwardus iij[clu}
crowned at Westmester the first day of Feverell, and in the xv yere ^{post Conquestun}
of his age; and this Kynge Edwarde was called the floure of knyghte-
hode of all Cristendome. And in the same yere, through counsell of
Quene Isabell and Sir Roger Mortymer, was Sir Edward of Carnarvan
broȝt from the castell of Kyllingworthe to Berkle, and fro thens to
the castell of Corffe; and ther he was mortherd betwene ij feþer
beddis, and an hote brenynge spitt put in his fondement, and so
brent his bodi with in; and that was on Seint Matheus daye in
Septembre; and tho was he enterred at Glowceter. And in the
nexte yere folowynge Kynge Edward spowsed Quene Phelippe, the
Erles doughter of Hennawde, at Yorke, upon the feste of Conver-
cion of Seint Poule, the yere of our Lord M^lCCCxxvij^o. And

while Kynge Edward was of tender age he suffred many prejudice done in Engelonde, for Quene Isabell and Sir Roger Mortymer ruled all Engelond as hem liked. But aftir King Edward redressed hit full wele bi his discrete counsell, and chastesid the traytors and the rebellis of Englond full wele and manfully. And in the third yere of his regne, Edmond of Wodstok, that was the kynges uncle, was be hedid at Wynchestre wrongfully, and all throwe Sir Roger Mortymer that was late made Erle of Marche; and sone aftir, for his grete covetise and falshede that he did to al the realme, he was drawen and hanged at Tiborne upon Seint Andres evyn, the v yere of his regne. After that, he went in to Scotlond, and conqured a yene all þe fewte and homage that the Scottes owid to the crowne off Englond. And in the vj yere of his regne was the batayle at Hayldon Hill besides Berwyk; and at that batayle was slayne xxxvm¹vijᶜ and xij of Scottes and nombred by herawdes, and of Englissh men but xxvij persones, thanked be God, for this was a grete victorye. And this was upon Seint Margaretes even, the yere of our Lorde m¹cccxxxij. And after that he conquered all Scotlond, and made the Kynge of Scottes his liege man, to do him fewte and homage as he ought of right. And in the xiiij yere of his regne Kynge Edwarde made him redy with a grete nombre of peple for to go in to Fraunce, for to chalange the crowne be. right tytell and erytaunce by his moder Quene Isabell. And Kynge Karoll died with oute issewe, and Phelipp Valeys, his emys sonne, ocupyed the crowne ayenes right. And so Kynge Edward and his oste were shipped taward Fraunce, and thought to lande in Flaundres ther as Phelippe of Valoys was with grete navye of dyverse nacions. And so Kynge Edward and his oste aryved with his navy in the haven of Skluse. And the viij day off Julii ther was a grete bataylle, and ther was slayne of the Frensshe partye xxxm¹ men, and oure kynge toke þer many grete shippis and cogges and hulkes. And so that tyme Kynge Edwarde hade a gracious victory, in the yere of our Lord m¹cccxl. And in the xviij yere of his regne the kynge made his eldest sonne Edward, Prince of Walys, Duke of Corn-wayle and Erle of Chester. And in the xxj yere of his regne wa

the bataylle of Cressey, the xxvj daye of August. Ther were slayne
and take many grete lordis of Fraunce, and the Frensshe kynge
was put to flight, the yere of our Lorde M^{l}cccxlvj^{ti}. And in the
therday of Septembre nexte folowing Kynge Edward laide sege to
Calys, the whiche contenewed unto the iij daye of August, the
nexte yere after, and than hit was yelden up for evir, bothe towne
and castell, the yere M^l.iijc.xlvij^{ti}. And in the same yere duringe
the sege was the Kynge off Scottes sore werrynge in Englond, and
robbed and revid the contre aboute Derham; and so ther was taken
Kynge David of Scotlonde, the Erle Mountyf, Sir William Douglas,
and many oþer, the whiche were brought to the Toure of London;
and than was the Kynge of Scotlonde taxed at an c.m^l. marke to be
paid in x yere daye. And in the nexte yere after was the grete
pestilence at London, from Michelmas to Lammas. And in the
xxv yere of his regne ther was a grete bataill on the see with the
Spaynardes upon the coste of Wynchilsey, and ther were taken
xxiiij^{ti} grete shippis off Spayne. And in the xxviij yere of his
regne was a corde made be twene Kyng Edward and the Frensshe
kynge, so that he shulde have Normandye, Gascoyne, and Gyane
in pees. And anone after died Phelippe of Valeys. Tho was his
sonne John made Kynge of Fraunce, and he did myche harme in
Gascoyne, and distroyed all the contre. Tho went Prince Edward
to Burdeux for to kepe the contrey. After the one and therty yere
of his regne was the bataylle of Peyters, the xx day of Septembre;
and ther was taken Kynge John of Fraunce and Phelipp his sonne,
and many oþer lordis, the whiche Prince Edward brought in to
Englond to Kyng Edwarde his fader; the whiche Kyng John
was taxed at iij melyons of scutis, that is to sey, vc.m^l.$li.$ of mony.
And in the xxxiiij yere of his regne Syr John off Gawnte, Erle of
Rychemond, that was Kyng Edwardes therde sonne, spoused Dame
Blanche, Duke Henryes doughter of Lancastre, by dispensacion of
the Pope, the xiiij day of Julij, and than was made pees be twene
Englond and Fraunce. And the nexte yere after was the grete
wynde upon Seynt Maurys daye in June, A^o M^l.cccxlj. Also the

same yere be for the grete wynde was þe secunde pestilence, in the
whiche died the noble man and myghty Harry, Duke of Lancaster.
And than was Sir John of Gaunte, Erle of Rychemond, made Duke
of Lancaster, for he hade spowsed Duke Henry doughter.   And in
the same yere Prynce Edward spoused the Countes of Kentt; also
in þe same yere Sir Lionell, Kynge Edwardes sonne, was made
Duke of Clarence, and Sir Edmond of Langley was made Duke of
Yorke, and Sir Thomas Wodstok was made Duke of Glowcester.
Alle thes v lordes were Kyng Edwardis sonnes.   And in the xxxix
yere of his regne came iij kynges in to this londe for to speke with
Kyng Edward, that is to sey, the kynge of Siprys, the kynge of
Fraunce, and the Kynge of Scotlond; and in the same yere died
Kyng John off Fraunce, in Engelonde, at Savoye, in þe Dukis
place of Langastre.   And in the xlj yere of his regne was Richard
Prince Edwardes sonne, born at Burduex; and in the xliij yere of
Kynge Edwarde dyed that noble Quene Philippe of Englond, and
lithe at Westmester enterred, the yere of oure Lord M¹ccc.lxix.
And in the same yere was a grete derthe in Engelond, a busshell of
whete was worthe xl d.   Also the xlvij yere of his regne the Duke
of Lancaster spoused the kynges doughter of Spayne, and the Duke
of Yorke spoused that oþer doughter.   And in the l. yere of his
regne dyed the noble Preince Edwarde, the viij day of Jun, in the
feste of the Trinite, and lieth at Caunterbury.   And in the nexte
yere folowynge died the noble conquerour Kynge Edwarde the iijᵉ,
of Wyndsore, flour of knyghthode, at Shene the xxj daye of June,
and lieth worthely enterred at Westmester, in the yere of our Lorde
M¹ccclxxvjᵉ.

·dus ijᵘˢ, filius
ιrdi Tercii.ᵃ
And in the lj yere of his regne regned Richard the Secounde,
the whiche was Prince Edwardis sonne after the right lyne, and he
was crowned kynge at Westmester the xvj day of Julij, in the yere

ᵃ The annotator here commits the gross blunder of representing Richard II. as
the son, instead of grandson, of Edward III.; and, not content with this inaccuracy
in the margin, he has written over " Prince Edwardis sonne " in the text the words
" Edwardus iijᵘˢ " above the line.

a forseyde, at the age of xj. And whiles the kynge was in yonge age certeyn lordis of the realmo ruled the londe as hem list; and so thei made an ordenaunce amonge hem in the iiij yere of his regne that every man, woman, and childe in this londe of the age of xiiij yere and above shulde paye to tallage iiij d., pore man and other; the whiche ordenaunce was cause of myche trouble and sorowe in this londe. Wherfor anone after in the somer folowinge for the comyns of this londe a resyn up in diverse parties of the realme and deden myche harme, the whiche was called the hurlyng tyme, The Hurlyng tyr the yere of our Lord M^l.CCC.lxxxj^e.

And the comenys of Kent and Essex rysen up and gaderd hem togeder, and came to London the xiiij day of Junij, and as it fell in the yere hit was the Fridaye after Corpus Christi daye, and they toke Sir Symond Sudbery, Erchebisshoppe of Caunterburye, and Sir Robert Halis, Priour of Seint Johnis, and a White Frere, that was the kynges confessore, and other mo, and brought hem to the Toure Hill and smoten of her hedis, and come a yene to London, and slowe men of lawe and false juges, and all the alyauntes that thei couthe owher fynde, and smoten of her hedis and toke awey ther godis, and wenten to Savey and distroyed and wasted all that was ther, and sett fyre on the place when they went, and dedyn moche harme in many placis with in the cite and with oute at Westmester; thei sparid none. And this horlynge endured iij dayes, and no man durst sett upon hem, the nombre was so grete. And þe Monday folowing William Walworthe, that tyme being Meyre Wylliam Walwo slow Jak Strawe of London, slowe Jack Strawe with his owne hondes, and lete smyte of his hede, and set it on London Brigge. And a none, as the capteyn was dede, every man fled a wey as hit had never ben thei. And the v yere of his regne Kynge Richard spoused Quene Anne, the kynges doughter of Beam and Emperour of Almayne, apon Seint Fabian and Sebastians daye, in the Abbaye of West-mester. And upon Seint Vincentes daye^a nexte folowynge she was

---

^a After "Seint Vincentes daye" about a line and a-half is crossed out, beginning "of May was the Erthe quake." The erased words occur in the text immediately below; which shows that the MS. is here a copy and that the transcriber had missed a line.

crowned. And in the same yere, the xxj daye of May, was the erthequake, the Wenesday a for Witsonday, the yer of our Lord M¹.CCC.lxxxij^ti. And in the nexte yere folowing Syr Richard Spencer, Bysshuppe of Norwyche, went over the see in to Flaundres with holy water stickys, and ther he gate the towne of Gravenyng, Borborowe, Dunkerk, and Newporte. And ther was done a grete bataylle be twene the Englisshe men and the Flemynges, but the Englisshe men had the victorye. And in the xj yere of Kynge Richarde v lordis of Englond a ryssen at Ratcote to brynge in the discenccion the rebellis þat were that tyme in the realme. The first was Sir Thomas of Wodstok, the kynges uncle and Duke of Gloucester, and Sir Richard, Erle of Arondell, and Sir Richard Erle of Warwyk, Sir Henry Bolyngbrok, Erle of Derby, and Sir Thomas Moubraye, Erle of Notyngham. And these v lordes seynge the myschefe and falssed of the Kynges Counsell, these v lordes thought to amend hit, and a none the chefe lordes of the kynges counsell fled over the see; that is to say, Sir Elysander Nevell, Erchebisshuppe of Yorke, and Sir Robert Vere, Marques of Develyn, the Erle of Oxenford, and Sir Michell Poole, Erle of Southefolk, and Chaunseler of Englond. And thes lordes went over the see and came no more a yene, for ther they dyed; sone after was Sir Robert Tresylyan, justice, Sir Nicoll Brembre, knyght and alderman of London, and Sir John Salysbury, knyght of the kynges householde, and Thomas Huske, sergeauntes of armes, and Thomas Blake, clerke of the kynges house, were drawen, hanged, and by heded at Tiborne. And Sir Symonde Beverle, a knyght of the garter, and Sir John Bechamp, knyght and stiward of the kynges housholde, a[nd] Sir James Berners, and oþer mo were be hedid at the Toure Hill. And in the xvij yere of his renge dyed the Quene Anne in þe maner of Shene upon Witsondaye, and lithe at Westmester, the yere of our Lord M¹.CCC.iiij^xx^xiiij^e.

And in the xx yere of his regne Kyng Richarde spoused Queue Isabell the kynges doughter of Fraunce in the towne of Caleys, and after she was brought in to Englond and crowned at Westmester the Sonday after Seint Clementes daye. And the xxv day of August nexte folowynge, by evill exitacion and false counsell, and for pure malice that Kynge Richarde had to his uncle and to other lordes, he rode to Plaschey, and ther Kyng Richard a rested hem with his owne bandes, Sir Thomas of Wodstock Duke of Glowcester, and comaunded him to Caleys, and there he was morthered betwene ij feder beddes; and on Seint Matheus day nexte after was Sir Richard, the gode Erle of Aroundell, be heded at the Toure Hill, and Sir Richard Erle of Warwyk and the Lorde Cobham were dampned at Westmester to perpetuell preison.   And in the same yere fell grete dissencion be twene the Erle of Derby and Sir Henry Bolyng-broke, the whiche was made Duke of Herfford, and the Erle Marchall, that was newe made Duke of Northefolke for serteyne poyntes, in so myche they waged batayll to have fought with in listes, and ther place was assigned at Coventre where þe batayll shulde be.   But at the last the kynge of his gode grace toke hit in his honde and wolde not suffre hem to fyght, but exiled the Duke of Herfford for the term of x yere and the Duke of Northfolke for ever.   And Sir Thomas Aroundel, Erchebisshuppe off Caunterbury, deposyd of his cee and exiled for ever.   Tho went thes lordes in to dyverse londes.   And a none Kyng Richard sett all Englond to ferme to iiij persones, to Sir William Scrowpe,[a] Busshe, Bagott, and Grene, the whiche broȝt in myche tene.   And Kyng Richard went him selffe in to Irelond.   Anone came tidynges in to Fraunce to Sir Henry Bollyngbroke whate governaunce was in Engelond, and anone he came downe to Caleys with his meyne that he had, and met ther with Sir Thomas of Arondell, þat was Erchebysshuppe of Caunterbery, and cam over the see in to Englond a yene, and londed at Ravonspor in the northe contre.   And when thei were londed all the contre fell downe to them and were joifull of his comynge in helpinge of hem and destroyenge of the fals rule and governaunce of the londe.   This was in the xxij yere of the regne of Kynge

[a] The original text read "Sir John Busshe;" but "John" is crossed through and "Wylliam Scrowpe" inserted in the margin by another hand, with a caret in the text after the cancelled word.

Richard.   Than came he home oute of Irlond in haste, and come
to the Castell of Flyntt, and thought to take his counsell whate was
best to done.   Anone all is men forsoke him and lefte him alone.
Tho was Kynge Richarde taken and doen in warde in the Toure
of London, and by comon assent of al the lordis of Englonde he
was deposed and put downe of this riall realme and kyngdome.
Tho he was put in to the Castell of Pomffrett and kept full streyte
terme of his lyfe.   And than was Sir William Scrowpe, Busshe,
Baggott, and Grene were done to dethe for her false covetise.[a]   Aftir
the deposinge of Kynge Richard the ij[de], Henry of Bolyngbrok, Erle of
Derby, Duke of Herford, and Duke of Lancaster, by all the Comyns

icus iiij[tus]

assent was made kynge for his worthines.   And so Henry the iiij[e]
was crowned at Westmester upon Seint Edwardis daye in Octobre,
the yere of our Lord M[l].CCC.iiij[xx]xix[e].   And a none after he made
Henry his eldist sonne Prince of Walys, Duke of Cornwayle and
Erle of Chester.   And in the fyrst yere of his regne Kynge Richard
died in the Castell of Poumffrett and was beryed at Langeley.   On
whose soule God have mercy.   And in the same yere the Duke of
Surrey, the Duke of Excester, the Erle off Salisbury, the Erle of
Glowcester, and oþer moo of ther affynite were accorded to sle the
kynge at Cristmas a twelffe nyght, with a momynge at Wyndsore.
But the kynge had knowlech ther of, and came to London in haste.
And thes lordes wiste wele that they were be wrayed and fled awaye,
and after they were taken and put to dethe.

William Conquerour.[b]

iam Conqueroure
ɔd xxj yere.

This myghti William, Duke of Normandie, as bokes olde maketh
mencion, be juste title and by chevalrye made kynge be conquest

---

[a] There is no stop here in the MS. the punctuation of which is evidently wrong.
The sentence ends with "Kynge Richard," the words "the ij[de]" being added by the
corrector's hand.   A mark is also put to indicate the beginning of a new sentence at
"Henry of Bolyngbrok."

[b] What follows is a corrupt text of Lydgate's Verses on the Kings of England
which I printed from another MS. in "Collections of a London Citizen" edited for
the Camden Society in 1876.   They are here printed precisely as they stand in this M

of Brutes Albyon, put oute Harrolde and toke possession, and bare
the crowne full xxj yere, buryed at Cane, thus saithe the crone-
klere.

Next in ordre succession William Ruffus, his sonne, crowned Wylliam Rufus
kynge with gode devocion, distroyed chirches of olde and newe yere.
bildinge for to make a forest plesaunt for huntynge; xiiij yere he
bare his crowne in dede; beryed at Wynchester, in the cronekle ye
may rede.

His broþer nexte, called the fyrst Henrye, was at London Herry the fyrst,
crow[n]ed kynge, as y fynde, whose broþer Robert, Duke of Nor- xxxiij yere.
maudye, be ganne on him to werre, the cronycle maketh mynde.
Reconciled, all rancoure sett be hynde, full xxxiij, be record of
writynge, yerys he regned; beryed at Redynge.

His cosyne Stephen, whan first Henry was dede, tawarde Eng- Stephyn, xix ye
lond can crosse his sayle; the Erchebysshope sett upon his hede a
riche crowne, beynge of his counsell; xix yere with sorowe and
grete travaile he bare his crowne, had he no rest; at Feversham
lithe heryed in his cheste.

Harry the Secounde, sonne to thEmpryse, was crowned nexte, Herry the ij^de, x
a full manly knyght, as bokes olde playnly dothe expresse; this yere.
saide Henry, be forwarde forse and myghte, slowe Seint Thomas for
Holy Chirche right; xxxv yere reyned, hit is made in mynde. Att
Fownt Everard lythe beryd, as I fynde.

Richard his sonne, next be succession, fyrst of that name, stronge, Richarde the fyr
hardy, and notable, was crowned kinge; called Cure de Lyon, with cal[led] Cure de
Lyon, ix yere.
Sarsyne hedis servid at his table; slayne at Gayliarde by deth full
lementable; the space of him regned fully ix yere; his herte beryed
at Rome^a at the high autere.

Nexte Kynge Richard regned his broþer John; after sone entred Kyng John, xvii
into Fraunce, lost Anjoye and Normandy anone. This londe entir- yere.
lited by his governaunce, and, as it is put in remembraunce, xviij
yers was kyng of this region; lithe at Worseter, dede with poyson.

Hanry the iij^e, his sonne, of ix yere of age, was at Glouceter Herry the iij^de,
lv[j yere].

^a So in MS., instead of Rone, i. e. Rouen.

crowned, as I rede; longe werr he had with his baronage, gretly delited in almesdede; lvj yere he regned I rede; beryed at Westmester, by recorde of writinge. The day of Seint Edward was made kynge.

ırde the fyrs[t,] ' yere, with the ̣ sh[ankes].

Edward the First, with shankes longe, was after crowned, that was a gode knyght; wanne Scotlond, magry the Scottes stronge; and all Walis, spite of her myght; durynge his lyve manteyne trouthe and right; xxxv yere he was kynge; lithe at Westmester for trouthe and no lesynge.

ırd the ij^{de}, d Edwar[de of] arv[on], xix

Edward, his sonne, called Carnarvan, succedinge after to make his alyaunce, as the cronekyll will recorde, wedded the doughter of the Kynge of Fraunce. Thomas Lancaster, by dethe he toke vengaunce; xix yere helde he his rigalye. Beryed at Glowcester as bokes specefie.

arde the iij^d, lij

The iij^e Edward, borne at Wyndsore, myche in knyght hode he hade gre preise; enherytor of Fraunce, with outen more, bare in his armes iij lyons and iij floures de lyse. And he gate Caleys with his prudent devyse. Regned in Englond lij^a yere, lyth at Westmester, this seith the Cronecle[re].

ıarde the ij^{de}, yere.

Sonne to Prince Edwarde, Kynge Richard the ij. In whose tyme was pees and plenty. Wedded Quene Anne, of Almayne, as it is fownde; Isabell of Fraunce, who lust to see; xxij yere, he regned here parde. At Langley buryed first, so stode the case. After to Westmester his body caryed was.

y the iiij^{th}, xiiij

Harry the fourthe, nexte crowned in certeyne, a famouse knyght and of grete semblenesse, from his exile whan he came home agayne, travaylled after with wer and grete sekenes; xiiij yere regned in sothnesse. Buryed at Caunterbery, in that holy place God of his mercy do his soule grace.

y the vth, ix yere.

The v^e Henrye, of knyghthode lodester, wyse and right manly to termyne right. Fortunate preved in pees and werre. Erthly expert and mercyall displyn, worthi to stonde a monge the worthie

---

a Corrected into "lj," the "i" being erased with the knife.

ix. Regned ix yere, who list have rewarde; lieth at Westmester not far from Seint Edwarde.

Harry the vj^e, crowned at Westmester and at Paryse; in his yonthe he had grete noblenes, bothe in Englond and Fraunce; and in his last daies ther fell grete distaunce through his false counsell that was covetowse, he was put downe from the crowne by all the comyns. So he regned kynge here all moste xxxix yere. Herry the vj^{to}, x yere.

The names of the Kepers and Baylyffes of the Cite of London in the tyme of Kynge Richarde the fyrst, the whiche was crowned iij daye of Septembre. Ricardus Primus

Henry Cornhill, Richard Remer, Baylyves A° primo.

The same day of the kynges coronacion all the Jewes that were fownde or myght be take were distroyed as well be nyght as by day.

John Herlyon, Roger Duke, Baylyves A° ij.

William Averyll, John Boknott, Bayllives A° iij^e.

Nicholas Dukett, Peter Newlyn, Bailyves the iiij^e yer.

Roger Dewke, Richard Aleyn, B. the v yere.

William FitzIsabell, William FitzArnulff, B. the vj.

The same yere the kynge comyng homard warde from Jerusalem was take wythe the Duke of Ostrych and was rawnsoned, and for to pay his rawnson enche other chalis throwe this londe was coyned in mouye.

Robert Besaunt, Jokerell Josue, Baylives the vij.

Gerrard Antilache, Robert Durant, B. the viij.

Roger Blont, Nicholas Dukett, B. the ix^e.

Costotinus Arnulff, Robert Lovell, B. þ^e x^e yere.

This yere dyed Kynge Richard, and lythe at Powntlarge.

The names of the Kepers and Baylyves in Kynge Johns tyme, the Assencion daye of our Lorde at Westmester. Rex Johaunes.

Arnolde Arnulffsone, Richard Darthy, B. þ^e j yere.

This yere the kynge had of every plowelond in þis lond iij s.

Roger Dosett, Jamys Darthy, B. the ij yere.

This yere died Seint Hugh of Lyncolne.

Water FizAlis, Simond Alderman, B. the iij yere.

Norman Blonden, John Ely, B. the iiijᵉ.

This yere Englond and Walys was enterdited, the whiche dured v yere.

Water Browne, William Chamburlayne, B. þᵉ v yere.

Thomas Averyll, Hamonde Bronde, B. the vjᵉ.

This yere began the Order of Frere Prechurs.

John Waldgrave, Richard Wynchestre, B. the vijᵉ.

John Holylonde, Edmond Gerrard, B. viijᵉ.

Roger Wychester, Edmond Hardell, B. ix.

This yere Henry the kynges sonne was borne, and the enter-dityng sessed.

' Regis Johannis,
o Domini 1210.
All presentes that was Kepers and Baylyves at that tyme were put downe, and chosyn Mayr and Shoreffes for the Cite of London.

us major, quia
fuerunt ballivi.

| Harry Allwyn, Mayr | Petyr Duke
Thomas Nell | Shoryffis | xᵒ. |

This yere the chirche of Seint Mary Overes was fyrst fownded.

iij.

| Harry Alwyn, Meir | Petir Joswe
William Glond | the xjᵉ. |
| | Adam Wittley
Stephen Legras | the xijᵉ. |

This yere the kynge wente in to Irelonde, and made the rebelles sogetis to hym.

iiij.

| Harry Alwyn, Meir | Josevus Petresson
John Garlond | Aᵒ xiijᵉ. |

This yere Sowthewerke, London, the Brygge, and the most part of the Cite of London, was brent.

, iiij.

| Harry Alwyn, Meir | Raff Holylond
Costantyne Joswe | the xiiijᵉ. |

This yere the stone brygge was fyrste be gon, and Castell Baynarde destroyed.

ꝓ, iiiij.	Roger Aleyn, Meir	Martyn FizAlis Petyr Batte	the xvᶜ.
. jᵒ	Serle Mercer, Meir	Salman Basynge Hugh Basyng	þᵉ xvjᵉ.
	William Hardell, Meir	John Travers Hugh Basynge	þᵉ xvijᵉ.

This yere, the morne after Seint Lukys day, dyed Kyng John, and is beryed at Wursceter.

The name of the Meyres and Shoreffes of London in the renge Henricus iijᵘˢ of Kyng Henry the iijᵉ, the whiche was crowned at Glowcester in thest ᵃ of Simond and Jude.

Jacob Alderman, Meir	Benet Coventre William Blunttravers	þᵉ j.
Serle Mercer, Meir	Thomas Bokerell Rauff Holylond	Aᵒ ijᵉ.
Serle Mercer, Meir	John Wayle Josevus Spicer	þᵉ iijᵉ.

This yere the kynge had of every plowe londe ij s. And the same yere Seint Thomas of Caunterbery was translatyd, 1 yere aftir that he was martred.

Serle Mercer, Meyr	Richard Wymbyldey John Waylle	A. iiijᵉ.
	Richard Renger Josevus Ruff	Aᵒ vᶜ.
	Richard Rengee Josevus Ruff	Aᵒ vjᵉ.

This yere the kynge was in purpose to caste downe the wallys of London.

Serle Mercer, Meir	Richard Renger Thomas Lamberd	the vijᵉ.

ᵃ So in MS.

| Richard Renger, Mair | { William Joyner / Thomas Lambard | } the viij^e |

This yere came Frere Mynours first in to Englonde.

Richard Renger, Meyre	{ John Travers / Andrewe Bokerell	} þ^e ix.
	Roger Duke / Martyn FizWilliam	} the x^e.
	Stephen Bokerell / Harry Cobham	} the xj.

This yere all the weerys that were in Temmes were distroyed by the kynges ordynaunce. And the same yere the kynge graunted to the Cite of London waren.

| Roger Duke, Meir | { Stephen Bokerell / Harry Cobham | } A^o xij^e. ^{a} |

This yere the kynge grawnted that eche Shereffe of London sholde have ij Clerkis and ij Sergauntes and no moo. Also the kynge graunted to the Citezeynes of London that thei shulde have a Comyne Seale, þ^e whiche shulde be in kepynge of ij Aldermen and ij Com[en]ers of the seid Cite. And that the seid seale shuld not be denyed to any comener of the seide Cite whan hit is resonablye asked. And nothinge be taken for the seid seale, &c.

| Roger Duke, Maire | { Water Wynchester / Robert FizJohn | } A^o xiij^e. |
| Andrew Bokerell, Mair | { Richard Watyr / John Wouborne | } A. xiiij. |

This yere was ordeyned that from that day forwarde shold never after Shoreff of London be in Office lenger then one yere.

| And[r]ewe Bokerell, Meyre | { Mighell of Seint Ellyns / Water of Denffeld | } A. xv. |

---

^{a} Owing to an erroneous entry before the last paragraph which is crossed out, this and all the subsequent years of the reign have been dated a year in advance and afterwards corrected, as far as the 39th year, originally written "xl", in which the numeral letters are simply crossed out without further correction.

Andrewe Bokerell, Mair	Harry Edylmetory Gerrard Batte	A° xvj°.
	Symond Marye Roger Bontt	A° xvij°.
	Rauff Ashewy John Norman	A° xviij.

This yere was a grete wynde and an erthequake.

Andrewe Bokerell, Maire	Gerrard Batte Robert Ardell	A. xix.

This yere the kynge spoused the eldest doughter of the Provynce [a] at Caunterburye.

Andrew Bokerell, Mair	Harry Cobham Jordeyn Coventre	A° xx.
William Juyn, Mair	John Tolesan Gervys Cordwan	A° xxj°.
Richard Date, Mair	John Wilhale John Saundres	A° xxij°.

This yere Edward the kynges sonne was borne.

Rauffe Grene, Maire	Reynold Bongey Rauff Ascheheme	A. xxiij°.
Richard Renger, Mair	John Gysors Myhell Truy	A° xxiiij.
Stephen de Bongey, Maire	John Wayle Thomas Durham	A° xxv°.
	John FizJohn Rauff Aschewy	A° xxvj°.
Rauff Ashewy, Mayre	Hugh Blunt Adam Bassynge	A° xxvij°.

This yere Newlyn Prynce of Walys meved wer a gayne the kynge, and Gryffyn, Newlyns sonne, fell oute of the Toure of London and brake his neck.

Michell Tony, Meir	Rauffe Spicer Nicolas Batte	A° xxviij.

[a] So in MS. The word " the " before " Provynce " is interlined in a later hand.

John Gysors, Mair	Robert Cornhill / Adam Bentley	A° xxix.
	Symond Mary / Lawrens Frowyke	A° xxx.
Roger FizRoger, Maire	John Wayle / Nicolas Batte	A. xxxj^e.
Michell Tony, Maire	Nicholas Joce / Geffrey Wynchester	A° xxxij^e.
	Raffe Ardell / John Tolesan	A° xxxiij^e.
John Nornya, Meir	Geffrey Basynge / William FizRichard	A° xxxiiij.

This yere the Cite of Damaske was won with Cristen men.

Adam Basynge, Maire	Lawrens Frowyke / William FizRichard	A. xxxv.

This yere be gan Frere Austines fyrst in Engelonde.

John Teson, Maire	William Durham / Thomas Wyndborn	A° xxxvj^e.
Nicholas Bamme, Maire	John Norhampton / Richard Pykard	A° xxxvij^e.
Rauff Ardell, Maire	William Asshewey / Robert Bylton	A. xxxviij.

This yere was Seint Peter of Melayne martered.

Rauff Ardell, Maire	Stephen Oystergate / Harry Walmote	A° [xl].^a
	Martyn Bokerell / John Mynor	A° xlj^e.
	Richard Ewell / William Asshewey	A° xlij^e.
	Thomas FizRichard / Robert Catlegre	A° xliij^e.
John Gesors, Maire	John Adryan / Thomas Cornhill	A° xliiij^e.

^a Crossed out.

This yere the kynge lete gader the scowtage, that is to sey of every knyghtes fee throw Englond xl s.

William Riche, Meir	Adam Brownyng / John Norhampton	A°. xlvᶜ.
	Rychard Pykard / Richard Coventre	A° xlvjᶜ.
Thomas FizThomas, Maire	Phelip Walbroke / Richard Taylor	A° xlvj.ᵃ

This yere was the bataylle of Lewys, and stella comata apered xv wekys.

Thomas Fiz Thomas, Maire	Robert Momplers / Osbern Bukessell	A° xlvij.
	Thomas Lampforde / Gregory Mukessell	A° xlviij.
	Edward Blunt / Peter Augre	A° xlviij.
John Ryche, Costos	John Lynde / John Walme	A° l.
Almanus Godich, Costos	John Adryan / Lucas Bradcourt	A° lj.
	Water Hermy / William Duranson	A° lijᶜ.
Hugh Thomas, Mair	Thomas Basyng / Robert Cornhill	A° liij.

This yere the kynge did translate Seint Edward in to a precious shryne, and in the same yere was the erþe quake.

John Adryan, Maire	Watyr Porter / John Taylor	A° lv.
	Gregory Rokisley / Harry Waleys	A° lvjᶜ.

This yere the stepill of Bowchyrche fell downe and did myche A° Doᶦ Mᶦ.ij.c.ii harme.

John Adryan, Maire	Robert Mylkotte / Petyr Cosyn	A° lvij.ᶜ

<hr>

ᵃ Corrected from "xlvij."

This yere died that noble kynge, whose bones ben buryed at Westmestre.

Thes bethe the names of the meyres and shereffes in the regne of Kynge Edwarde the First.

William Hervy, Meir	{ John Horne { Water Porter	} A° primo.
Harry Walleys, Meir	{ Nicolas Wynchester { Harry Coventre	} A° ijᵉ.
Gregory Rokysley, Meire	{ Lucas Madcourt { Harry Frowycke	} A° iijᵉ.

This yere was a grete erthe quake.

	John Horne Rauff Blunt	} A° iiijᵉ.
Gregory Rokysle, Meire	Robert Bras Raff Fyner	} A° vᵉ.
	John Adryan Water Langley	} A° vjᵉ.
	Robert Basynge William Morle	} A° vijᵉ.

This yere the house of Frere Prechours was first founded at Castell Baynarde.

Gregory Rokysley, Meire	Thomas Box Raffe More	} A° viijᵉ
	William Farendon Nicolas Wynchester	} A° ixᵉ.
Harry Walleys, Meire	William Meyre Richard Chykwell	} A° xᵉ.
	Rauff Blunte Ankyrtyn Betle	} A° xjᵉ.

This yere Newlyn Prince of Walis was take and beheded.

Harry Walleys, Meire	{ Jordane Godechepc { Martyn Box	} A° xijᵉ.

Roger Rokesley, Meire	Stephen Cornhill Robert Rikysle	A° xiij^e.
	Watyr Blunt John Wade	A° xiiij^e
	Thomas Gros William Antony	A° xv^e.
Rauffe Southe, Meir	William Harfford Thomas Stanys	A° xvj^e.
	William Betayne Thomas Caunterbury	A° xvij^e.
	Fult Edmond Salmon Langfford	A° xviij^e
Cartsteyne, Meire	Thomas Romayne William Lyre	A° xix^e.

This yere the kynge ordeyned that all the Jewes that were dwellinge in this londe shulde be exiled for evir.

Rauffe Blunt, Maire	Rauffe Blunt Hamond Box	A° xx^e.
	Harry Belle Ellyse Russell	A° xxj^e.
Sir John Kyrton, Costos	Martyne Ambreshire Robert Rokysley	A° xxij.
	Richard Glowestre Hary Box	A° xxiij^e.
	John Donstable Adam Alyngbury	A° xxiiij^e
	Thomas Southe Adam Fulham	A° xxv^e

This yere the kynge toke the towne and castell off Berwyke, and ther were slayne many Scottes.

Sir John Kyrton, Costos	William Stafford John Stafford	A° xxvj^e.

This yere the kynge did a grete batayll in Scotlonde.

Harry Walles, Meire	Richarde Soperlane Thomas Cely	A° xxvij°.
Elys Russell, Meire	Harry Fyngreth John Anetres	A° xxviij°.
Syr John Blunt, Meire	Lucas Averyng Richard Cambe	A° xxix°.
	Robert Taylor Petyr Basynge	A° xxx°.
	Hugh Froude Symond Parys	A° xxxj°.
Sir John Bluntt, Meire	William Commate John Burfford	A° xxxij°.
	Roger Paryce John Lyncolne	A° xxxiij°.

This yere the lordis of Scotlond were sworne liege men to the kynge of Engelonde.

| Harry Wales | Reynold Underle
William Cosyne | A° xxxiiij°. |
| | Symond Benett
Geffrey Conditt | A° xxxv° |

This yere died the noble kynge, whos bonys ben buried at Westmester.

Thes bethe the names of the Meires and Shereffes of the Cite of London in the tyme of þe regne of Kynge Edwarde the Secunde.

ırdus ij^{dus}

| Thomas Romayn,
Maire | William Furney
Nelle Drury | A° primo. |

This yere the kynge spowsed Isabell, the kynges doughter of Fraunce, and in the same tyme proffessied the holy chanone of Brydlyngton.

| Thomas Romayne,
Maire | William Basynge
John Boteler | A° ij°. |

Nicolas Faryngdon, Meir	{ Roger Palmer John Edmond	} A° iij^e.
Richard Bosham, Meire	{ Symond Cropp Petyr Blakeney	} A° iiij^c
John Gysors, Meire	{ Symond Morwade Richard Wilfford	} A° v^e.

This yere was Edward the kynges sonne borne at Wyndsore on Seint Bricys daye.

| Nicholas Faryngdon, Meir | { John Lambuy
Richard Lutkyn | } A° vj^e. |
| | { Adam Burton
Hugh Gayton | } A° vij^e. |

This yere the kynge went in to Scotlond with a riall power.

| John Gysors, Meir | { Stevyn Abyngdon
William Bedyngham | } A° viij^e |
| Stephen Abyngdon, Meire | { Hamond Goodchepe
William Bedyngton | } A° ix. |

This yere the towne and the castell of Berwyk was lost throwe treson of Peris of Spaldynge [a whom the kyng had put there to kepe the towne with many burgesys of the same towne, where fore the chyldren that were put in hostage thorugh the burgesys of Berwyke folowde the kynges marchalse many dayes fetterd in strong yrens. And after that cam two cardynals in to Englonde to make peace be twene Englond and Scotland. And as they went toward Durham to have consecrate one Master Lewys of Beamount Bysshop of Durham they were robbyd uppon the more of Wynglesdome, of whiche robrye Syr Gylbert of Mytton was atteynt, take, drawne, hangyd, hys hed smyt of, and quarterde. And the same tyme be fel many myscheves in Englond, for the pore people dyed for hungre, and so faste that uncthe men myght bury them. For a

* This between brackets has been added by the Corrector at the top of the page, fo. 24*b*.

quarter of whete was then at xl s., and two yere and *di.* whete was
at x marke a quarter, in so moche that pore people stole chyrdern
and ete them, and all so ete howndes, hors, and cattes.]

John Wyngrave	William Palmer Ranff Gawston	A° x^e.
	John Pryour William Furnex	A° xj^e.
	John Pulteney John Dollynge	A° xij^e.

This yere the kynge helde his Parlement at Yorke, and Sir
Hugh Spencer sone was made chefe Chamburlayne of Inglonde.

Hugh Chykwell, Meyr	Symond Abyngdon John Preston	A° xiij^e.

This same yere was bothe Lord Spencer and his sonne exiled
oute of Ingelond, and, sone after, the kynge commaunded ayene
to the Lordis governaunce.

Nicholas Faryngdon, Maire	William Fordon Reynold Condyt	A° xiiij^e.
Hamond Chykewell, Mair	Rychard Costantyne Richard Akeney	A° xv^e.
	John Grantham Roger Ely	A° xvj^e.
Nicholas Faryngdon, Maire	Adam Salysbury John Oxynford	A° xvij^e.
Hamond Chykwell, Maire	Benett Fullham John Gawston	A° xviij^e.

This yere the Bysshoppe of Exceter,[a] that tyme was[a] Tresorer
of Inglonde, was be heded at the Standarde in Chepe.

Rechard Betey, Meyre	Gilbert Mordon John Cotton	A° xix.

In the left margin:

yere were the
nobles, *di.* nobles,
arthynges of gold
:, for a fore this
there was no
' but sterlyng.

---

[a] The original reading was " Oxenford," which has been corrected into " Exceter"
by a later hand.

This yere the kynge was deposed and Edward his sonne made kynge.

The names of the Meire and Shereffes of London in þᵉ yere of ^{Edwardus iijᵘˢ} the regne of Kynge Edwarde the iij°

| Hamond Chikwell, Maire | { Richard Deryng Roger Chaunceler | } A° primo. |

This yere the kynge spoused the Erlis doughter off Henawde. And in the same yere the kynges fader was morthered at the castell of Berkele.

Hamond Chikwell, Meire	(Richard Deterynge Harry Darcy	} A° ijᵉ.
	Richard Deterynge Roger Chaunceler	} A° iijʳ.
John Grantham, Maire	{ Symond Fraunces Harry Chamburleyne	} A° iiijᵉ.

This yere was Roger Mortymer honged for holding of the Queue.

Symond Swanlond, Mayre	{ Richard Later Harry Gesors	} A° vᵉ.
John Powntney, Maire	(Robert off Ely Thomas Herwolde	} A° vjᵉ.
	John of Mokkyng Andrew Aubry	} A° vijᵉ.

This yere was Berwik yolden to oure kynge.

John Powntney, Maire	(Nicholas Pyke John Howsbonde	} A° viijᵉ
	William Haunsed John Haunseyd	} A° ixᵉ.
Reynold Condit, Maire	{ John Hyngeston Watyr Turke	} A° xᶜ.
John Powntney, Maire	(Watir Mordon Rauff Upton	} A° xjᵉ.
	William Beklesworthe John Northhalle	} A° xijᵉ.

Harry Dacy, Maire	Watyr Neell Nicholas Crane	A° xiij^e.
	William of Pounfret Hugh of Markeber	A° xiiij^e.
Andrewe Awbrye	William Thorney Roger of Forsham	A° xv.

This yere was the bataylle of Slews in Flawndres.

John of Oxynford, Maire	Adam Lucas Bertilmewe Denmarke	A° xvj^e.
	Richard of Berwyk John Rokysle	A° xvij^e.
Symond Frawnces, Maire	John Lovekyn Richard of Kyllyngbury	A° xviij^e

In this yere was an erthe quake.

John Hamonde, Maire	John Sewarde John of Haylham	A° xix^e.

This yere began the knyghtys of the Garter a yene.

John Hamonde, Maire	Geffrey Wyngham Thomas Legge	A° xx^e.

This yere was the kynge of Scotlonde take and broȝte in to Ingelonde.

Richard Lacer, Maire	Edmond of Evynhall John of Glowcester	A° xxj^e.

This yere was the Batayll of Cressy and the Sege of Caleys, be gonne 1346.

Geffrey Wychyng- ham, Maire	William Clapton John Croydon	A° xxij^e.

This yere was Calys wonne and yelde to Kynge Edwarde.

Thomas the Gaye, Meir	Adam Brabanson Richard of Basyngstoke	A° xxiij.

This yere was the fyrst Pestelence.

Harry Loffkyn, Meire	Harry Pykard Symond Dolseley	A° xxiiij^e.

John Turke, Maire	{ Adam Bury { Rauffe of Lynne	} A° xxv°.

This yere was the grete Pestelence.

Richard Beslyng- bury, Maire	{ John Nott { William of Worseter	} A° xxvj°.
Andrewe Aubry, Maire	{ John Wrothe { William Styryntrope	} A° xxvij°.
Adam Fraunces, Maire	{ John Peche { John of Stody	} A° xxviij°.ᵃ
	{ William of Welde { John Lytell	} A° xxix°.
Thomas Legge, Mair	{ William of Tudham { Richard of Smolt	} A° xxx°.
Symond Fraunces, Mayre	{ Watyr Frost { Thomas of Lardon	} A° xxxj°.

This yere the kynge of Fraunce was brought in to Ingelonde prisoner, the whiche Prince Edwarde toke in þᵉ felde at the Batayle of Peyters. And the Crow[n]e off Scotlond yelden to oure kynge.

Harry Pycard, Maire	{ Richard Notyngham { Thomas Dolsle	} A° xxxij°.
John Stoody, Maire	{ Stephanus Caundiche { Bertilmewe Frestlynge	} A° xxxiij°.
John Lovekyn, Maire	{ John of Burys { John of Banys	} A° xxxiiij°
Symonde Dolse Maire	{ Symond of Bodyngton { John of Chechester	} A° xxxv°.

This yere was the threde Pestelence.

John Wrothe, Maire	{ John Denys { James Andrewe	} A° xxxvj°.

* The following note occurs in the margin opposite the 28th year: " This yere were the fyrst g[ro]tes and *di.* grotes, that is to s[aye] iiij d. and ij d. of sylver made, [and] afore ther was no monye b[ut] the noble, the half noble, the [far]thyng of gold and sterlyng o[f] sylver."

John Peche, Maire $\left\{\begin{array}{l}\text{William Holbeche}\\\text{Jamys of Tame}\end{array}\right\}$ A° xxxvij^e.

This yere was a grete wynde on Seint Mawres daye.

Stephen Candysh, Meir $\left\{\begin{array}{l}\text{John de Seint Albonis}\\\text{James Andrewe}\end{array}\right\}$ A°xxxviij^e.

John Notte, Maire $\left\{\begin{array}{l}\text{Richard of Croydon}\\\text{John Hiltoft}\end{array}\right\}$ A° xxxix^e

Adam of Bury, Maire $\left\{\begin{array}{l}\text{Symond of Mordon}\\\text{John of Medfford}\end{array}\right\}$ A° xl^c.

Adam of Bury, Mair to þ^e xvij day of Janyuer $\left\{\begin{array}{l}\text{John Brekyllesworthe}\\\text{Thomas Irelonde}\end{array}\right\}$ A° xlj^e.

John Lovekyn, Maire $\left\{\begin{array}{l}\text{John Warde}\\\text{Thomas Atlee}\end{array}\right\}$ A° xlij^e.

James Andrewe, Maire $\left\{\begin{array}{l}\text{John Tornegold}\\\text{William Dikeman}\end{array}\right\}$ $\left\{\begin{array}{l}\text{A° xliij}^e\\\text{stella}\\\text{comata.}\end{array}\right.$

This yere was the fourthe Pestilence, and in the monthe of Marche apperid.[a]

Symond Mordon $\left\{\begin{array}{l}\text{Adam Wymondham}\\\text{Robert Gurdeler}\end{array}\right\}$ A° xliiij^e.

This yere went Sir Robert Knollis in to Fraunce with a grete power.

John Chcchester, Maire $\left\{\begin{array}{l}\text{John Pyll}\\\text{Hugh Holbech}\end{array}\right\}$ A° xlv^e

This yere was called the grete dere yere, and that same yere was a quarter of whete at iiij nobles.

John Bernys, Maire $\left\{\begin{array}{l}\text{William Walworthe}\\\text{Robert Gayton}\end{array}\right\}$ A° xlvj^e.

John Pyell, Maire $\left\{\begin{array}{l}\text{John Philpott}\\\text{Nicholaus Brambyll}\end{array}\right\}$ A° xlvij^e.

[a] So in MS. Doubtless the words " stella comata " written above under the regnal year ought to have been inserted here.

John Bernys, Maire { Robert Hattfeld / Adamo Stable } A° xlviij°.

This yere was John Norword, mercer, slayne att the Blacke hethe at a wrestelynge.

Adam of Bury, Maire { John Aubrye / John Fysshehed } A° xlix°.

William Walwothe, Maire { Richard Lyons / William Woodhows } A° l.

John Warde, Maire { John Hadley / William Newport } A° lj.

This yere was the wode Satyrdaye for the Duke of Lancaster at Sir Johnis Inne of Prys; the same yere was the v pestelence. This yere dyed Prince Edwarde, and lithe at Caunterburye.

Adam Staple, Maire { John Northehampton / Robert Launde } A° lij°.

This yere was Adam Stable deposid of his meyralte by John Duke of Lancaster on Palme Sondaye eve, that is to sey the xij day of Aprile. And in his stede was made Nicholas Bremble. And on the same day was John Mynsterworthe hangged and heded. And on Seint Albones even dyed Kynge Edwarde [the thirde],[a] and is enterred at Westmester.

Thes bethe the names of the Maires and Shoreffes of the Cite of London in the tyme of the renge of Kyng Richard the ij°. Ricardus ij[dus]

Nicholas Bremble, Maire { Andrewe Pykeman / Nicholas Twyfford } A° primo.

This yere every man, woman, and childe after the age of xiiij yere payd to the kynge iiij d.

[b] John Philpot, Mayre { Thomas Cornwales / John Basham } A° ij°

[a] The words between brackets are inserted by the Corrector.
[b] The names and heading for this year are supplied by the Corrector at the foot of a page.

This yere was a bushell of whete at vj d.   And a galon of white
wyne at vj d. and a galon of rede wyne at iiij d.

John Hadle, Maire   { John Aylsdon
                      William Bareyte   } A° iij^e.

This yere was the Parlement at Northampton, and ther was
Kyrkeby drawen and hanged for the dethe of Marshaunt Janyn.
And in the same yere, be for the feste of Seint Michell, were the
gallyes in Temmes brent at Gravysende; and for the same cause was
Sir Rauffe Ferres appellyd.   In the same was a bataylle at Westmester be twene Sir John Aunsell, knyght, appellaunt, and Thomas
Katerton, defendaunt.   And in this yere come a grete peple oute
of Kentt and Essex to London and brent the Savey and a parcell
of Seynt Johns and the maner of Heybury.   And so entryd in to
London and fette oute of the Toure the Erchebysshoppe of Caunterbury, the priour of Seint Jonys, and a Frere Robert Halys, and
Frere William Appylton, and a Frere Menor, and John Legge, a
sergeaunt of armes, and Richard Somner, were be hedid at Towre
Hill.   And Richard Lyons behedid at the Standard in Chepe.   And
on the morowe after was William Walworth, Nicholas Brembyll,
John Philpott, and Robert Lawnde, made knyghtis in Smythfeld.
And uppon Samfford Hill was the Erle Marchall, and the Erle
Pembroke, and Syr Nicholas Twyfford and Sir Adam Fraunces,
knyghtes, with in a shortt tyme.   And this was called the Hurlynge
tyme.

William Walworthe, { Watyr Begette
    Maire   John Knyghtcott   } A° iiij^e.

This yere the kynge hade of every man and woman be twene lx
and xvj yere xij d., for the whiche þe rysinge afore be ganne.

John Norhampton, { John Rote
    Maire   John Hende   } A° v^e.

This yere, the vij day of Janner, on a Saterdaye, Quene Anne
came to the Toure of London, and the Sonday followinge she was
weddid to Kynge Richard the Secounde.   And the xxiiij day of
Maye was a grete Erthe quawe.

A post Dunstanum post tempore meridianum
C circulum vixi terre motum tibi dixi.[a]

| John Norhampton, Mair | { Adame Bamme John Cely | } A° vj^e. |

This yere the Bysshoppe of Norwyche went in to Flaundres and slewe many Flemynges. This yere was John Norhamton, John More, John Norbury, dampned in the Toure of London for certeyne congregaciouns that were made a yenes þe pese.

| Nicholas Bremble, Mair | { Nicholas Exton John Fresche | } A° vij^e. |

| Nicholas Bremble, Maire | { Symond Wynchecombe John More | } A° viij^e. |

This yere the kynge wentt in to Scotlonde with a riall power and distroyed all the londe to the Scottes see.

| Nicholas Bremble, Maire | { John Orgon John Churcheman | } A° ix^e. |

This yere went the Duke of Lancaster in to Spayne for to cha lange the crowne.

| Nicholas Exstone, Meir | { William Staunton William More | } A° x^e. |

This yere was the Erle of Arondell mad Amell of the see, and toke in that yere lxxx^xx [b] shippis of enmyes and mo with xiiijм^l ton wyne.

| Nicholas Exston, Mayre | { William Venor Hugh Fasthalffe | } A° xj^e. |

This yere was a grete dissencion amonge the lordis, that is to sey, the Duke of Glowcester, the Erle of Derby, the Erle of Arondell, the Erle off Warwyk, and the Erle of Notyngham, a gayne the Erle of Oxynford, and the Erle of Southfolke, and the Erehe-bysshope of Yorke, Sir Robert Tresylyan, and Sir Nicholas Bremble, the whiche Sir Robert and Sir Nicholas were drawen and hanged, and the Erle of Oxynforde and the Erle of Southefolke fled in to

---

[a] I confess the meaning of these lines is beyond me.—*Editor.*
[b] "lxxx^xx." So in MS.

Braband, and ther died, and the Erchebysshuppe of Yorke fled in
to Scotlonde and ther died, and all ther godes fell in to the kynges
hande.

| Nicholas Twyffor, Mair | { Thomas Austyn
{ Adam Carlhill | } A° xij^e. |
| William Venor, Maire | { John Walcotte
{ John Loveney | } A° xiij^e. |

This yere was a grete Pestylence.

| Adame Bamme, Maire | { Thomas Vyment
{ John Fraunces | } A° xiiij^e. |
| John Hende, Maire | { Harry Vanner
{ John Shodworth | } A° xv^e. |

This yere was the Mayre and bothe the Shoryves were putt
downe of her offyce, and Syr Edwarde Delyngrege made wardeyn
by the kynge. And after him Syr Bawdewyne Radynton in the
xv yere of the kynge and Gebonde Mandfeld and Thomas Newnton
chosyn Shoreffys, and London rawnsoned at a M^l marke.

| William Staunton | { Gylberd Mansfeld
{ Thomas Neunton | } A° xvj^e. |
| John Hadle, Maire | { Drue Barentyn
{ Richard Wytington | } A° xvij^e. |

This yere on Witsondaye dyed Quene Anne and lithe at Westmester; and in the same yere the kynge wentte in to Irlonde and
toke all the rebelles of that londe.

| John Fresshe, Meire | { Thomas Knollys
{ William Bramton | } A° xviij^e |

This yere came the kynge oute of Irlande.

| William More, Maire | { Roger Elys
{ William Heryngham | } A° xix^e. |
| Adame Bamme, Maire | { Thomas Welford
{ William Perker | } A° xx^e. |

This yere Quene Isabell was wedded to Kynge Richard at
Caleys. And also the same yere, the xxi day of June, was the Duke
of Glowcester, the Erle of Arondell, the Erle of Warwyke, the

Lord Cobham, Sir Thomas of Arondell, the Erchebysshoppe of Caunterburye were a rested, and the Duke of Glowcester was sent to Caleys and ther mortherd, and the Erle of Arondell behedid at the Toure Hill on Seint Matheus Eve.   And the Erle of War-wyke, the Erle of Arondell, the Lord Cobham, and Sir John Cheyne, were dampned to perpetuall prison.

Richard Wytington,   William Ascame
Maire   John Wodcok $\}$ A° xxj^e.

This yere the kynge made v Dukes and a Markes and iiij Erlys. Fyrst was the Erle of Derby was made Duke of Herforde, and the Erle of Rutlonde Duke of Arondell, and the Erle of Kent Duke of Surre, the Erle of Hontyngdon Duke of Excester, and the Erle Marchall Duke of Northefolke, the Erle of Somersed Markes of Dorsett, and the Lord Spencer Erle of Glowceter, the Lord Nevell Erle of Westmerlond, Sir Thomas Percy Erle of Worseter, and Sir William Scroope Erle of Wilshire.

Drew Baryngtyn, $\{$ John Wade
Mayre $\{$ John Warner $\}$ A° xxij^e.

This yere dyed the Duke of Lancaster and is buryed at Seint Poules in London.   Also the Friday after Seint Peter and Poule the Duke of Lancaster after his fader disses came in to Englonde, with him his sonne Thomas Arondell that was Erchebysshoppe of Caunterbury, and they londed in the northe contre at a place called Ravenspore, to whom came in haste the Erle of Northehomberlonde and his sonne Sir Harry Percy, and many other lordis with grete power, and thei went to Brystowe wher thei fonde Sir William Scrope, Tresourer of Engelonde, and Sir John Busshe, and Sir John Grene, and all were be heded.   And in þ^e mouthe of Septem-bre the kynge resseyved his dignite in the Toure of London.

Thes bethe the names of the Maires and Shoreffes of the Cite off Henricus iiij^{tus} London in the regne of Kynge Henry the iiijth, the whiche was crowned at Westmestre in the daye of Translacioun of Seint Edwarde, the yere of our Lord M^{l}iij^{c}lxxxxix.^{a}

^{a} The words following "Seint Edwarde" are added by the Corrector.

Thomas Knollys,	William Walden	A° primo.
Maire	William Hide	

This yere the vj day of Feverell were all the seales of blanke chartours brent at the Standarde in Chepe, and the xth day of Marche Kynge Richarde the Secunde [a] was brought from Pomfret Castel whereyn he decessyd [a] to London in to Powles, and the nexte day after he was caryed to Langley to be buryed there yn a howce of freers.[b]   And in the same yere was the Erle of Kent, the Erle of Salisbery, be hedid at Susseter.[c]   And Sir Thomas Blunt, Sir Rauffe Lomney, Sir John Cely, and Thomas Venter, were be hedyd at Oxenford.   And Sir John Holond and the Duke of Excester were be hedyd at Plaschey.   And the Lord Spencer was be hedid at Bristowe.

John Fraunces,	John Wakele	A° ij[e].
Maire	John Gnotte	

This yere was the Batel at Halydon Hyl.[d]

John Shadworthe,	William Venor	A° iij[e].
Maire	John Frelyngham	

This yere the kynge spoused Dame Jane, Duches of Brettaynge. And the same yere apperyd stella comata v wekys in Leynte.   Also the yere the Priour of Launde and Sir Roger Claryngton and viij Frerys Menoures were drawen and honged upon a day.

John Walkott,	Richard Marlowe	A° iiij[e].
Maire	Robert Checheley	

This yere, on Mary Mawdelen day,[e] was the Bataylle of Shrowysbury, and ther was Syr Harry Percy slayne and Syr Thomas Percy his eme take, and ij dayes after he was drawe and hanged, and the Erle of Stafford slayne under the kynges baner.

---

[a] The words " the Secunde " and " from Pomfret—decessyd " are inserted by the Corrector in the margin."

[b] " there—freers."   These words are inserted by the Corrector.

[c] Cirencester.   [d] This sentence is inserted by the Corrector in the margin.

[e] "on Mary Mawdelen day."   These words are inserted by the Corrector.

William Askam, { Thomas Faukener \
Maire { Thomas Polle } A$^\circ$ v^c.

This yere was William Serle, that mordered the Duke of Glow-cester at Calleys, drawen, hanged, quarterde, and beheded[a] at London.

John Hende, Maire { William Lowthe \
{ Stephyn Spilman } A$^\circ$ vj^e.

This yere on the Monday in Witsonweke Syr Roger Scrope, Erchebysshoppe of Yorke, and the Erle Marchall, were behedid at Yorke. The same yere was a grete frost that endured xv wekes and m[o].[b]

John Wodcok, { Harry Barton \
Maire { William Crowmer } A$^\circ$ vij^e.

Richard Wityngton, { Nicholas Wotton \
Maire { Geffrey Brooke } A$^\circ$ viijth.

This yere the Erle of Kent spoused the Duches doughter of Myllayne.

William Stawnton, { Harry Poumfrett \
Mair { Harry Halton } A$^\circ$ ix^e.

This yere the Erle of Nothehomberlonde and the Lorde Bardollff was be hedid. Also the same yere was a stronge frost that duryd xv wekys, and the Erle of Kent was slayne in Brettayne.

Drengh Barentyn, { Thomas Duke \
Mair { William Norton } A$^\circ$ x^e.

Richard Marlowe, { John Lane \
Meire { William Chechiley } A$^\circ$ xj^e.

Thomas Knolles, { John Penne \
Maire { Thomas Pyke } A$^\circ$ xij^e.

This yere came Enbassatours from the Duke of Burgoyne to have men a gayne the Duke of Orlyance. And the Prince sent over the Erle of Arondell and the Lord Cobham with other dyverse lordes.

---

[a] "and beheded." Added by the Corrector.\
[b] This sentence beginning " The same yere" is added by the Corrector.

Robert Chechiley,   { William Reynwell   } A° xiij^e.
Maire   { John Cotton   }

This yere Thomas the kynges sonne was made Duke of Cla
rence, and he wente over the see with a faire mayne in help ynge
of the Duke of Orlyaunce a gayne the Duke of Borgoyne. Also
the same yere the kynge lete smyte a newe mynte the noble lesse
wight than the olde noble by halfe apeny wight of gold.

This yere in one day were iij floddys yn the Temmys water.^a

William Waldren,   { Rauffe Lovenam   } A° xiiij^e.
Maire   { William Sevenoke   }

And in this yere dyed the kynge, and lithe enterred at Caunterbury.

The names of the Maires and Shoreffes of London the whiche
were in the tyme of the regne off Kynge Henre the v^the, the whiche
was crowned at Westmestre the ix^th day of Aprel, the whiche than
was Passyon Sonday and a grete raynye daye.^b This yere the
kynge lete fetche frome Langley the bonys of Kyng Richard the
ij^de c to Westmestre in to the tombe that he did make him selffe for
hym and his Quene Anne. And the same yere Sir John Oldcaste
was a rested in to the Towre, and after brake oute of prison.

Wylliam^d Crowmer,   { John Sutton   } A° primo.
Mair   { John Nicoll   }

This yere Sir John Oldecastell with many oþer lordes and
heritikes had emagened the distruccion of the kynge and of Holy
Chirche, but the kynge with stode hem and toke many of them,
which were drawe and hanged and brentt, galowes and all, to the
nombre of xlij^ti persones, but Sir John Oldcastell scapyd.

^a This sentence is added in the margin by the Corrector.
^b The words following "Westmestre" in this sentence are added by the Corrector
and carried out into the margin.
^c "the ij^de" is interlined by the Corrector.
^d The name was "John" in the text, but it is crossed through and "Wylliam"
is written over. The Corrector has added the following note in the margin, relative
to the year of his mayoralty: "Primo, quia bis fuit maior civitatis."

| Thomas Fawkener, | { John Michell | } A⁰ ijᶜ. |
| Mair | { Thomas Aleyn | |

This yere was brent in Smythfeld John Claydon, Skynner, and Richarde Gutmyn, Baker, for herytckys. Also the same yere the kynge toke his jorney toward Normandy, and at Southehampton the Erle of Cambryge and the Lorde Scrope and Sir Thomas Graye were be heded for conspirynge of the kynges dethe. And þan the kynge passed the see with iiijᶜ. shippes. And the xvj day of August he landed a litell from Hareflete and leide a sege to the towne, and conteneued to the xx day of Septembre, and than was the towne yolde to oure kynge. And than the kynge wente towarde Caleys, and on Crispine Crispianis day at Agyncortte all the rialte of Praunce come be for the kynge to lett him of his wey. And the kynge faughte with hem and discomfid them and slewe many lordis and other peple, and toke many prisoners, Dukes, Erlis, and othir lordes. And on the xxiiij day of Novembre the kynge with his prisoneres came to London.

The Batel of A_| corte in Pycard} the day of Crys| and Crispynian Fryday.

| Nicholas Wotton, | { Aleyn Everarde | } A⁰ iijᵉ. |
| Maire | { William Cambryge | |

This yere the Empour of Almayne came in to Engelond and was at Seint Georges fest. And at the procession the kynge went a bove him, and at the masse the kynge sate a bove him, and at the mete the kynge sate on the right honde of the emperoure. And the Duke of Bedforde, Chaunsler of Englonde, sate on the lifte side of the Emperour, and the Beshuppe of Dyvelyn and dukys that came with the Emperour sate on the right honde of the Kynge. And the first sotilte that came on the table was our Lady armyng Seint George and an angill doinge on his sporys. The secounde sotilte was Seint George fightynge with the dragon, and the spere in his honde. The therde sotilte was a castell, and Seint George and the kynges doughter ledyng the lambe in to the castell gate. Also this yere Duke William of Holond came in to Engelonde.

[E]mperowre of Allmen.

| arr Barton, | { Robert Wityngton | } A° iiij^th |
| H Mayre | { John Coventre | |

This yere the kynge sailed in to Normandy and londed the first
day of August be syde Towcke and toke the towne and castell sone
after; on our Ladye day the Nativite the kynge wan the towne of
Cane, and sone after the castell.   Also the Duke of Clarence beseged
the towne of Bayne and wan hit.   And the same yere the kynge
wan many other townes and castelles and stronge abbeyes longe
be for the fest of Seint Edward in Octobre.

| Richard Merlowe, | { Harry Rede | } A° v^e. |
| Maire | { John Gedney | |

This yere the generall counsell was endyde atte Custaunce, and
an unyversale pece made in Holy Chirche and a Pope chosyn,
whiche was called Martinus quintus.   Also Sir John Oldcastell
was take and dampned at Westmestre, drawen and brentt, galows
and all.   Also the same yere the kynge besegide the towne and
castell of Falloyes and gate hem bothe ; also the towne and castell
of Shirebrough yelden to the Duke of Glowcester.   And after the
kynge gatte Pountelarge and many other streynthes.   And a boute
Lammas the kynge layde sege to Rone.

| William Sevenoke, | { John Pernesse | } A° vj^e |
| Maire | { Rauff Barton | |

This yere on Seint Wolstones day the towne and castell of Rone
was yolde to oure kynge.

| Richard Wityngton, | { John Boteler | } A° vije. |
| Maire | { Robert Wytyngham | |

This yere the kynge came to Troyes in Champayne where he
was worthely resseyved of all the lordys spirituall and temporall.
And on the morowe the kynge mett withe the Quene of Fraunce
and Dame Kateryne hir doughter and the Duke of Boyrgoyne in
the body of Seint Petris churche; and after they went up to the
auter and there the articles of the pees were redde and othes made
on eyther syde.   And then was the kynge and Dame Kateryne
ensured togeder.   And on the morowe after Trinite Sondaye, that

is to sey the iij day of June, he spoused Dame Kateryne in the seide chirche of Seint Peter in Troyes, and the kynge was made Regent and Eyre of Praunce.

William Cambryge, Maire — John Wellis / John Botler — A° viij^{e}.

This yere the ix day of Peverell the kynge and the Queue Kateryne came to London, and the xxj daye of the same mo[n]the she was crowned at Westmester, and the fest was holden in the grete hall.

The Coronacyon Quene Kateryne.

Off the Feste of þᵉ Cronacioun of Quene Kateryne and of Service. Fyrst, the quene sate in hir astate, and the Erchebysshoppe of Caunterbury and the Bysshoppe of Wynchester satte upon the righ[t] honde of the quene, and the Kynge of Scottis sate in his estate upon þₑ lyfte hand of the quene. And the Duches of York and the Countes of Huntyngdon sate upon the same side. And att every course nexte the quene the Bysshoppis were servid, covered as the quene, and than the Kynge of Scottis and other lordis. And the Duke of Glowcester was Surveour, and the Erle Marchall knelyd in the right side of the quene holdyng in his honde upryght a septure, and the Knyght Marchall holdyng a noþer septure on the lifte syde of the quene. And the Countesse of Kente sittinge on the right fote of the quene. And the Countesse Marchall sytting on the lifte fote of the queue.

Also this same yere sone after Wytsonday the kynge sayled in to Praunce and laide a sege to the Cite of Mewes Embrye[a] and contenewed forthe. This yere was a new wedercok set u[p] on Powles stepyl.[b]

Robert Checheley, Maire — Richard Goslynge / William Weston — A° ix$^{\circ}$.

This same yere on Seint Nicholas day Henry the kynges sonne was borne at Wyndsore, and in the monthe of Maye the Cite of

Henricus vj^{tus} na yz. [vj] die Dec bris, hoc est die S Nicholai episcop Domini M^{lo}iiij^{c}x?

[a] Meaux en Brie.
[b] The last sentence is added by the Corrector in the margin.

Mewes in Brye was yolden to the kynge.   Also the same monthe
the quene shipped at Hampton, and so passed the see in to Fraunce.

·icus quintus
10 Augusti diem
]sit e[xtre]mum.
c vixit post
itatem filij sui
[ici] vj^{ti} xxx^{ta}
to septimanas
fere duos dies.
Also in this yere the last daye of August dyed Kynge Harry the
vth at Boys Vynsent with oute Parys, whos bonys the viijth day of
November at Westmester were enterred.

The names of the maires and shoreffes of the Cite of London in
the tyme of the regne of Kyng Henry the vjth

| William Waldren, Mair | William Estffeld Robert Tetersalle | A° primo. |

This yere the xxj day of Octobre (betwene vij and viij of the
clok a fore none in the Cite of Parys ^a) dyed Kynge Charles of
Fraunce.   Also the first day of Marche William Tayler was brent
in Smythfeld for eresy.   Also the secounde day of March Pownt-
melayne was yolden to the gode Erle of Salysbury.   Also John
Duke of Bedford, the kynges uncle, Regent of Praunce, spoused the
Dukys sister off Burgoyne.

| William Crowmer, Maire | Nicholas Jamys Thomas Wandisfford | A° ij^e. |

This yere the xxj day of Octobre was the Parlement holden at
Westmester.   And the xxvj day of Novembre the kynge was brought
in to the Parlement.   And the same daye the kynge remevid to
Waltham, and the Parlement was engorned in to the xx day after
Cristmas.   This yere the xiiijth day of Feveryere dyvers bylles were
cast in London and in the subbarbys of the same a yenst mer-
chantes strawngers.^b   Also the xiiij day of Feverell Sir John Mortymer was dampned be Parlement, hanged, drawe, and quarterd for
brekynge of prison.

| John Michell, Maire | Symond Seman John Bewatyr | A° iij^e. |

---

^a This parenthesis is inserted by the Corrector.
^b This sentence is inserted by the Corrector in the upper margin of the MS.

This yere in the mouthe of Octobre the Duke of Glowceter and his Duches sayled to Caleys and so forthe in to Henaude wher was his wiffes eritage, where he was at the fyrst worsshupfully resseyved, but after they sett nott by him, and so came home and lefte his lady at Moynys in Henaude. And then the Duke cf Burgoyne beseged hir and wanne the towne and brought hir to Gawnte in Flaundres, but she scaped from thens and came in to Holonde, and there longe tyme helde wer a yenes the Duke and put him dyverse tymes at the worste.

| John Coventre, Maire | { William Mildred John Brokley | } A° iiij^c. |

This yere on Witsonday the kynge was made knyght at Leyseter of my Lorde of Bedford, and the kynge made xxxiiij^ti other knyghtis. Also the same yere was a grete dissencioun be twene the Duke of Glowcester and the Bysshoppe of Wynechester that tyme Chauncyler, for the whiche all London a rose with the Duke a yenest the for-saide Bysshoppe.

| John Reynwell, Maire | { Robert Arnold John Hygham | } A° v^e. |

This yere be for Shroftide the Bysshoppe of Wynchester saylled over to Caleys, and sone after the Duke of Bedford and his Duches. And upon our Lady day the Annonciacion the Bysshoppe of Wynechestre was made cardenall in Seint Mary chirche of Caleys, beyng ther present the Duke of Bedfford and his Duches. And be for the masse be gan, the whiche the Bysshoppe shuld doo, the popis cosynne brought in the cardenalles hatte, and with grete reverence sett it upon the auter, and ther hit stode all the masse tyme. And whan the bysshoppe had songe and was un revessed, ther was done on him an habite in maner of a freres cope off fyne scarled furred with puryd graye. And than he knelid downe upon his kneys befor the auter, while the Popis bullys were red to him. And the first byll was his charge, and the secounde byll was that

the pope confermed that he shulde have still all the benefies that
he hathe in Englonde. And whan this was done the Duke of
Bedforde went up to the auter and toke the cardenales hatt and
sett it on the bysshoppys hede and abeyed to hym, and afterwarde
toke him all wey above him. This yere Wylliam Wa[we] was
drawen, hanged, [and] quarterde.[a]

| John Gedney | Harry Frowyk | A° vj[e]. |
| Maire | Robert Otley | |

This yere the Duches of Holond, whiche longe tyme was besegid
and vexid by the Duke of Burgoyne, understondynge that no
remedy nor helpe was ordeyned for hir in Ingelonde, and also
cosiderynge that the Duke of Glowcester hadde for sake hir and
spowsed a noþer woman, by gode and wyse consayll submytt to be
governed afterward by the Duke of Borgoyne. Also the same yere
the Cardenale came to London upon Seint Gylis daye, and the Meir
Shoreffes and the craftis of London rode a gaynes him in a gode
a raye.

| Harry Marton, | John Abbott | A° vij[e]. |
| Maire | John Duffhous | |

This yere sone upon Midsomer the Cardenall saylled over the
see with a fayre mayne waged to werre upon the lordis of Prage.
But a lite a for the departynge of the Cardenall oute of Englonde
the Erle of Southefolke, the Lord Talbott, the Lorde Sealys, and
many oþer lordys, knyghtis, and squiers were taken, and many
slayne at the sege of Orlyaunce, and the sege broken.

| William Estffeld, | Rauff Holond | A° viij[e] |
| Maire | John Russe | |

This yere on Seint Lenardes[b] daye in Dessembre the kynge was
crowned at Westmestre (the dominical letter B[c]).

---

[a] This sentence is added by the Corrector.

[b] Corrected from "Lauernce." The Corrector ought also to have noticed that
"Dessembre" should have been November.

[c] The parenthesis added by the Corrector.

| Nicholas Wotton, Maire· | { Water Churchesey
Robert Large | } A° ix^c. |
| John Wellis | { Stephen Browne
John Aderley | } A° x^c. |

This yere the kyng went in to Fraunce and the xiij day of Decembre was he was crowned in Parys.[a]

This yere the kynge came oute of Praunce in to Ingelonde in savete to the Cite of London. And the Maire, Aldurmen and Shoryvis with all the comenalte of the Cite him resseyved right worthely.

| John Perneys, Mair | { John Padysley
John Olney | } A° xj^e. |

This yere was a gre clepes on Seint Botholles daye.

| John Brokley, Maire | { Thomas Chalton
John Lynge | } A° xij^e. |
| Robert Otley, Maire | { Thomas Barnwell
Symond Eyre | } A° xiij^e. |

This yere was a grete froste, the whiche dured from Seint Katerynes daye to Seint Volantynes daye. And the vintage of wyne came ovir Sheters Hill in cartys from Gravisende.

| Harry Frowick, Maire | { Robert Clopton
Thomas Catworthe | } A° xiiij^e. |

This yere hit was oppenly knowen that the Duke of Burgoyne was forsworne unto the Crowne off Engelonde, for in this yere he laide sege unto Caleys, and he lete make a grete bastyle, the whiche bastile oure men of Calleys wanne, and toke ther in many prisoners, and slowe all the remnante, and forthe with brent it. And that tyme the Duke of Glowcester, the Duke of Northfolke, the Erle of Huntyngdon, þe Erle of Stafford, the Erle of Warwyck, and many oþer erles, baronez, knyghtes, and sqwyers, were poynted to goo to Calleys to breke the sege. But the peple of Calleys had broke the sege or they were redy, and þat tyme every lord founde a cer

---

[a] This sentence is added in the margin by the Corrector, who has also interlined under the names of the mayors and sheriffs, " The kyng was crowned in Parise.'

teyn meyne on her owne coste, and every bysshoppe, abbay, howsell
of religiouns, and every gode towne fonde a certayne of men. And
London sent a for that v sowdyors for to kepe Calys. And yet
London yave to the werrys M¹ *li.* And so my Lord of Glowseter
toke his shippe with many other lordes at Wynchelsey, and so
sayled to Calleys with all his oste, and his shippis waitinge on the
see coste off Flawndres upon our Oste. And so the Duke of
Glowseter toke his jorney taward Flaundres the Monday after Seint
Lauerence daye, in the yere of our Lorde M¹.CCCC.xxxvij^{the}, and lay
that nyght at Sparkys place be syde Oye; upon the morne he
passed the water of Gravenynge at **x** of the clokke, with l.M¹ men
nombryd. And ther he made dyverse knyghtis. And so passyd
forthe to Mardyke and brent hit and Poperynge and Bell, and so
distroyed all West Flawndres. And our shippis brentt a gode Ile
whiche is called Cagent, and sone after the Duke with all his oste
retorned to Caleys, and so came a yene in to Englond.

John Michell, Maire	{	Thomas Morsted	}	A° xvᵉ.
		William Gregory		

This yere fell downe the Towre of London Brygge with ij arches.
And the same yere dyed Quene ª Kateryne, þᵉ whiche is buryed at
Westmester.

William Estfeld, Mair	{	William˙ Halys	}	A° xvjᵉ.
		William Chapman		
Stephen Browne, Maire	{	Hugh Dyke	}	A° xvijᵉ.
		Nicholas Yoo		

This yere the Duke of Orlyaunce went over the see to Caleys
with a certayne lordys, and so was delyverd by composicioun made;
and in that yere the Erle of Hontyngdon was sent in to Gascoyne.
And in that yere whete was worthe throwe the londe xvj d. a
busshell. And in that yere was ordeyned that all the comyn strom-
petes sholde were raye hodis and white roddis in her hondes.

ª Above these words is written by the Corrector: "uxor Henrici quinti."

| Robert Large, | { Robert Marchall | } A° xviij^e. |
| Maire | { Phelyppe Malpas | |

This yere the water condyt was in Flete strete fyrst made.[a]

This yere hit was ordeyned by Parlement that all maner strangers shulde go to Oste. In that yere were two men honged in Temmes by yonde Seynt Katerynes, for they had rubbed vitalers in Temmes. And in this yere was Sir Robert White, some tyme vicorye of Depfford, and anoþere seculer man, dampned for heresye, and brent at Toure Hill in a mornyng at vij of the cloke.

| John Padysle, | { William Whetnalle | } A° xix^e. |
| Maire | { John Sutton | |

This yere the Duke of Yorke was made Regent of Fraunce and Normandy for v yere, and went overe þe see with a ryall power. And in that yere was a chalange made of a knyght of Spayne and Sir Richarde Wodfelde, knyght, whiche was done in Smythfeld a for the kynge and the lordys. And the kynge toke it in his honde with in iiij strokes, and so was ended. And in that yere Dame Elynore Cobham, Duches of Glowseter, and a clerke of hires that was called Maiste Roger Bultyngbroke, throwe nigrymancye, and a wyche of the Eye, by wychcrafte, had conspired the kynges dethe. All thre were a rested and put in holde.

Elynor Cobham, Duches of Glo[cester].[b]

| Robert Clopton, | { William Combys | } A° xx.^c |
| Mair | { Richard Riche | |

This yere Dame Elynor Cobham a for wreten was made to go throwe London, openly beryng a taper in hir hande by pennaunce enjoyned by the Chirche and the Kynge, and after hir body to perpetuall prison. And the clerke was dampned to be hanged, drawe, and quartered, and þe wiche was brent in Smythfelde for the treson afor wretyn. And this yere was a chalange previd with in lystis in Smythfelde a for the kynge of a knyght of Aragon and John Assheley, squyer, the whiche Assheley had the felde, and of

---

[a] This sentence is inserted by the Corrector.
[b] To this note is added in a hand considerably later: "and the wytche of Eye."

the kynges honde was made knyght in the felde for his wele
doynge.   And the lorde of Aragon after that offerd up his harneys
at Wyndsore.

John Athirle, Mayre { Thomas Bemond
                        Richard Northern   } A° xxj°.

This yere the Duke of Somersed went in to Fraunce with x m¹
men, and that yere came the Cardenalle Erchebysshope of Rone,
Chaunseler of Normandy and Bysshoppe of Hely, in to Englond
and here dyed, &c.

Thomas Catworthe, { Nicholas Wyffolde
Maire   John Norman   } A° xxij°.

This yere came the Duke of Somersed oute of Fraunce, þᵉ whiche
had lost myche of his peple.   And that yere the Erle of Southefolk, and the Prevey Sealle,[a] and Sir Robert Roose, the kynges
secretory, went on enbassetory in to Fraunce to trete for pees, and
to make a maryage for the Kynge with the Dukys doughter of
Angios, whiche pees was made for xviij monthes, and seuerte hadde
of the maide for maryage a for recorde of all the riales of Fraunce
in presens of oure enbassetours.   And so they came a yene in to
Engelond, presentyng the kynge this tythinges, for the whiche was
made bothe in Inglonde and Fraunce grete solemnyte.   And in that
yere died the Duke of Somersett.   And in that yere was ordeyned
that no markett sholde be holde on the Sonday.   And this yere the
Erle of Stafford was made Duke of Bokynham, þᵉ Erle of Dorsett
was made Markes of Dorsett, the Erle of Southefolke Markes of
Southefolke, the Erle of Warwyke made Duke of Warwyke.

Harry Frowyk,   { Stephen Foster
Maire   Hugh Wiche   } A° xxiij°.

e Margaret, the
: of Angyos
hter, cam fyrst
Englonde, A°
1444.

This yere Quene Margeret came in to Englond with grete rialte
of the kynges coste.   And the xxix daye of Maye all the craftes of
London with the Meire and Aldermen met with the quene on
hors backe in blewe gownes browdered and rede hodis, and brought
hir to the Towre of London ; and on the same day was made xlvij

———
[a] Adam Moleyns, afterwards Bishop of Chichester.

knyghtis of the Bathe. And on the morowo all the craftes of London in her best a ray brought hir to Westmester, and all the forsaide knyghtes a for ridynge. And the xxx day of May (the whiche was than the Sonday next after Trinite Sonday[a]) she was crowned at Westmestre. And iij dayes after open justynge to all tho that wolde come. And in this yere the priour of Kylmayne of Irlonde apeled the Erle of Ormond. And in this yere came ser- teyne enbassetours oute of Fraunce to trete for pees to be badde generall whiche duryd not but xij monthis after the xviij monthis a for wretyn. And in this yere was the translacioun of Seynt Edward made holy throwe London; and Poules stepyll sett on fire with lyghtnynge.

Coronacio Regin Margarete uxori Henrici Sexti.

The Translacior Seyn[t] Edward made halyd[ay].

| Symond Eyre, Maire | { John Derby
Geffray Feldyng | } A° xxiiij°. |
| John Olney, Mayre | { Robert Horne
Geffrey Boleyn | } A° xxv°. |

This yere was the Parlement at Bury for the Duke of Glowcester with grete treison wrought a yenes him comyng thedir, and was logcd in the Ospitale, for whom was raysed lx m¹ men. And as he sate at soper, lordis of dyverse degreis came to him in the kynges name dischargeynge him of the kynges presense, and of all other maner of answeres. And so they a restid him of hie treyson. And þat he mekely obeyed, and all his men were avoyded from him full hevely. And sone after he dissesyd, the sykenes howe God knowith. And xxxij of his men were sentt to dyverse persones, and afterward v of his men were broʒt to London. And ther thei were dampned to be drawe, hanged, and quarterd; and so they were drawe to Tiborn. And thes bethe ther names: Arteys the Dukys bastard sonne, and Herberd squyer, Medilton squyer, and Sir Roger Cham-burlayne knyght, and Nedame yoman. And ther thei were hanged and lette downe quycke; and ther was the Markes of Southefolke, and shewed a chartour generall for hem all; and so they were par-doued and had lyfe and godes.

The Parlament : Saynt Edmundes Bury, and Hum. Dewke of Glowc and regent of En there was slayne Domini 1446, vi die Januarij.

---

[a] The parenthesis is inserted by the Corrector in the margin below.

John Gedney, Meire $\left\{\begin{array}{l}\text{William Abraham}\\\text{Thomas Scott}\end{array}\right\}$ A° xxvjᵉ.

This yere the xxij day of Marche the water brake in oute of Temmes be syde Lymeoste, and in a noþer place in Temmes, and dide myche harme. And in the same yere was an herytik brent at the Toure Hill.

Stephen Browne, Maire $\left\{\begin{array}{l}\text{William Cantlowe}\\\text{William Marowe}\end{array}\right\}$ A° xxvijᵉ.

Thomas Chalton, Maire $\left\{\begin{array}{l}\text{Thomas Canynges}\\\text{William Hewlyn}\end{array}\right\}$ A° xxviijᵉ.

This yere the kynge helde his Parlement at Westmester. And that same yere was all Normandy loste. And also in the terme of Cristmas while the Parlement was at Westmester the Duke of Southefolke was a rested and sent to the Toure of London. And with in a moneth after the kynge sent after the duke frome the Toure to the towre at Westmestre, and a yenes Ester the Parlement was enjorned to Leyseter, and the kynge toke with him the Duke of Southefolke. And whan the kynge and the comenys were come to Leyseter the comenys saide that they wolde have excusyon don upon the traytors that badde solde Normandy, Gyan, and Gascoyne, and were causes of the dethe of the Duke of Glowcester, for the whiche the Duke of Suthefolke was named chefe, and the Lord Saye and Danyell squyer, and many other. And so the comenys cryed so sore on the Duke of Southefolke that at the laste the kynge did exile hym oute of the londe. And so the duke shepped and was forwarde in the see, and ther mett with him a shippe calles[a] Nicholas of the Toure, and toke the duke and smote of his hede in the see the first day of Maye. And so he was brought to Dovyr a londe, and forthe with the Parlement was ended. And than the comynes of Kent a rose and hade chosen hem a capteyne the whiche namyd hym sylfe John Mortymer, whose very trew name was John Cade, and he was an Iresheman;[b] and so he come to the Black

Cade.

---

[a] So in MS.

[b] " whose—Iresheman." This clause is inserted by the Corrector.

hethe withe the comynes of Keutt. And the kynge with all his
lordis made hem redy with all her power for to with stonde him.
And the capteyn hiryng that the kynge was comynge, and so the
nyght a fore the capteyne with drowe him and his peple; and so the
xviij day of June the kynge toke his wey taward the Blacke Hethe.
And Sir Umfrey Stafford, knyght, and John Stafford, squyer, with
her peple went in the fowarde, and they were slayne and myche of
her peple. And the kynge came to the Blacke Hethe with his
lordys. They hirynge of þis jorney a none the lordis meyne went
togeder and said, but the kynge wolde do excussyon on suche
traytors as were named else they wolde turne to the capteyn of
Kent. And than the kynge grawnte hem that they shuld have
ther entent, and bade hem name suche persones as were fectyffe, and
they shulde have as lawe wolde. And than the lordis men saide that
the Lorde Saye was one, the Bysshuppe of Salysbury, the Baron of
Dudley, the Abbott of Glowcester, and Danyell, and many moo.
And the Lord Saye was a rested in the kynges presence, and sent
to the Toure of London ; and so the kynge went to Grenewiche, and
so to London by water, and ther was ij or iij dayes, and than made
him redy to remeve to Kyllyngworthe. And the Meire of London
with the comynes of the cite came to the kynge besekynge him that
he wolde tarye in the cite and they wolde lyve and dye with him, and
pay for his costes of housholde an halff yere; but he wold nott, but
toke his jorney to Kyllingworthe. And whan the kynge was gone
the capteyn with the comynes of Kent came a yene to the Black hethe.
And the iij^{the} day of Juyll he came to London; and as sone as thei
entred in London they rubbed Phelippe Malpas. And the iiij day of
Jule he behedid Crowmer and a noþer man at Myle Ende; and the
same day at after none the Lorde Say was fett oute of the Toure to
the Yelde Hall to for the meire to have jugement, and whan he came
befor the meir he saide he wolde be juged by his perys. And
then the comenes of Kent toke him from the officers and ledd him
to the Standart in Chepe and there smote of his hede. And than the
capteyn did do drawe him thorowe London, and over London brige,

and to Seint Thomas Watring, and ther he was hanged and quartered, and his hede and Crowmers hede and a noþer manes hede were sett on London brige.   And after that he smote of ij oþer menes hedis in Sowthewerke.   And the vth day of Jule at nyght (and beyng Sondaye [a]) the comynes of London sett upon the comynes of Kent, for they began to rubbe. And all the men of Kent that were in London that nyght they went to her capteyne in to Sowthewerke. And the same nyght the Meir and Shoreffes and my Lorde Scalys and Mathew Gowghe and the comynes of London went to London Brygge, and ther they faughte from ix of the cloke at eve till ix on the morowe, and at the laste the capteyne fired the drawe brigge. And forthe withe went the Chaunseler [b] to þe capteyne and sessed him and yave him a chartur and his men a noþer, and so with drowe hem homward.   Than the xij daye of Juyll was in every shire proclamed that whate man that couthe take the forsaide cap-teyne shulde have a M^l marke and brynge him to the kynge quycke or dede, and as for any man that longed to him, x marke; for hit was openly knowe that his name was nott Mortymer, his name was John Cade, and þerfor his chartor stode in no streynthe.   And so one Alexandre Iden, a squyre of Kent, toke hym in a garden yn Sowthsex the xiij day of Jule; [c] and in the takynge of him he was hurtt and died that same nyght, and on the morowe he was brought in to the Kynges Bynche, and after was drawe throwe London and his hede set on London brige.

batel on London
e by twene men
)ndon and Kent-
men, Jak Cade
g capten of Kent.

ı Cade taken yn
;, and so hurt yn
akyng that he
the same nyght.

| Nicholas Wyffold, Maire | { William Dere John Medilton | } A° xxix^e. |

This yere the kynge went in to Kent to Caunterbury and sate and did grete justice upon tho that rose with the capteyne, and ther dyed viij men upon a daye.   And in oþer places in Kent the kynge did grete justice; and so þe kynge wentt in to Southsex, and so

---

[a] This parenthesis is added in the margin by the Corrector.
[b] Cardinal Kemp.
[c] This passage has been altered by the Corrector. The sentence originally stood: "And so the xiij day of Jule John Cade was take in Keutt."

westwarde to Salisbery, and ther as the Bysshoppe of Salysbery [a] was slayne. And the same yere stode at ones xiij hedis on London brige. And this yere was Burdeux lost.

Burdens lost.

| William Gregory, Maire | Mathew Phelipp | A° xxx°. |
| | Krystofer Water | |

This yere Richard Duke of Yorke came oute of Walys by Kyngeston brygge unto the Blacke Hethe with a grete power to clere him selfe a gaynes Kynge Henrey of all maner poyntes that the kynge was his hevy lorde fore. And the kynge came ridinge thorowe London with a riall power agayn the sayde duke. And ther the lordis bothe spirituall and temporall toke the mater in honde and entretid hem of rest and pees; the whiche the seid duke at the last agred to on this condission, that his peticiouns for the wele of the kynge and the realme myght be badde and his enemyes to the Toure to abide the lawe; and so were the lordis agreed and sworne enche to other. A none the duke sent home his men ayen, and him selfe mekely obeyed the kynge at the Black Hethe, and his adversaryes stode present contrary the poyntment and othis. And so they brought him thorowe London ungirde by twene two bysshopis to his owne place, and after that made him sworne on the sacrement at Powles after ther entente, and putte him from his gode peticiouns.

| Geffrey Feldynge, Maire | Richard Lee | A° xxxj°. |
| | Richard Alley | |

This yere was the queue delyverde of a sonne, the whiche was called Edwarde, that tyme called Prince.

The byrthe of Edwarde, the so of Kyng Henry vj[te]

| John Norman, Maire | John Walden | A° xxxij°. |
| | Thomas Cooke | |

This yere the ridynge of the Mayres to Westmester was for done, and John Norman, Draper, was the first maire that went to Westmester by barge.

[a] William Ayscough, who was murdered in the preceding year.

| Stephen Foster, Maire | John Felde William Taylor | A° xxxiij^e. |

'yrst Batel at Albons.
This yere the Lord Egrymond was take by Sir John Nevell, my Lorde of Salysburys sone. And in the same yere (the xx^th day of May, beyng Thyrsday ^a) was the fyrst ^b batayll at Seint Albonys; and ther was slayne the Duke of Somersett, the Erle of Northe-homberlonde, the Lord Clyfforde, with oþer mo under the kynges baner. And the Duke of Yorke, the Erle of Warwyke, the Erle of Salysburye wanne the felde, and so came with the kynge to London with mycche ryalte. And this yere the Kynge of Scottys with the rede face layde sege to Berwyke bothe by water and londe. But he was dryve thensse, and all his ordenaunce and vitayle that was on the watir syde lefte be hynde them.

| William Marowe, Maire | John Yonge William Holgrave | A° xxxiiij^e. |

This yere was a grete horlynge be twene the mercers and Lombardes; and then the kynge helde his Counsell at Coventre. And Cauntelowe, mercer and alderman, was sent fiore to come a ffor the kynges Counsell; and as sone as he came he was a rested by the kynges commaundement, and the Baron of Dodley had him in kepinge in the Castell of Dudley for the mater a for wretyn.

| Thomas Canynges, Maire | Rauffe Verney John Stewarde | A° xxxv^e. |

This yere Sir Thomas Percy brake oute of Newgate. And in the same yere was an hurlynge by twene mercers with oþer craftes a yenes Lombardes. And after that by comaundement of the kynge xxviij^ti mercers men and other were sent to Wyndsore Castell, and the Lorde Fakonbrige had the kepynge of them till thei came to the kynges presence. And in this same yere the Sencyall of Normandy, Sir Peers the Brasyle,^c and Flokket,^d came with iij м^l

---

^a Inserted in margin by the Corrector.

^b "the fyrst." Interlined by the Corrector in place of "a," struck out.

^c Pierre de Brézé, Seigneur de la Varenne.

^d Robert de Floquet, bailiff of Evreux. See Monstrelet, iii. 71.

men and londyd be syde Sandwyche, and toke the towne and spoyled
hit, and toke a way myche goode, and slewe dyverse persones, and
toke many prisoners; but the contre came downe and drove hem
a wey, and in her fleynge to shippe ther were drowned mo than
vj^{xx} men of the Frensshe parties.

Geffrey Bolleyn, Maire	John Reyner / William Edward	A° xxxvj^e.

    This yere as the Duke of Yorke and the Erle of Salysbury lay
peasablye in London, than came to London the Duke of Somersett,
and the Erle of Northehomberlond, and the Lord Egrymond, and
other lordes of ther affynite, and loged hem from Tempill Bar to
Westmester, with myche people all aboute to Seynt Gylis; and they
came in that entent for to fight with the Duke of Yorke. And in
the meane tyme came from Caleys the Erle of Warwyke with a
godely fellaueshippe to helpe the Duke of Yorke and his fader,
but the Meire off London with a godely fellaueshippe of men of
armes kepte the pees. And in the same yere Bysshoppe Pecok Bysshop Pecok.
was acusyd of heresye, and many of his bokys brent, and he put in
holde to the Erchebysshoppe of Caunterbury. And the same yere
the Erle of Warwyke destressed the Flete of Spayne taward
Flawndres. Also a none after he toke xvij hulkes with oþer smaler
vesselles laden with salt for be cause they wolde not strike in the
kinges name of Inglond.

Thomas Scott, Maire	Rauffe Josselyng / Richard Medam	A° xxxvij^e.

    This yere was a grete fraye be twene the Cite of London and A grete fray in
men of Cowrte, which were drevyn with the Archeres of the [F]letestrete he [t]he Cyte and
Cite from the Standarde in Flete strete to ther innes, the xiij day of men of Corte.
Apreill, and some were slayne and some were taken, where for
William Tayllour, Alderman of the same warde, was sent to
Wyndsore to a byde the kynges grace, and ther thei bode till
Hewlyn was Meire, and so thorowe his prayer thei had grace of the
kynge. And þis same yere the kynge and the queue and ther
lordes lete make a grete gaderynge in the northe contre, where of

was grete noyse. And the Erle of Warwyke came from Caleys thorowe London, and the Erle of Salysbery went from Medlame for to mete withe the Duke of Yorke and Warwyke his sonne with iiij M^l men, and the quene lay by the wey with xiiij M^l men to stoppe his wey. And he toke a felde manly at Blorehethe the xxiij day of Septembre, and faught and slowe many and put the remnant to flight, and helde forthe his wey in purpos to Ludlowe, where Kynge Henry came with l M^l men a gayne the Duke of Yorke, the Erle of Marche, the Erle of Rotlonde, the Erle of Warwyke, the Erle of Salysbury, the whiche never entendid to be oþerwyse then feythefull and trewe liege men to the kynge, but crowelly were banysshed oute of this londe and not excepte like as thei were worthi. And so ther departed the Duke of Yorke and his sonne Rotlond thorowe Godis helpe in to Irelonde; and the Erle of Marche, the Erle of Warwyke, and the Erle of Salysbury, and Sir John Wenloke in a litell vessell, Almighti God gided hem oute of the Weste Contre by the see to Caleys.

| William Hewlyn, Maire | John Plomer John Stocker | A^o xxxviij^e. |

This yere the kynge graunted the Duke of Somersett for to be Capteyne of Caleys. A[nd] anone he made him redy thedirwarde; but the Erle of Warwyke was þer a fore, and kepte him that he myght not londe there; and so he was conveyed to Gynes and his pepylle, and assone as he was with in the castell he made stronge werre a gaynes Caleys, and they of Calys a gaynes him. And than he sent in to Englonde to the kynge for more pepull. And so the kyng sent the Lorde Ryveres and his sonne Antony with iiij^c men for to strenthe the Duke of Somersett. And as they were at Sand-wyche the Erle off Warwyke had knowleche, and a none he made a sawte over with a godely fellaweshippe and londed at Sandwyche, and toke the Lorde Reveres and his sonne and distrussyd all his pepull. And so they were brought to Caleys a yenes her will. And this yere a for this tyme the Duke of Exceter was syned for kepe the see a yenes the Erle of Warwike, but his viage turned to

nought; and or he went to the see he toke a gentilman of the
Temple that was called Nevell, and John Goode felane, vinter, and
oþer viij persones, and bare hem on honde that they were going to
Caleys to the Erle of Warwyke with bowestrenges and arowes
heded. And here upon thei were dampned of treison, and her
hedis sett on London Brige, and ther quarters on the yatis aboute
the towne. And this yere Judde, that was maister of the kynges
ordenaunce, as he caried ordenaunce to the kynge warde, a litell
beyonde Seint Albonis, he was slayne on Seint Albones daye. And
þat same tyme Moumfford was made capteyne of iiij^c men for to
goo to helpe the Duke of Somersett. And as they were at Sandwiche the Erle of Warwyke had knowleche of them, and a none
he made oute a pussaunce of pepulle and beseged Sandwyche, and
wanne the towne, and toke Moumford, and many of his men slayne;
and so they led him to Caleys, and so led him to Rise banke, and
ther the shipmen smote of his hede, and ij of his menes hedis. And
sone after came the Erle of Marche, the Erle of Warwyke, the Erle
of Salysbury, and Sir John Wenlok, and the Lorde Audeley from
Caleys, and londid at Sandwyche; and so they came to London
warde, and ther mett with hem the Lorde Cobham and oþer statys
and comyns of Kentt, and so they came to London. And the Lorde
Scalys was that tyme in London, and he desired to be capteyn of
the cite but the comenys wolde not have him. Than the Lord
Scalis, the Lord Lovell, the Erle of Kendale, Thorpe, and Browne
of Kentt, and many galy men, with oþer peopulle, went to the
Toure of London, and made grete werre a yenes the cite. And in
the mene tyme thes oþer lordes sent to the meire and to the statis
of the cite for to have all ther hertes. And a none ther was sent
sertayne aldermen and comynes for to well come them; and so they
came with all ther pussaunce of pepull in to Sowthwerke. And
on the morowe they came, to the nombre of xlM^l, to London Brigge,
and toke downe suche hedis as were there, and beryed them at Seint
Mangnus; and so they rode forthe to Seint Powlys and ther offerd.
And þere mett with them the Erchebysshoppe of Cawnterbury,

withe many other bysshoppes, and the meire and the aldermen,
with all the statis of the cite; and ther was declared all the poyntis
and pardon to all the realme.   And than all thes lordis went to the
Grey Frerys and helde ther a counsell on the Thorsday.   And on
the Fryday they went to the Gelde halle, and ther was endited
many persones and putt in presone.   And sone after rode the Erehe-
bysshoppe of Caunterbury, the Bysshoppe of Excester, and many
other bysshoppis, and a legett,[a] and the Erle of Marche, and the
Erle of Warwyke, the Lord Faconbryge, the Lorde Bowser, and
his sonnes, with myche other pepull of Kent, Southesex, and Esex,
tawarde the kynge with grete ordenaunce; and the Erle of Salysbury, the Lorde Cobham, and Sir John Wenlock, were lefte in the
cite of London with the meire.   And forthe with the Lord Cobham
and the shoreffes went and laide grete ordenaunce a yenes the Toure
on the towne syde, and Sir John Wenlok, an[d] Harow mercer,
kept on Seint Katerynes side, and myche harme done on bothe
parties.   And in all placis of London was grete watche for doute of
tresoun.   And then they skyrmysed to gedir, and myche harme
was done dayly.   And on the Thorsdye, the ix[th] [b] day of Julle, was
the batayll be syde Northhampton in the Newfelde be twene Har-
syngton and Sandyfforde, and ther was the kynge take in his tente.
And ther was slayne the Duke of Bockyngham, the Erle of Shrovys-
bury, the Vycounte Bemonde, the Lord Egremonde, and Sir
William Lucy, and many other knyghtes and squyers, and many
comyners were drowned.   And than the Erle of Marche, and the
Erle of Warwyke, with oþer lordis, brought the kynge to Northampton with myche rialte.   And so the kynge with his lordis came
to London, with him the Erle of Marche; þe Erle of Warwyke
bare the kynges swerde.   And ther came with the kynge the
Bysshoppe of Caunterburye, withe many other bysshoppes and
lordis.   And the Erle of Salysbury rode a yenes the kynge withe
myche rialte; and then was called and sett a Parlement.   And on

[a] Francesco Coppini, bishop of Teramo.
[b] Should be the 10th, which was Thursday.

the Fryday after the kynge herde the masse of Jesus at Poulys, and so went a processyon thorowe the cite. And on that same daie was the Towre yolden. And on the Satyrday Sir John Wenlok and Harowe mercer were sent to the Toure to put hem to warde that were gilty, and so thei dide; but they sent the Lord Sealys a wey prevely. And that was perceyved by the shippmen, and they laide watche and toke him, and slowe him and leyde him naked in Seint Mary Overes chirche yerde. And forthe with the Erle of Warwyke rode to the Toure, and ther he made a proclamacion, and all a boute the cite, chargynge that no maner of persone shuld not sle, nor stelle, nor morder, on peyne of dethe. And the same day dyned all the bysshoppes and lordis with the meire. And on the Wenesday aftir the lordis and the meire went to the Gildhall, and they comaundid the shorevys to fette the prisoners from the Toure, and so they feghte Senkeler, and Browne of Kent, Okeley, Monkys, Davy John, Fawkoner, with oþer, whiche were reyned, and some were dampned of tresoun, and were drawe and hanged, and her hedis smytten of. And this yere Thorpe was goinge a wey, and he was disgysed, but he was take and brought to London a yene with a newe shave crowne, and so brought to the Erle of Salysbury place, and afterwarde sent to the Toure of London. This yere came the Duke of Yorke and his sonne Erle of Rotlonde oute of Irlonde to Westmester, to the forsaide Parlement, on a Friday, the x day of Octobre, cleymynge his right and titell, where in the lordis were a yenes him, but that was afterward full dere bought. And ther it was argued and prevyd be twene Kynge Harry and the seid duke, with all ther wise counsell, spirituall and temporall, in the seid Parlement, that þe right of the crowne is of Inglond and of Fraunce to þe seid duke and his eyres perteyneth and longethe, and to none othir. And yett they be liege men a yene to Kyng Henry for his lyve tyme, and eche to oþer sworne to be trewe, and hit was proclamed.

The Lorde Scal
slayne the xxth (
July, Aº D'ni M'
lx.

Richard Lee, Maire { John Lambard
                      Richard Flomynge } Aº xxxixᵉ

This yere the Duke of Yorke, the Erle of Rotland, and the Erle of Salysbury, with myche oþer pepull, rode northewarde to kepe her Crystmas.   And there lay in her wey at Wakefelde to stope hem the Duke of Excester, the Duke of Somersett, the Erle of Wilde-shire, the Lord Roose, with other lordys and myche other pepull, and so fell upon hem and slowe the Duke of Yorke, the Erle of Rotlonde, the Erle of Salysbury, and Harowe and Pekerynge, mercers, and myche other pepull; and this was done on newe yeris evyn.   And a none after the quene reysed all the northe and all oþer pepull by the wey, compelled, dispoyled, rubbed, and dis-troyed all maner of cattell, vetayll, and riches to Seint Albones, where þᵉ Duke of Northefolke, the Erle of Warwyke, and many oþer lordis with Kynge Harrye and grete multitude of comyncs and ordynaunce mett with hem with batayle, and slewe myche pepull on bothe the parties.   And there Kynge Henry brake his othe and grement made be twene hym and his trewe lordis, and so wyckedly for sworne went to the contrary parte of the northe, and disseyved his trewe lordis that stode in grete jopardy for his sake, Northeffolke, Warwyke, with other moo, whiche were full fayne to scape with her lyves, and the Lorde Bonvyle and Sir Thomas Kyryell, that bode with the kynge and trusted on him, for he graunted to save them; and they were be hedid evyn a for the quene and prince so called at that tyme.   And so the kynge and the queue purposed for to come to London and do excucion upon suche persones as was a yenes the quene; but the comynes of the cite wolde not suffer hem, nor none of herrys, to entyr in to London; and so they torned northewarde. ' And the Erle of Marche kept his Crystmas at Glowceter.   And when tythinges came that my lorde his fader and his brother with many oþer lordys falsely was mortherd and slayne, to hym the grettes hevynes that might be, and how the northe was reysed like as it is a for wretyn com-mynge southewarde, than a none he dide sende in to dyverse shires of knowlache, and sone after he badde xxx Mˡ of gode men commyng to fyght with hem.   Than came sodenly oþer tidynges

felde on new vyn.

ecunde Batell Seynt Albons.

Erle of
he, fyrst so
d, after was kyng,
ᵈ Edwarde the

that the Erle of Wildshire and the Erle of Pembroke by see were
come in to Walys with Frensshemen and Brettons, and Iresshe
men, comynge and reyson Walys thorowe purposynge hem for to
distroye hym, and he with all his men torned a yene bacwarde in to
Walis and mett with hem at Mortymers Crosse, where that hit was _{Mortymers Cross}
saide on a Sonday Candilmasday by the morowe appered the sonne _{Walys.}
as iij sonnys sondry on hym in the este and closyd a yene to geder.
And than he kneled doune on his kneis and made his prayers and
thanked God. And anone fresshly and manly he toke the felde
upon his enemyes and put hem at flyght, and slewe of them iij m¹,
and some of ther capteyns were take and be bedide, but Pembroke
and Wildshire stale a wey prevely disgysed and fled oute of the
contrey.   And a none forthe with he made him redy a gayne in the
marche of Walis, and on the Thorsday the first weke of Lenten he
came to London with xxx m¹ men of Westren men and Walsshmen,
Kentes men and Esex men togeders, and so in feld and towne
everychone called Edward Kynge of Ingelond and of Fraunce. _{Md. Kyng Edw:}
And the iiijth day of Marche he rode to Westmester and resseyved _{the iiijth at West}
the septor with his dignite. And also that tyme Sir Baudewyn _{mynster the iiij^t}
Fulforde, knyght, and Haysond, squyer, were saylenge on the see <sub>of Marche toke t
hys septor with l
dignite, but not</sub>
taward Brettayne for to reysse pepull agaynes Kynge Edwarde, but _{crowne.}
they were take and brought to Bristowe, and ther were drawe,
hanged, and quartered, and Sir Baudwyns hede caryed to Excester
and sate upon the castell yate. And than our Kynge Edwarde _{Palme Sonday f}
made him redy with hym the Duke of Northeffolke, the Erle of <sub>called York feld
xxixth day of M:</sub>
Warwyke, the Erle of Kent, with oþer lordis, knyghtes, and _{Aⁿ D'ni M¹.iiijᶜ.l}
squyers northewarde, and hem folowed grete multitude of pepull,
and thei mette be side Shireborne with the lordes of the northe on
ether syde lyke an c. m¹. And ther was slayne on bothe partes
xxxvj m¹. vijc. lxxvij. And ther wan Kynge Edwarde the felde
thanked by Jesu. And than rode the kynge to Yorke and ther he
was rialy resseyved. And ther he in the castell toke the Erle of
Devynysshyre and oþer mo, and did lett smyte of her hedes. And
Kynge Harrye fled with his quene and dyverse lordis with hem to

Berwyke, and they delyverd that towne and many oþere castelles
in the northe to the Scottis and to the Frensshemen for to have
socoure of hem.   And after that Kynge Edward came a yene to
London, and ther he was rialy resseyved, and forthe with he was
crowned at Westmester the xxviij daye of June on Seint Petirs
evyn.   And there he made his ij brethern dukys, that is to sey,
Lorde George Dukè of Clarence, the Lorde Richard Duke of
Glowcester, and he made many knyghtes and squyers.

nācio Edwardi
28 die Junii, Aᵒ
1461.

Thes bethe the names of the Maires and Shoreffes of the Cite of
London in the tyme of the regne of Kynge Edward the Fourthe.

ırdus iiijᵗᵘˢ

Hugh Wyehe, Maire $\left\{\begin{array}{l}\text{John Locke}\\\text{George Irelond}\end{array}\right\}$ Aᵒ primo.

This yere was imagened and wrought grete treyson a yenes the
kynge by the menys of the Erle of Oxenford and his sonne Aubry,
with oþer knyghtes and the kynges rebelles, traytors and adves-
saryes with oute the londe, the whiche tresones God sent the kynge
hym selfe knowleche, and anon they were taken and juged to dethe.
Fyrst the Lorde Aubrye was drawe the xx daye of Feverell thorowè
London to the Toure Hill, and ther he was behedid ; and the xxiij
day of Feveryll was Sir Thomas Tudnam, knyght, and Sir William
Tyrrell and John Mongomery, squyer, drawe from Westmester
thorowe London to the Toure Hill, and ther was be hedyd upon a
scaffolde.   And the xxvj day of the same monthe was John Veer
the Erle of Oxynford led thorowe London to the Toure Hill, and
ther was be heded on the same scaffolde.   And the fyrst d[a]y of
Marche was Sir William Kenedy, knyght, led from Westmester
thorowe London to the Toure Hill, and ij other men with him, and
ther were be hedid on the same scaffold.   Also this yere the Egill
on Poulis stepell was take downe for hit was broke, but whan hit
shulde be set up a yene he that shulde have set it up fell downe and
was dede, and so anoþer man was hired and sett up the Egyll the
iij daye of Juyll.   This yere was dyverse of the castelles in the
northe yolden a yene to Kynge Edwarde.

| Thomas Cooke, Maire | William Hampton Bartilmewe James | A⁰ ij^c. |

This yere Quene Margaret toke Bamburgh, Anwyke, and Don-synburgh with the nombre of vj M^l of Frensshemen; and in this same yere the kynge did make grete gunnes and other grete ordy-naunce at London, and did do cary hit in to the northe contre. And ther the kynge with thes lordis laide sege to thes castelles a for wreten; the whiche were yolden, savynge Bambrough wold not yelde till the wallys were betten downe; and ther in was take Sir Rauffe Graye, knyght, and he was be heded at Yorke. Also this yere Thomas Routhe, squyer, and ij oþer men, were be hedid at the Toure Hill for treson. Also this yere the Duke off Somersett be came the kynges liege man and sworne, but he kepte not his othe, for he went a yene to the contrary parte.

| Matheus Philippe, Maire | Thomas Muscehamp Robert Bassett | A⁰ iij^e. |

This yere came diverse lordes and gentillez to Exham of the quenes affynete, and the Lord Mountegew with other knyghtes an squyers had knowleche of them, and ther thei toke the moste parti of them, that is for to sey: Harry the Duke of Somersett, the whiche was be heded the xv day of May at Exham; Sir Emonde Fyssh, knyght, Bradshawe, Rawlyne Honte, and Blacke Jackett, were be heded at Yorke the xv day of May; and the xviij day of May was be hedid Sir Thomas Hull, knyght, John Marfyn, late servaunte with the quene, John Botler, John Gosse, late kerver to the Duke of Somersett, Roger Water, late purcer to Kynge Henry that was, Harry Docfford, William Dawson, William Pryce, Thomas Hegge, Thomas Fenwyck, and John Champyon; at Midlam were be heded Sir Philippe Wynterworthe,[a] knyght, Sir William Ponyngton, war-deyne of Topclyff, Olyver Wyntworthe, William Spyller of Yorke, Thomas Honte, late yoman with the queue that was. Also at Newcastell the xxvij day of May were beheded the Lord Honger-

---

[a] Wentworth.

ford, the Lorde Roose, Sir Thomas Fyndorne, knyght, Bernarde
Delamore, Nicholas Massy, and the xxviij day of May was other vj

ete drought, for
ver reyned from
ıyddys of Marche
ıe morow after
somer day.

persones be heded.   Also this yere was a grete drouthe, the whiche
duryd from myddes of Marche till the morne after Mydsomer day
that never reyned.   And this yere whete was worthe iiij d. a
busshell, and all maner of vetaille grete chepe, and wyne grete
chepe, and grete skarssete of money.   Also this yere was a grete
pestilence thorowe all the realme.

Rauff Josselynge, Maire	{ John Tate { John Stone	} A⁰ iiijᵉ

This yere there was a grete frost and grete snowne, where
thorowe mych cattell of bestis and shepe for fawte of mete were
distroyed.   Also this yere the kynge spoused the duches doughter

a i   of
e Elyzabeth.

of Bedford, þe whiche was crowned at Westmcster the Sonday a
for Wytsonday, that is to sey, the xxvj day of Maye, att the whiche
coronacion was made xlvij Knyghtes of the Bathe, where of were
foure men of London, þat is to sey, Rauffe Josselynge, draper,
that tyme beynge maire, Hugh Wiche, mercer, John Plomer,
grocer, Harry Waffer, draper.   Also this same yere Kynge Harry
was take in the northe contre, and ij doctors with him, the whiche
wer called Doctor Mannynge and Doctor Beden, the whiche were
all thre brought to London.   And by the wey the Erle of Warwyke mett with hem at Islyngdon by the kynges comaundement,
and ther a rested the forsayde Kynge Hanry upon serteyne poyntes,
and so brought him in att Newgate and thorowe Chepe side, and
so thorow all London to the Toure, that is to sey, on Seint James

be gan fyrst the
l of x s. callyd
yal.

evyn the xxiiij day of Jule.   Also this yere the kynge lete smyte
a newe noble with a roose standyng there as the crosse shulde at
the value of x s. ster.   And the olde nobill was valued, and so to
goo for vııj s. ıııj d.   And ther was newe grotes and pensse made
after the valewe of the nobyll, that is to sey, lighter then they were
a fore.   Also he lete make a pece of golde valued at vj s. viij d.,
that is to sey an angell, and oþer smaller peces of golde of les
valure, &c.

HISTORICAL MEMORANDA

IN EARLY HANDWRITINGS,

FROM THE SAME MS.

The first of these articles is in a fifteenth century hand. The handwriting of all the others is a little later. Nos. V. VI. and VII. are in a handwriting of the time of Henry VIII. being that of the annotator and corrector of the preceding Chronicle. Nos. II. and III. are apparently contemporary with the events related, and No. IV. may possibly be so too. No. VII. consists of entries written inside the cover at the beginning of the book.

I. *Siege of Calais*, 1346.

(At f. 139.)

Her begyneth the retenewe of the dowty kynge, K. Edward the thirde, and howe he went to the sege of Callis with his oste, and to the partes of Fraunche and of Normandye, and howe he layde sege to the towne and castall of Callys be water and londe in the yere of oure Lorde God a M^{li}.iijc & xlvj. And in the iij day of Septembur the good Kyng Edward the thirde laide his segge to þe towne and castell of Callis, and ther contenewide his sege be water and londe unto the iij dai of Auguste next folowing, at the whiche dai, moynant the grace of Almyghty Jesu, the saide towne and castell were delivered unto the saide good Kynge Edward at his owne welle, &c.

Item, furst Edward, prince of Wallys, and the Bischope
    of Dyvelyn they brought with theym erlys a .   xj
Barones and baneretes .   .   .   .   .   xlvij

And of knyghtes they brought . . . . . xc.lxiij

Squyers, constablys, receyvers, and leders of men with
    the oste . . . . iijм^{li}.vjc

Item, in venterars and archers on horsbacke   vм^{li}.iiijc

Item, of hobelares . . . . vjc

Item, archers on fotte . . . . . . xvм^{li}.шjc.шj^{xx}

Item, of masones, carpentrs, smythis, engyners, pavy-
    landrs, armorars, goners, and macker of artorie . шjc.шj^{xx}

      Some of þe nombur of þe men be forsayde comythe
      to . . . . xxvjм^{li}.vc.iiij^{xx}j

Item, of mayster schepmen, constalars, schepmen, and
    pages, schepis forstaged, barges and ballyngrs, and
    vetylars diverse, the some of men beforseide, xlvjм^{li}.iiijc.iiij^{xx}xij

And some of the schipes and schipmen and vetellers
    comyth to . . . . xvjм^{li}

Theys bene the names of þe seide retenewe of Prince Edward
and with hym in his retenewe.

Item, baneretes x

Item, with him of knyghtes . . . . . . ijc

Item, with him of squyrs . ijc.iij^{xx} & iiij

Item, with him archeres on horsbake ijc.iiij^{xx}iij

Item, with him archeres on fote . . . . iij^{xx}ix

                             ixc.xxvj.

The yerle of Lancaster.

Item, with him of kny3ts baneretes . . . . xj

Item, with him of knyghtes bachellers iiijc.xj

Item, with him of squyers . . vc.xij

Item, with him archres on fote vc

         Summa, м^{li}.iiijc.xxxiiij.

Sir William Becheham, Erle Notingham.[a]

Item, with him knightes baneretes . ijc
Item, with him knyghtes bachelers xlij
Item, with hym of squyrs . . . . . . cxij
Item, with hym of archeres . . . . . . cxlj

Summa, iiijc.iiij[xx]xv.

Sir William Bechamp, Erle of Ware.[b]

Item, with him knightes baneretes . . . . iij
Item, with him knyghtes bachelrs . xlij
Item, with him squyers . . . . . . cxij
Item, with him of archres . . . . . . cxlj

Summa, ijc.iiij[xx]xviij.

Sir Richard, Erle of Arndell.

With him kny3ts baneretes . . . . . . iij
With him kny3ts bachelers . . . . . . xlj
With him of squyers . . . . cvj
With him of archers . . . . clij

Summa, iijc.ij.

Syr Robert Dafferd,[c] Erle of Soffolke.

With him kny3ts baneretes . . . . . . j
With hym knyghtes bachelers . . . . . xxxvj
With hyme of squyers . . . . lviij
With him of archers . . . . lxiiij

Summa, vij[xx]xix.

Sir William Elynton,[d] Erle of Huntyngtoun.

And with him knightes baneretes . . . . . ij
And with him kny3tes bachelers xxx
And with him of squyers . iiij[xx]xiij
And with him of archers . . . . . iiij[xx]viij

Summa ijc.xiij.

---

[a] There was no such title in those days, and even the surname appears to be erro-neons. Sir William de Bohun, Earl of Northampton, is probably the person intended.

[b] Sir Thomas Beauchamp, Earl of Warwick, appears to be the person intended.

[c] d'Ufford.   [d] Should be Clynton.

Sir John Vere, Erle of Oxenford.

With hym knyȝtes baneretes	j
With him knyghtes bachelers	. xxij
With hym of squyers	xliiij
With hym of archers	iijˣˣiiij
	vijˣˣ & xj.

Sir Lawraunce Hastingis, Erle of Penbrocke.

With him knyghtes baneretes	j
With him knyȝtes bachelers	. j
With him of squyers	xxiiij
With him of hoblers	xxviij
With him of archers	xxvj
	Summa, iiij score.

Theys bene the names of diverse lordes withholden in the kynges retenewe that ben straungers and not empresed in the nombur afforseyd:

Lowes, emperoure of þᵉ Normaynes, to him delliverd
in prest at diverse tymes for his wages and his
mens . . . . . . viijᴍˡ.ijᴄ.xxvij*li.* xij*d.*
To Machony, William Juillian, and to his men viijᴍˡ.ixᴄ.lxij*li.* x*s.*
To Reynold, Ducke of Melder, and his meney iiijᴍ.vᴄ.xij
To John, Duck Brabant, and his meny . vᴄ*li.*
To William, Erle of Henawde, and his men . . iijᴍˡⁱ.ᴄ.
To Threder, Lorde Frankmownde, and his men iijᴍˡⁱ.viijᴄ.
iijˣˣiiij*li.* viij*s.* iij*d.*
To Charles of Maroke, brother to the Bischope of Legges,
to hym and his men . . . . . vijᴄ*li.*
To Bartold, Erle of Baspiche, Mark of Bradisbourch,
and to other knyghtes and squyres, and straungers
with holdyng a bowte the kynge and his housholde
Summa, iijᴄ.xlj*li.* xvj*s.* viij*d.*

Item, to Bawdwyne, Ersbischope of Thyne, and his meny vjc.vj$li.$
Item, to the Ersbiship̄e of Magondenentes,[a] and his meny iijc.l$li.$
Summa totalis prestez xxxjM^{li}.lxiij$li.$ v$s.$ xj$d.$

The sume total of þᵉ saide exspencēs, as wil for wage, prestis, as for þᵉ exspencis of þᵉ Kyngis house as for other giftes and rewardes, and for schipes, and for other thynges neserers in þᵉ saide partis of Praunce and Normandy, and before Calis durynge the sege there, as it apperithe in the compe of Wil Norwell, keper of þᵉ kyngis warddrope, from the xij day of Juylii, the yere of þᵉ reigne of þᵉ saide Kynge Edward, unto the xxvij daie of Maye, in þᵉ yere of his reigne the xiiijth, that is to saie be a yere and iij quartres and xlj days, þat ys to saie, iijc.&xxxvijM^{li}.c.iiij$li.$ ix$s.$ iiij$d.$

In the yere of oure Lorde God a M^{li}.iijc xlvj, and in the iij dai of September, the good Kynge Edward the iij^{de} laide his sege to the towne and castill of Calis, and contenewed his sege be water and londe unto þᵉ iij dai of Auguste next folowynge, at the whiche day, moynant þᵉ grace of our Lorde God, the saide towne and castill were delliverd unto the saide good Kynge Edward at his owne will.

II. *Edward IV. at Bristol*, 1461.[b]
(At f. 132.)
The Receyvyng of King Edward the iiijth at Brystowe.

First, at the comyng ynne atte Temple gate there stode Wylliam Conquerour with iij lordis, and these were his wordis:

Well come, Edwarde, our Son of high degre,
Many yeeris hast þᵘ lakkyd owte of this londe.
I am thy fore fader, Wylliam of Normandye,
To see thy welefare here thrugh Goddys sond.[c]

Over the same gate stondyng a greet gyaunt delyveryng the keyes.

<hr>

[a] Maguntineusis, *i. e.* of Mayence.
[b] This fragment has been already printed by Mr. Halliwell in the appendix to Warkworth's Chronicle, p. 32.
[c] *i. e.* by a mission from God.

The Receyvyng atte Temple Crosse next folowyng.

There was Seynt George on horsbakke uppon a tent fyghtyng
with a dragon, and the kyng and the queue on hygh in a castell,
and his doughter benethe with a lambe. And atte the sleyng of the
dragon ther was a greet melody of aungellys.

III. *Capitulation of Granada,* 1492.
(III. At f. 141.)

Be hyt had yn mynde that the cite of Garnartho, the whiche
sometyme was Crysten, and after were renegates, and so contynued
ᵃthe space of vijc. yere unto the tyme hit plesed God the Crysten
Kyng of Spayne layd sege to the sayde cyte, and so famysshed
them, in so moche as the fyrst day of January, the yere of our Lord
Mˡ.iiijᴄ.iiijˣˣxj,ᵃ the sayd cite be poynt ment was yelde up and
deliverd to the forsaid Kyng of Spayne, every Sarazyn to have as
moche of his owne stuf as he cowde bere on hys bak at oon tyme,
harnes, gold, sylver, and wepyn oonely except.

Item, whan the fyrst man entred the cyte they founde xxxᵗⁱMˡ.
payre of bryganders, where of vjMˡ. were coverd with clothe of gold
and sylk nailed with gilt nailes. Item, thei fownd iiijMˡ. peire of
white harnes complete, xxijMˡ. crossebowes with alle thapparrell to
them belongyng, xxiiijMˡ. swerdes, where of xMˡ. were gylt and
harnest with sylver, eche of them to the valeue of l.s. sterlynges.
Item, ther was founde in the saide cite, at soche tyme as it was yeld
up, the nowmbre of xxiijᵗⁱᴄ.Mˡ. and xMˡ. people betwext the age of
xij and iijˣˣ yere, be side children and very olde people. Item, in
the chefe tempyll were iijᴄ. laumpes of gold, the worst ofᵇ them to
the valew of xxiiijᵗⁱ *li.* sterlynges. In the same temple also were
iiij chayres of gold, and xxijᵗⁱ sylver setys for the kyng, the quene,
and other lordes. In the same temple also was founde grete plente

---

ᵃ 1492 according to the historical year which begins on the 1 Jan.
ᵇ *of* repeated in MS.

of gold and sylver redy coyned, which the Kyng of Spayne left
there styll to byld therewith a chyrche, where as afore was the
tempyll of ydolatrye. Item, in one of the castels where as the kyng
and the queue of Garnartho logged, the walles of the halle and
chambers were of marbel, crystall, and jasper, set with precious
stones, and more over there was fownde grete and innumerable
ryches. Item, or thei wold yeld up the citee for lak of vytalles,
thei ete hors, dogges, and cattes, ijᶜ. Crysten men ther beyng
prisoners.

IV. *The Battle of Flodden*, 1513.ᵃ

(At f. 204.)

Here folowyth the batyll be twyxte the Kyng of Scottys callyd
Kyng Jamys and the noble Eerele of Surrey, foughten yn Bramton
Felde the ixᵗʰ day of Septembre, in the fyfte yere of Kyng Henrye
the viijᵗʰ [he then beyng in his warres in Fraunce.] ᵇ

Fyrste whan bothe armyes were met with yn iij myles togedyr,
the Erle of Surrey sent an offycer of armes called Roger Crosse ᶜ
un to the Kyng of Scottes desyryng hym of batell, and he answerde
he wolde abyde hym batell tyll the Fryday at noone. The Lorde
Howarde at xj of the elok the same day passyd over the brydge of
Twyssell with the fowarde and artyllerye, and the Erle of Surrey
folowde with the rewarde. The armye was devyded yn to ij batelles,
and every batell ij wynges. The Kyng of Scottes armye was devyded in to fyve batelles, and every batell arowe shote from another,
and all yn lyke farnes from the Englyssh men, and they were in
greet plompes, parte of them were quadrant, some pykewyse, and
were on the toppe of the hyll, beyng a quarter of a myle from the
foote ther of. The Lorde Howarde cawsed his vowarde to scale yn

---

ᵃ This account is nearly the same as that printed in the State Papers of
Henry VIII. vol. iv. p. 1, from a MS. in the Public Record Office, but there are
material variations, especially towards the end.

ᵇ Added in a different hand.

ᶜ MS. Rog' crosse, *i. e.* Rouge Croix.

a lytell valey tyll they were ——— [a] of the wynge of hys batell; and then bothe wardes yn oone avaunced ageynste the Scottes; and then they cam downe the hyll and met with them yn good ordre after the Allmens manner, with owte spekyng of any wordes. The Erele of Huntley ——— [b] and Crafford with theyre hoste cam uppon the Lorde of Howard with vjᴹ¹. men, and shortley theyr bakkes were turned and the most parte of them were slayne. Then the Kyng of Scottes cam with a grete poysaunce uppon the Erle of Surrey, havyng on hys lyfte hande the Lorde Dacars son,[c] whych two bare all the brounte of the batell; and there the sayde kyng was slayne with yn a speere-length of the sayde erele and meney noble men with hym, and no prisoners to these ij batelles. And yn the tyme of theyr batell theerle of Ly——[d] and Argylle with theyre puysaunce yoyned with Sʳ Edwarde Stanley, and he boldely met with them and put them bothe to flyte. Edmónde Howarde had with hym ᴹ¹. Chesshyre men and vᴄ. Lankyshyre men, and meny gentyllmen of Yorkshyre on the ryght wyng of the Lorde Howarde. The Lorde Chamberleyn of Scotlonde, with many other lordes, dyd set on the forsayde Edmunde; and the Chesshyre men and Lankysshyre men never abode stroke, and verey few of the gentylmen of Yorkshyre abode but fled. Master Grey and Sir Umfrey Lyle be prisoners and Rycharde Harepotell slayne; and the seyde Edmunde Howarde was twyse fellyd, and to hys relyfe cam the Lorde Dacars with xvᴄ. men and put to flyte all the Scottes, and of hys men were slayne abowte the nomebre of viijᴄ.; in whyche batell a gret nomebre of Scottes were slayne. The batell begɪn be twene iiij and v of the elok at aftyrnoone, and the chase lastyd iij myle, with mervylous slawter of men; and yf the Englyssh men had be horsyd to have pursuede the chase they had slayne xᴍ¹. mo Scottes than there were

[a] Blank in MS. The reading in the Record Office MS. is, "tyll the rerewarde were joyned to oon of the wynges."

[b] Blank in MS. The Record Office MS. reads, "Arell" (i. e. Erroll).

[c] The Record Office MS. reads, "my Lord Darcy son."

[d] The latter part of the name is left blank in our MS. That in the Record Office reads, "therles of Lynewes (i. e. Lennox) and Argyll."

slayne, for the Scottes were above iiij score M^l. And borederars not oonely stale awey horsys, but allso the oxen that drew the ordnaunce, and cam to the pavylions and toke awey all the stuffe there yn, and slew meny of them that kep the same. The Kyng of Scottes body is karryd to Berwyke. Allso on the morrowe after that the felde was fawght the Lorde Howarde went yn to the felde ageyne, where that the Scottes ordynaunce lay, with a smawle companye of men. And then cam viijc. Scottes on hors bak presupposyng to have had awey the ordynaunce which they lefte behynde them the day before; and when they sawe the Lorde Howarde they set apon hym, and there they began a sore fray, for then were meny men slayne on bothe partys; there were ijc. of Scottes slayne, and of Englyssh men I can not tell. There was slayne oone gentyll man callyd Morres Bakley, and oone othyr callyd Warcoppe, with maney other whyche be not yet knowen.

V. *Books prohibited,* 1531.

(At f. 65.)

Memorandum, the first Sonday of Advent, in the yere of our Lorde M^l. fyve hundreth and xxxjth, these bokes folowyng were opynly at Poules Crosse, by the autorite of my lorde of London[a] under his autentycal siale, by the doctor that that day prechide, prohibite, and straytely commaunded of no maner of man to be used, bought, nor solde, nor to be red, under payne of suspencion, and a greter payne, as more large apperyth in for sayde autoryte. The first boke ys this:—

1. The disputacion betwixte the father and the son.
2. The Supplicacion of Beggars.
3. The Revelation of Antechriste.
4. Liber qui de veteri et novicio[b] Deo inscribitur.

[a] John Stokesley.
[b] The word *novo* occurs before *novicio,* but is erased.

5. Pie Precaciones.

6. Economica Christiana.

7. The Burying of the Masse, in English yn ryme.

8. An Exposition in to the vij chapter to the Corinthians.

9. The Matrimony of Tyndal.

10. A. B. C. ayenst the Clergye.

11. Ortulus Anime, in Englisshe.

12. A Boke a yenst Saynt Thomas of Caunterbury.[a]

13. A Boke made by Freer Roye a yenst the Sevyn Sacramentes.

14. An Answere of Tyndal unto Sir Thomas Mores Dyaloge yn English.

15. A Disputacion of Purgatorye, made by John Frythe.

16. The Firste Boke of Moyses called Genesis.

17. A prologe in the ij^{de} Boke of Moyses called Exodus.

18. A prologe in Thyrde Boke of Moyses called Leviticus.

19. A prologe in the $iiij^{th}$ Boke of Moyses called Numeri.

20. A prologe in the vth Boke of Moyses called Detronomye.

21. The Practyse of Prelates.

22. The Newe Testament in Englissh with a Introduction to the Epistle to the Romaynes.

23. The Barable of the Wyked Mammonde.

24. The Obediens of a Chrysten Man.

25. A Boke of Thorpe, or of John Oldecastell.

26. The Some of Scripture.

27. The Prymer in Englissh.

28. The Psalter in Englissh.

29. A Dyalog betwyxt the Gentylman and the Plowman.

30. Jonas in Englissh.

And all other suspect bookes, bothe in Englissh and in Laten, as well now printed or that here after shall be printed, and not here afore namyd.

---

[a] The words " in Englissh " were here added, but are struck out.

VI. *St. Peter's Cornhill*, 1435.

(At f. 202 *b.*)

A decre and statute made by the honorable cownseyle of the Cite of London for the gevyng of the benyfice of Seynt Peters in Corne hull.

Where some tyme there was greate contraversy and stryfe betwixt the Mayre of London, the Aldermen, and the Commen Counsayle of the same Cite of London, for the gyfte and presentacyon of the saide benifyce and parissh church of Seint Peters in Corne hull; and for to avoyde, exscue, and put away the greate stryfe and con traversy be twyxte the scyde Mayre, Aldermen, and the Commen Cownseile, and to set them in a peaceable order, it was enactyd, statuted, and decrede by all the hole counsel of the saide cite, which counsaile was kept in the tyme of Henry Frowyke, then beyng mayre of the sayde cite, and the aldermen of the same cite, holde and kept the xxvij[th] day of the moneth of Octobre, the yere of the reygne of Kyng Henry, the Syxt aftir the Conquest, xiiij[th], by the foresaide mayre, aldermen, with the hole assent, mynde, and grement of the comynalte godly and holsomely to be provided from that day for evermore, that whan so ever the sayde churche chaunceth to be voyde, that as then fowre clerkys famous and seculer clerkes dwellyng with in the seide cite or a myle a bought the same cite, able yn maners and scyens, to be assigned and chosyn by the sayde Mayre and Aldermen for the tyme being to name to the Comen Councel, foure persones after ther consciens, moste mete in maners and conyng to the same cure and benyfice, of which foure thus namyd by the foure clerkes, they must be doctors of holy divinite or ellys bachylers of the same. And the persons thus named they must be seculer persons and not promoted. And of these maner of foure persons thus named, one of them, which semyth moste appte and expedyent bi the saide Mayre, Aldermen, and the

Comen Counseyle, to be take and presented to the same cure, pro-
mysing to them to keep residence there in the same cure, and so
canonically there to be institute and inducte.

VII. *Notes of various Occurrences.*

(Inside the Cover.)

The listes that Anthony Lord Scales and Anthony the Bastarde
of Burgoyne justyd yn in Smythfelde, the tymbre and workman
shippe ther of cost ijc. marke, and was of six of the thryftiest car-
penters of London bought and made. The length vj^{xx} taylours
yardes and x foote, and iiij^{xx} of brede and x foote, dowbyll barred;
the inner barres were mytche gretter then the utter, and be twixt
bothe v foote. The justes began the Thirsday next after Corpus
Christi Day, Anno Domini M^{l}.iiijc.lxvii, and in the vijth yere of
Kyng Edwarde the iiijth, Thomas Howlegrave, skynner, then beyng
mayre of London.

Below this is a catalogue of the mayors of London, giving generally the mere
names with hardly any dates appended, beginning with William Taylour, Mercer,
who was mayor in 1468-9. In one or two cases, however, important memoranda
are added, which are here transcribed. Opposite the name " Johannes Stokton,
mercer," is the marginal note " Barnet feelde." Three lines lower down occurs
" John Tate with the powlyd hed." Under the name " Stevyn Jenyn " occurs the note
" Henricus Septimus hic moriebatur," and the succeeding entry is as follows :

Thomas Bradbery, mercer. Capel successit pro residuo anni,
quia Bradbery moriebatur.

It is remarkable that the death of Bradbury and succession of Capel are not mentioned by Fabyan. Three years later we have the following entry:—

1512-3].   Copynger, fysshmonger, moriebatur. Richard Haddon, secundo
successit pro residuo anni.

And immediately after—

1513-4].   Wyllelmus Browne, mercer, moriebatur, et dominus Johannes
Tate, miles, successit pro residuo anni.

Then passing over two mayoralties we come to the following entries, the first of which refers to the riot known as Evil May day:—

John Reste, grocer. In whose tyme on May Evyn at mydnyght [A.D. 1516-17] a grete nowmbre of mennys servauntes and prentis of London rose and spoyled the alyentes of Seynt Martens and of Blaw[n]chapylton; and also one Nutas,[a] the kynges Frenche secretary, dwellyng in the parsonage at Saynt Andrew Undershafte, was put to flyte.

Exmewe, goldesmyth. Here cam in the legate[b] from Rome, and [A.D. 1517-18]. the amerall[c] and lordes of Fraunce.

A little lower we read:—

On the xvij[th] day of May, beyng Fryday, in the xiij[th] yere of Kyng Henrye the viij[th], ————————[d] Duke of Bokyngham was behedyd at the Towre Hyll of London, be twene xj and xij afore none, and his hede and body forth with put in a cofyn and borne to the Austen Freers of London upon vj freers bakkys of the same place.

Next after Burges, draper, Mr. Mylborn, draper, Mundy, gold- [A.D. 1522-3]. smyth. The xviij[th] day of June, in this yere, the Kyng of Den- marke cam to Gre[n]wyche [1523].

Baldry, mercer. [A.D. 1523-4].

Syr Wylliam Bayly made knyght at Bryde wel by K. H. the [A.D. 1524-5.] viij[th], the xix[th] day of Feveryere, beyng Sonday.

Memorandum, the vij[th] day of Septembre, in the xviij[th] yere of Kyng Henry the viij[th], the proclamatyon was made in London of the enhawnceyng of gold.

[a] His true name was John Meautis.
[b] Cardinal Campeggio.
[c] William Gouffier, Sieur de Bonnivet
[d] Blank in MS.

HISTORICAL MEMORANDA

IN THE HANDWRITING OF JOHN STOWE,

FROM THE SAME MS.

———————

A proclamation made by Jacke Cade, Capytayn of y Rebelles in Kent.*   Anno M.iiijc.l.[a]

Thes be the poyntys, causes, and myscheves of gaderynge and assemblinge of us the Kynges lege men of Kent, the iiij day of June, the yere of owr Lorde M.iiijc.l., the regne of our sovereyn Lorde the Kynge xxix[ti], the whiche we trust to All myghte God to remedy, withe the helpe and the grace of God and of owr soverayn lorde the kynge, and the pore commyns of Ingelond, and elles we shall dye there fore:

We, consyderyng that the kynge owre sovereyn lorde, by the insaciable covetows malicious pompes, and fals and of nowght browght up certeyn persones, and dayly and nyghtly is abowt his hynesse, and dayly enforme hym that good is evyll and evyll is good, as Scripture witnesseth, *Ve vobis qui dicitis bonum malum et malum bonum.*

Item, they sey that owre sovereyn lorde is a bove his lawys to his pleysewr, and he may make it and breke it as hym lyst, withe owt eny distinction.   The contrary is trew, and elles he shuld not have sworn to kepe it, the whyche we conceyvyd for the hyghest poynt

———————

[a] This heading is struck through with the pen, and below is written in small characters: "An othar copi hathe 1460 at y[e] comyge in of y[e] Erles of Marche, War-wyke, and Sarum, with y[e] Lordes Faconbridge and Wenloke, from Calais to y[e] battayll at Northampton." But this note is likewise cancelled.

of treson that eny soget may do to make his prynce renn in perjury.

Item, they sey that the commons of Inglond wolde fyrst dystroye the kynges fryndes and afftarwarde bym selff, and then brynge the Duke of Yorke to be kyng, so that by ther fals menys and lyes they make hym to hate and to distroy his frendys, and cherysythe his fals traytors. They calle themselves his frendys, and yf ther were no more reson in y⁰ worlde to knowe, he may knowe they be not his fryndes by theyr covytysnes.

Item, they sey that the kyng shuld lyve upon his commons, and that ther bodyes and goods ben the kynges; the contrary is trew, for then nedyd hym nevar perlement to syt to aske good of his comonys.

Item, they sey that it were gret reproffe to the kynge to take ageyne that he hath gevyn, so that they woll not sufere hym to have his owne good, ne londe, ne forfeture, ne eny othar good but they aske it from hym, or ells they take bribes of othar to gett it for them.

Item, it ys to be remedied that the fals traytours wyll sofre no man to come to the kynges presens for no cawse with out bribes where none owght to be had, ne no bribery about the kynges persone, but that eny man myght have his comynge to hym to aske hym grace or jugement in such cas as the kynge may gyve.

Item, it is a hevy thynge that y⁰ good Duke of Gloucestar was apechid of treson by o fals traytour alone and so sone was morderyd and myght nevar come to his answer; but the fals traytur Pole was apechyd by all the holl comyns of Ingelond, the whiche nombre passyd a quest of xxiiijM., and myght not be suffryd to dye as y⁰ law wolde, but rather the sayd trayturs of the affinite of Pole that was as fals as Fortager ᵃ wolde that the kynge owre soverein lord shuld hold a batayll with in his owne realme to dystroy his pepyll and aftarward hym selffe.

ᵃ *Sic* MS.

Item, they say that whom ye kyng woll shall be traytur and whom he woll shall be non, and that apperyth hederto, for yf eny of the traytours about hym wolde malygne ageynst eny person, hyghe or low, they wolde fynd fals menys that he shuld dy a traytor for to have his londes and his goods, but they wyll sufer the kynge nethar to pay his dettes with all, ner pay for his vytaylls ner be the rychar of one peny.

Item, the law servyth of nowght ellys in thes days but for to do wrong, for nothyng is sped almost but false maters by coulour of the law for mede, drede, and favor, and so no remedy is had in ye cowrt of conscience in eny wyse.

Item, we sey owr sovereyn lord may understond that his fals cowncell hath lost his law, his marchandyse is lost, his comon people is dystroyed, the see is lost, Fraunce is lost, the kynge hym selffe is so set that he may not pay for his mete nor drynke, and he owythe more then evar eny Kynge of Yngland owght, for dayly his traytours abowt hym wher eny thyng shuld come to hym by his lawes, anon they aske it from hym.

Item, they aske jentylmens goodys and londes in Kent and call them rysers and traytors and the kynges enimys, but they shall be fond the kynges trew legemen and best frendys with the helpe of Jesu, to whom we cry day and nyght with many M. mo that God of his grace and rytwysnese shall take vengawnce and dystroy the fals govournors of his realme that hath brought us to nowght and in to myche sorowe and mysery.

Item, we wyll that all men knowe we blame not all the lordys, ne all tho that is about ye kyngs person, ne all jentyllmen ne yowmen, ne all men of lawe, ne all bysshopes, ne all prestys, but all suche as may be fownde gylty by just and trew enquery and by the law.

Item, we wyll that it be knone we wyll not robbe, ne reve, ne stelle, but that thes defautes be amendyd, and then we wyll go home; where fore we exort all the kyngys trew legemen to helpe us, to support us, for what so evar he be that wyll not that thes defawtes be amendyd, he is falser than a Jewe or Sarasyn, and we shall with as good wyll lyve and dye upon hym as apon a Jewe or a Sarasyn, for who is a genst us in this casse hym wyll we marke, for he is not the trewe kyngys legeman.

Item, his trewe comyns desyre that he wyll avoyd from hym all the fals progeny and affynyte of the Dewke of Suffolke, the which ben openly knowne, and that they be p[u]nyshyd afftar law of lond, and to take about his noble person his trew blode of his ryall realme, that is to say, the hyghe and myghty prynce the Duke of Yorke, exilyd from owre sovereyne lords person by the noysyng of the fals traytore the Duke of Suffolke and his affinite. Also to take about his person the myghte prynce, the Duke of Exceter, the Duke of Bokyngham, the Duke of Norffolke, and his trewe erlys and barons of his lond, and he shall be the rychest kynge crystyn.

Item, the trewe comyns desyryth the punyshement upon the fals traytours, the which conterfetyd and imagenyd the dethe of the hyghe and myghtfull and excellent prynce the Duke of Glowcester, the which is to mych to reherse, the which duke was proclaymyd at Bery openly in the parlement a traytur, upon the whiche qwaryll we purpose us to lyve and dye that it is fals; allso owre fadyr the cardenall, the good Duke of Exeter, the nobyll prynce the Duke of Warwyke, the wiche ware delyveryd by the same menys untrew; allso the realme of Praunce lost, the Duchy of Normandy, Gascon, and Gyan, and Anjoy demayn [a] lost by the same traytours, and owr trew lordys, knyghtes, and squyres, and many good yemen lost and wer sold or they went, the whiche is gret pyte and gret losse to our sovereyn Lord and to all the realme.

Item, they desyre that all the extorsiners myght be leyd downe, that is to say, y[e] grene wexe, the which is falsly used to the per-petwall hurt and distructyon of the trew comyns of Kent; also the extorsiners of the Kynges Benche, the which is ryght chargeable to all the comyns with owten provysyon of owr sovereyn lord and his trew cowncell.

[a] *Sic.*

Item, takynge of whet and othar greyns, beffe, motton and other vytayll, the which is inportable hurt to the comyns, with out pro-vysyon of owr sovereyn lord and his trew councell, for his comyns may no lengar bere it.

Item, the statute upon the laborers and the gret extorsiners of Kent, that is to sey, Slegge, Crowmer, Isle, and Robert Est.

Item, where we meve and desyre that same[a] trew justyce wyth certeyn trew lords and knyghts may be sent in to Kent for to enqwere of all such traytors and brybors, and that the justice may do upon them trew jugement, what some evar they be; and that owr soverayn lorde dyrecte his lettars patentes to all the pepull ther universall opynly to be rede and cryed, that it is owre sovereyn lordys wyll and preyar of all his peple trewly to enquere of every mans govarnawnce and of defawtes that reygneth, nother for love, favor, dred ne hate, and that dewe jugement shalbe forthe with and ther upon. The kynge to kepe in his owne handes theyr londes and goodys, and not gyve them aweye to no man but kepe them for his rychesse, or ells owre soverayn lorde to make his emarme[b] in to Fraunce, or ells to pay his dettes; by this owr wrytynge ye may conceyve and se whethar we be the fryndes ethar enimys.

Item, to syt upon this enqwerye we refuse no juge except iij chefe juges, the which ben fals to beleve.

Item, they that be gylte wyll wrye ageynst this, but God wyll brynge them downe, and that they shall be ashamyd to speke ageynst reson, but they wyll go to the kynge and say that yf they be taken fro hym that we wyll put hym downe, for the traytours wyll lyve lenger, and yf we were disposed ageynst owr sovereyn lorde, as God it forbyd, what myght then the traytowrs helpe hym?

Item, thes defawtes thus dewly remedyd, and from hens forthe no man upon peyne of deth beyng abowt the kyngs person shall take no maner of brybe for eny byll of petysyons or caws spedynge or lettynge, owr sovereyn lord shall regne and rewle with gret worshipe, and have love of God and of his people, for he shall have

─────────────

[a] "same." So in MS. for "some."   [b] So in MS.

so gret love of his people that he shall with Gods helpe conqwere
where he wyll; and as for us, we shall be all weye redy to defend
owr cuntre from all nacions with our owne goods, and to go withe
owr sovereyne lorde where he wyll commaunde us, as his trew
legemen.

FINIS.

Here folowythe a dyrge made by the comons of Kent in the tyme
of ther rysynge, when Jake Cade was theyr cappitayn.[a]

> In the moneth of May whan gres growes grene,
> Fragrans in there floures with a swet savor,
> Jake Napis in the see a maryner for to bene,
> With his clogge and his cheyne to sell more tresowr.
> Suche a thynge prykkyd bym, he axid a confessour.
> Nycolas of the Towre[b] seyd I am redy here to se;
> He was holde so hard, he passyd the same houre.[c]
> For Jake Napes sowle *placebo* and *dirige*.

> Who shall execute y[e] fest of solempnite?
> Bysshoppis and lords as gret reson is,
> Monkes, chanons, and prestis, with all y[e] clergy,
> Prayeth for hym that he may com to blys,
> And that nevar such anothar come aftar this.
> His interfectures blessid mot they be,
> And graunt them to reygne with aungellis,
> For Jake Napys sowle *placebo* and *dirige*.

---

[a] Another version of this satirical dirge has been printed by Ritson in his Ancient
Songs and Ballads (p. 101, Hazlitt's edition), and by Wright in his Political Poems
(ii. 232), from the contemporary Cottonian MS. Vespasian, B. xvi. f. 1. But it consists only of nine stanzas, of which the first seven agree pretty nearly with the first
seven in this transcript.

[b] *Nicholas*, of the Tower, was the name of the ship by which the Duke of
Suffolk's vessel was stopped upon the sea.

[c] The Cott. version reads: "that he ne passede that hour."

Placebo, begynneth the Bishop of Hereforthe.[a]
Dilexi, quod y[e] Bisshop of Chester,[b] for my avaunse.
Hew michi, seyd Salysbery,[c] this game gothe ferforthe.
Ad Dominum cum tribularer, seyth y[e] Abbot of Glocester.[d]
Dominus custodit, thus seyth y[e] Bisshoppe of Rowchestre.[e]
Levavi oculos meos, seyth Frere Stanbery.[f]
Si iniquitates, seyth y[e] Bysshope of Worcestre.[g]
For Jake Napis sowle *de profundis clamavi.*

Opera manium[h] *tuarum,* seyth y[e] cardinall[i] wysely,
Hath wronge *confitebor* for all Jake Napis wisdome.
Audivi vocem, seyd Jhesus on hye.
Magnificat anima mea Dominum.
Now to this *dyryge* most we nedys come.
This joyfull tyme to sey brevely,
ix spalmes ix lessons to sey all and sum.
For Jake Napys sowlle *placebo* and *dirige.*

Executor of this office dirge for to synge,
Shall begynne y[e] Bisshope of Seynt As.[k]
Varba mea auribus, seythe the Abbot of Redynge,
For all our hope and joy is come to allas.
Convertere Domine, for us wantyth grace,
Thow Abbot of Seynt Albonys full sorely synge ye.
The Abbot of the Towre Hyll, with his fate face,
Tremelyth and quakythe, for *Domine ne in furore.*

[a] Richard Beauchamp, who was translated to Salisbury the same year.
[b] The Bishop of Chester, *i. e.* of Coventry and Lichfield, at the time was William Booth.
[c] William Ayscough, Bishop of Salisbury, who was murdered soon after Suffolk, 29 June, 1450. He was clerk of the Council to Henry **VI.**
[d] Reginald Butler, or Boulers, who was made Bishop of Hereford, 23 Dec. 1450.
[e] John Lowe.
[f] John Stanbury, a Carmelite, Provost of Eton, who was nominated by the King to the Bishopric of Norwich in 1445, but set aside by the Pope.
[g] John Carpenter.   [h] So in MS.
[i] John Kemp, Cardinal Archbishop of York.
[k] Thomas, Bishop of St. Asaph, whose surname is not known.

Master Watyr Lyard[a] schall sey *ne quando.*
The Abbes of Seynt Alborghe,[b] *Domine Deus meus, in te speravi.*
Requiem eternam, God grawnt hem to,
To sey a patar nostar, the Bysshop of Seynt Davi,[c]
For the sowles of thes wyse and wurthy,
Adam Molens,[d] Suffolke, Sir Robert Ros,[e] thes thre.
And specyally for Jake Napis sowlle that evar was sly,
For his sowle *placebo* and *dirige.*

Rys up, Lord Say, and rede *Parce michi, Domine,*
Nichil enim sunt dies mei, that shalt thow singe.
The Bysshope of Carlyll[f] seyth *credo videre*
All fals traytors to come to evyll endynge,
Dwelle[g] thow shalt withe grete mornynge,
Rede *Tedet animam meam vite mee,*
Manus tue, Danyell,[h] thow shalt synge.
For Jake Napis sowle *placebo* and *dirige.*

Qui Lazarum resussistasti, Trevilyan[i] shall singe;
Hungerford, *manus tue fecerunt me,*
Uby me abscondam, for dred this day.
John Say synge *Dominus regit me ;*
Nichyll michi deerit for owt that I can se.
Ad te Domine levavi, Master Somerset shall rede.
John Penycoke, *Delycta juventutis mee,*
Allas, whythar may I fle for dred?

---

[a] He was Bishop of Norwich at this time, or else this is a namesake. A little later (1467) we find that a Walter Hert (undoubtedly the same name) was a Prebendary of St. Paul's.

[b] The Cott. MS. here reads " The Abbot of Westmynstre."

[c] John Delabere.

[d] Adam Molcyns, Bishop of Chichester, who was murdered in January 1450.

[e] He was associated with Bishop Moleyns in delivering up Maine to the French.

[f] Nicholas Close.

[g] "Dwelle." Probably a transcriber's error for "Dudley." The Cott. MS. reads: "The Baron of Dudley, with grete mornynge."

[h] Thomas Daniel, one of the most unpopular of the King's councillors.

[i] John Trevilian, alluded to as "the Cornish Chough " in another political poem.

Dominus illuminacio help, for now is ned.
Seyth Maystar Wyll Say, I trow it wyll not be.
Credo videre, Sir Thomas Stanle take hede.
For Jake Napis sowle *placebo* and *dirige*.
In memoria eterna, seyth Mayster Thomas Kent.
Now schall owre treson be cornicled for evar.
Patar nostar, seyd Mayster Gerveyse, we be all shent,
For so fals a company in Englond was nevar.

The Abbot of Barmundsey, full of lechery,
Quantas habeo iniquitatys take for thy lesson.
Gabull of the Chancery begynyth *Hew michi*,
That is his preve bande and detent of treson.
Homo natus de muliere, seyth yᵉ Master of Sent Laurence,
Repletur multis miseriis, and that shall he wayll,
Of Jake Napes sort that hath don gret offence,
And ever whill he lyvyd cheffe of his counceyll.
Ne recorderys, Stephen Shegge ª shall synge.
Quis michi tribuat for wichecraft, seyth Stace,
Domine, non secundum actum meum, for then shall I hynge
For Jake Napys sowle *placebo* and *dirige*.

Expectans expectavi, seyth Sir Thomas Hoo.
Complaceat tibi, begynneth John Hampton.
Beatus qui intelligit and dredit also,
Seyth John Fortescw, all this fals treson.
Sana Domine owre wittes with reson,
The Lorde Sudeley devoutly prayth.
Quem admodum desiderat, yᵉ Lord Stowrton,
Sitivit anima mea, for hym lyeth.
The Lord Ryvers all onely seythe
Requiem eternam, God grawnt us to se.
A pater nostar ther must be in feyth,
For Jake Napis sowle *placebo* and *dirige*.

ª So in MS., but qu. Slegge? See p. 98.

Spiritus meus attenuabytur, Blakney shall begyn.
Pecantem me cotidie, seyth Myners.
Pelle me consumptus carnibus[a] to the nynne,
Robart Horne, alderman, that shall be thy vers.
Requiem eternam for the respons.
Phylip Malpas be thow redy to synge,
It wexyth derke, thow nedyst a scons,
Com forth, Jude,[b] for thow shalt in brynge.

Quare de vulva eduxisti?
Ser Thomas Tudnam, that rede ye.
Abbot of Westmystar, com stond by
In thy myter and cope, and sey *libera me*.

Arys up, Thorp and Cantelowe, and stond ye togeder,
And synge *Dies illa, dies ire*.
Pulford and Hanley, that drownyd yᵉ Duke of Glocestar,[c]
As two traytors shall synge *ordentes anime*.[d]
And all trew comyns ther to be bolde
To sey *Requiescant in pace*.
For all the fals traytors that Engelond hath sold,
And for Jake Napis sowlle *placebo* and *dirige*.—Finis.
    Amen. Writn owt of David Norcyn his booke by John Stowe.

---

[a] " Pelli meæ consumptis carnibus adhæsit os."—Job xix. 20.

[b] Probably John Judde, an officer of the ordnance to Henry VI. See Stevenson's Wars of the English in France, ii. 512.

[c] This is a most extraordinary statement, as the Duke of Gloucester, whether murdered or not, certainly died in his bed.

[d] " Orde'tes a'i'e," MS.; qu. " ardentes "? 1 can find no corresponding psalm or antiphon.

The Cristenynge of Prince Arthure, sonne to Kynge Henrie y[e] VII. at Sent Swithins in Winchestar.

Fyrst my Lady Cecily[a] bare my lord prince to churche; my Lord Marques[b] and my Lorde of Lyncoln ledde my Lady Cecily; my Lady Marques, and afftar Cheyne as chamberlyn, bare the trayne of y[e] mantyll; my Lady Anne y[e] quens sister bare y[e] crysom. The hole chapell met with my lord prynce in y[e] qwens great chamber. My Lord Laware, my Lord Widvell,[c] my Lord John of Arondell, and Mastar Awdley bare y[e] clothe of astate. The torches unlight met hym at the steyre foote of y[e] qwenes great chamber, and so went by fore hym unlyght to the chirche. Many ladyes and gentyl-women folowyd hym. Knyston, Geddyng, gentilmen usshers, and Piers Wratton and John Amyas, yomen usshers, had y[e] rewle of y[e] conveyaunce of the torches. The sergeaunt of the pantry was redy with a ryche salt, and my Lord of Essyx bare y[e] same salte by fore my lorde prince to the churche. The sergaint of the ewrey was redy with a payre of coverd basons and a fayre towell lyeng ther upon, and my Lord Straunge bare them to the churche. Syr Rychard Gyldford, Knyght Constable, and Mastar Troblefylde, had the kepynge of the churche dores with his meyne. Fowre gentylmen and yowmen of the crowne had the kepynge of y[e] barryers a bowt the fonte, for y[e] comynge in of the preas. Ser Davy Owen, Master Poynes and iij othar knyghts and gentylmen, had y[e] kepynge and charge of the funte. Two gentylmen usshers had y[e] kepynge of y[e] travers by the fonte where my lord prynce was dysaparilyd, and aftar his cristynynge arrayed, and ther fyar

[a] Cecily, daughter of Edward IV.
[b] Marquis of Dorset.
[c] Sir Edward Woodville, called Lord Woodville by courtesy, who was slain at the battle of St. Aubin, in Britanny, in 1488.

and fumygacions and many royall thyngs don. My Lord Marques, my Lord of Lvncolne, and my Lord Strawnge, served Qwene Elisabethe [a] at wayshyng aftar y[e] cristinynge, and Mastar Weste, my Lorde Laware is brother, and Syr Roger Cotton, servyd the remnaunt of the gossoppes. My Lord Nevyll bare y[e] taper byfore my lord prynce aftar the cristinynge to the hygh awllter. Aftar all y[e] observaunces was gyven spicis and wyne to the states. My lord prynce was had frome the hyghe aultar to Sent Swithins shrine and there ofyryd, and ther was songen *Te Deum Laudamus*. All the torches lyght browght my lord prynce to his chamber. All the harolds went before bothe to the churche and home agayne. And the trompitis blewe afftar his cristenynge byfore hym home to his chamber. Ser William Stonnar, Ser Charles Somerset, and Sir John Wyngfeld bare thes gyfftes that y[e] gosyppis gave to his chamber byfore hym. The gyfftes were thes : Qwene Elisabeth gave a cuppe of gold set with stones, my Lorde of Derby a salte of gowlde, my Lorde of Oxenford a payre of basons with a cuppe of assay all gylt, my Lorde Matrevys a cofer of gold set with stones. All the great body of Seynt Swethyns churche to the hygh aultar was hangyd with arras. Ther was made an hyghe stoke for a fonte with grecis round abowght, and the fonte was of sylvar browght from Cawnterbery and a royal canapie over y[e] same. The gossyppes ben thes: Quene Elizabethe, godmothar, my Lord of Derby and my Lorde Matravers at y[e] fonte, and my Lord of Oxenforde at y[e] confirmacion. My Lord of Worcestar cristenyd hym, and his name is Arthure, doughtles a fayre prince and a lorge of bones; owre Lord save hym! Ther was present v mytars, that is to say: my Lord Sarum, my Lord of Excestre, my Lord of Worcestre, y[e] abot of Hyde, and y[e] pryowr of Seynt Swythynes.

---

[a] Not the queen of Henry VII., but her mother, the widow of Edward IV., who was godmother to the child.

The maner of makynge Knyghtes aftar ye custome of England in tyme of peace, and at the coronacion, that is to say, Knyghtes of the Bathe.

When an esquier commythe in to courte for to receyve ye order of knyghthode in tyme of peace, after ye custome of England, he shalbe worshipfully receyvyd of ye offycers of the cowrte, as of ye stywarde or chamberleyn, yf they be present, and ellys of ye marshall and usshers, in ye absence of ye stwwarde and chamberlyne.   And then ther shalbe ordeyned ij worshipffull esquyers, wise and well noryshid in curtesye, and experte in ye dedes of knyghthode, and they shalbe govowrnowrs to hym to serve and ordeyn what shall longe to hym for the tyme.   And in case that the esquire come before dyner he shall serve the kynge of watar, or of a dyshe onely of the fyrst course.   And that is do to take leve of service of esquires.   Then his govornowrs shall lede hym in to his chamber with owten eny more to be sene that daye; and at even the govern- owrs shall sende aftar the barbowr, and he shall make redy a bathe in the best wyse that he kan, the fatt with in and with owt wrapped with lynnyn clothe clene and white, and coveryd with thikke carpites for colde of the nyght.   Then shall the esquers berd be shave and his hede rounded; which done ye govornowrs shall goo unto ye kynge and to hym say thus : "Moaste myghtye prynce, owr soverayne lorde, lo it wexithe nere unto the eve, and owr maystor is redy unto the bathe when it pleasythe yowr royall majestye."   And uppon that the kynge shall commaund his chamberleyne to go unto the esquiers chamber that is to be made knyght, and to take with hym the moste worthy and wityeste knyghtes that bene then present to thentent that they shall the same esquier trewly councell, enforme, and teache wysely of ye order of knyghthode.   And so with that othar yonge esquiers of the howsholde with mynstrells syngynge and daunsyng shall go be fore the chamberleyn and ye sayd knyghtes unto the tyme that they come unto the chambre dore of y᷄ᵉ said esquier that is to be made knyght. When the govornowrs herythe noyse of mynstrills, anon they shall make naked theyr master, and all nakyd shalbe put in to the bathe. The mynstrells be fore the entrie of the chamberleyne and other noble knyghtes shall abyde and be styll with owtyn noyse, to gyder with the sayde esquires levynge theyr noyse for the tyme; which thynge done the chamber-lyne with y᷄ᵉ sayd noble knyghtes shall enter privelye with owten noyse in to the chamber of the seyd esquire; and when they enter everyche to otbar shall than do reverence and worshype whiche of them shalbe the fyrst for to counsell y᷄ᵉ esquier in the bathe of y᷄ᵉ order and y᷄ᵉ makynge to performe y᷄ᵉ kyngs commaundement. And whan they bene accordyd than shall y᷄ᵉ fyrst goo in to the bathe, and there he shall knele be fore y᷄ᵉ bathe, sayenge secretely to y᷄ᵉ esquier thus: " Ryght dere broder, great worshype be this order unto yow. Allmyghty God gyve yow y᷄ᵉ preysynge of knyghthod, lo this that order be ye stronge," &c.[a] Whan the esquire is councellyd the same knyght counselour shall take in his hond watar of y᷄ᵉ bathe, and shall put it uppon y᷄ᵉ shulders of y᷄ᵉ esquiers and take his leve to go and departe. And the governowrs at all tymes shall keppe y᷄ᵒ sydes of y᷄ᵉ bathe. In this wyse shall all the orders of knyghtes aforesaye do everiche aftar othar in the best wyse that they can, and this done the knyghtes with owt noyse shall go owte of the chamber for the tyme; then shall theyr govornors take their maister owt of the bathe and laye hym saftlie in his bed to drie. And y᷄ᵉ bede shall not be of great valewe, but with owtyn cowlowrs and curtyns. And when y᷄ᵉ esquier is well dryed he shall ryse owt of his bed, and shall clothe hym warme for the wache of the nyght. And uppon all his clothes he shall have a cope of blakke russet with longe sleves, and the hode sewyd unto y᷄ᵉ coppe in maner of an heremyte. The esquier thus arrayed and made redye, y᷄ᵉ barbar shall put awaye y᷄ᵉ bathe; and all thynge that is abowt y᷄ᵉ bathe, also well with owt as with in, the barbowr shall take all for his fee. And

[a] See note at the end of this article, p. 113.

all so he shall have for his shavynge lyke as it foloythe here afftar. That is to wete, yf he be a duke, an erle, a baronne, or a bachelowr, aftar y[e] custome of y[e] courte everiche shall have aftar his estate, and principally yf judgement be requiryd it shalbe then at y[e] will of y[e] kyngs majestie.   Aftar this y[e] govornors shall open the dore of y[e] chamber, and y[e] knyghtis shall entar in agayne with mynsteryles playnge in ther instrumentes and esquiers before them syngynge and daunsynge shall lede the esquicr in to the chapell.   Ther shalbe ordenyd spicis and wyne for y[e] knyghtes and esquiers; whiche thyng done, the governours shall lede thies knyghtes aforne thes squeres[a] for to take there leve, and he with silence shall thanke them of their labours and worshypes that they have done unto hym. In that wyse they shall goo owt of y[e] chapell, the governours shall shitte the dore till y[e] dawnynge wex clere and y[e] daye come, and ther shall abyde none in y[e] chapell but y[e] esquier, governours, and y[e] wayte his chaplyne chaundeler.   In this wyse shall y[e] esquier all nyght tyll it be day abyde ever in his prayers, praynge and besechyng Almyghty God and y[e] blesyd Virgyn Marie his moder that thylke passynge temporall dignyte he may receve to his worshipe and praysynge of God and y[e] blessyd Virgyn Marie his moder, holy churche and the order of knyghthode.   And when y[e] dawnynge comythe he shall have a prest and be con- fessyd if it will lyke hym of his synns and trespas; whiche thynge done he shall have his mattyns and masse and be comynt yf he will. Aftar his entre in to y[e] chapell he shall evar more have a serge or a tapir of wax brenynge afore hyme.   And when masse is begonnen, on of y[e] governours shall holde a taper brenynge afore hym unto the tyme of y[e] gospell be begonne, and then he shall be take it unto his maister whiche shalle holde it in his hands tyll y[e] gospell be endyd, allwaye his hede beynge coveryd; and at y[e] end of y[e] gospell the governowr shall reseyve the taper agayne and putt it afore his maister unto thend of the masse.   And at y[e] levacion of the sacrament one of y[e] govornowrs shall put of the hode of his maister, and aff[t]ar

        [a] Should be "the squire."

ye syght of ye sacrament he shall do it on agayne tyll *In principio* be begunne; and then one of his governours shall put of his hode and make hym stonde and holde ye sayd taper in his honde, havynge in ye sayde taper stikynge a peny nye to the light; and when ye priste saythe *Verbum caro factum est* he shall knele downe and offer ye taper and ye peny to ye worshipe of God, and ye peny to ye worshipe of hym that shall make hym knyght. Thes thynges done, ye govowrnors shall lede hym agayne in to his chamber and lay hym agayne in his bede till it be forthe dayes. And ther shall he take ye rest that ye wache of ye nyght made wery. So than ye bedde shall be amendyd and refresshed before ye tyme that his mastar wake, that is to wete with covertwr of clothe of golde callyd *seclecon* ; [a] and that shall be lynyd with carde. And when they se tyme thay shall goo to ye kynge and saye to hyme thus: " Most victoriws prince, when that it lykythe unto yowre mayestie, owr maister shall a wake." And ther uppon ye kynge shall commaund ye knyghties squere to wake hym, arraye hym and clothe hym and brynge hym in to ye hall before ye kynge hym selffe. But before ye comynge of ye knyghts in to ye esquiers chambre ye govowrnors shall ordeigne all manar necessaries redie by ordre for to be delyvered unto ye knyghtes. And whan thes knyghtes be commen unto theyr chambre they shall enter softlye with owt eny noyse and say to ye esquier, " Ser, good daye, it is tyme to aryse." And with that ye govornowrs shall take and arayse hym uppe by ye armes. Than ye moaste worthy and moste wyse knyght shall take to hym his sherte, and othar next worthye his breche, ye third his dowblett, ye fowrthe shall clothe hym with a gowne of redd tarteryn; othar ij shall lyfte hym owt of his bedd; othar ij shall doo on his hossyn, whiche shall be of blake sylke or blake clothe, wher of ye sowlls shall be of blake lethar sowyd to them ; ij shall boten his sleves ; one otbar shall girde hym with a gyrdle of white ledar with owt bernys of eny mettall and ye brede of an ynche ; an otbar shall kembe his hedd; an othar shall gyve hym his mantylle, of ye sewite of ye kyrtyll of rede

———

[a] Spelled *Siglyton* here in the Cottonian original, and afterwards *Siglaton.*

tarteryn fastenyd with a lace of white silke, with a payre of whit
gloves hangynge at yᵉ ende of yᵉ lace, but he shall have of the
chaundeler of yᵉ howsholde yᵉ corse girdill and yᵉ gloves, and on
yᵗ otharsyde yᵉ chaundelar shall take for his fee all yᵉ garments
and all yᵉ arraye with all yᵉ necessaries in yᵉ which yᵉ esquyre was
arrayd and clothid that day he enteryd into yᵉ courte for to take yᵉ
ordre, togedre with yᵉ bedd in yᵉ whiche he laye first aftar yᵉ bathe,
as well yᵉ clothe of golde called *secleton* as yᵉ othar necessaries
towchynge yᵉ sayd bedd; and, this fully done, this wyse knyghts
shall lede this esquiere on horse bake unto yᵉ kyngs hall, at all
tymes yᵉ mynstrells beynge before, makynge theyre mynstrellsye.
Ther horse shall be arrayed in this wyse; he shall have a sadell
coveryd with blake leder, yᵉ arsons of whit tree fowre sqware, and
blake stiroppes with gylde irons, and his sadell shall have no cropar
but a paytryll of gilt patee before, hangynge uppon yᵉ brest of yᵉ
horse, his bridle shall be blake lethar playne, with longe reynes in
ye guyse of Spayne, and a crosse patent in yᵉ forhede.   And ther
shall be ordaynyd a yonge gentyll esquier for to ride before this
esquiere that is to be made knyght.   And he shall be open hede,
and shall bere yᵉ swere of yᵉ esquire yᵉ poynt downwarde, with
sporrs hangynge uppoon yᵉ swerd, and yᵉ swerd shall have a white
scabard and frett with yᵉ gerdle and scales, with whit ledar, with
owt eny hernesse, and yᵉ yonge gentill esquiere shall holde yᵉ
swerde by the poynt.   In this wyse they shall ride to yᵉ kyngs
hall, all tymes yᵉ sayd governers beynge redye to yᵉ maystar as it
is fittinge to be.   And the forsayd noble and wyse knyghtes shall
soberlye lede this esquire as they awen.   And when yᵉ esquier
commythe before yᵉ hall dore, yᵉ marshalls and usshers shall
be redye afore hym in yᵉ moste honest wise that they can, saynge
thus, " Come downe." And than he shall come downe. The marshall
for his fee shall take yᵉ hors, or ccˢ· This thyng so done, these wise
knyghts shall lede yᵉ esquier in to yᵉ hall or in to yᵉ great chambre
unto his table, and forthe with he shall be put at the begynynge
of yᵉ second table tyll that yᵉ kynge come, the sayd knyghtes

abowght his person as one on every syde, and ye yonge squiere swerd berar before hym, standynge with ye swerde betwixt ye ij govournowrs aforesayd. When ye kynge comythe in to ye hall and perseyvythe ye esquer redy to take ye ordre in dwe wyse he askythe for ye swerde and ye spurs. Y^e kynges chamberleyne shall take ye swerde and ye spurrs owt of ye handes of ye yonge squiere, and shall take and shewe hym unto ye kynge. The kynge shall receyve ye ryght spure and betake it unto one of ye most worthy that standyth abowte, commaundynge hym that he put it on ye ryght hele of ye esquier, and by ye kyngs commaundement that lorde knelynge on ye one kne shall take ye esquier by ye ryght legg and putte ye foote uppon his kne, and shall putte ye spurr apon his helle, and he shall make a crosse uppon ye kne of ye esquer and shall kysse it. Then shall an othar lorde putt uppon that othar hele an othar spurr on ye same wysse that ye othar dyd; then ye kynge of ye mekenesse of his hieghe myght takynge ye swerde in his hands shall ther with girde ye squier. Than shall ye esquier lyft upp his armys on hieghe, and ye kynge shall putte his armys aboute ye neke of ye esquier, and lyftynge upp his right hand he shall smyte ye esquier in ye nekke saynge thus, " Be ye a good knyght," kyssynge hym. Afterwarde these noble and wyse knyghtes afore seyde this newe knyght shall lede in to ye chapell as it is to fore wnto ye hyghe awtar, and ther he shall unknyte hym and his swerde with prayers and devocions shall offer to God and to Holy Churche moste devowtly, beschynge God that thilke ordre moste worthy dewlie he may kepe unto his ende. Thes thyngs so done he shall take a sope in wyne. And in ye goynge owte of ye chapell ye master coke shall be redy to do of his spwrrs, and shall take them to hym for his fee; and ye reson is this, that in casse that ye knyght do afftar eny thynge that be defame or reproffe unto ye ordre of knyghthode, the master coke then with a gret knyfe, with whiche he dressethe his messes, shall smyt of his spurrs frome his heles; and therfore in remembraunce of this thynge ye spurrs of a new knyght in ordre takynge shall be fee unto ye mastar coke perteynynge dwely unto his office. Than shall this wyse knyghtes afore sayde lede this newe knyght in to ye hall agayne, the whiche beginynge ye table of knyghtes shall syt to mete; and ye sayd noble and wyse knyghts shall sett abowte hym at ye table, and ye noble knyghts shall be servyd lyke as other bene; and as for that tyme he shall not ete nor drynke at ye table but yf grete nede be, nor he shall not meve hym, nor loke hidre or thedar more than a wyfe newe weddyd; and evarmore one of his ij govornowrs shall stand by hym with a kerchyffe, of ye whiche, yf eny nede come, he may serve hym.   And whan ye kynge arrysythe from ye table and goythe in to ye chamber ye knyght shall be ledd unto his chambre with greate multytwde of knyghtes, squires, and mynstrells yonge syngynge and dawnsynge in to ye entre of his chambre.   And there ye knyghtes, esquiers, and mynstrills shall take thare leve, and ye newe knyght shall go to eate, the dore shall be closyd, and he shall do of his arraye, whiche shall be gyven to ye kyngs of armes; and also ye sayd kynges and haurawds shall have thoffice of armes of every duke, erle, baron, and bachiler aftar thayr estates, and at ye leste xx^s for theyr honors to shew them in ye kyngs presence and in ye sayd cowrte, ye graye cope shall be unto ye wayte or a noble for it. And aftar this mete this noble new knyght anon shall be arayed with a robe of blewe with streyght sleves, and he shall have uppon ye lefte shwldar a whit lace of sylke hangynge, and that lace he shall kepe in y^s wyse above his clothynge with owt forthe frome that daye hensforthe contynewally unto that tyme he gete sum maner of worshype by deservynge by wytnes of worthye knyghtes and squers of armes and herawdes dewlye afftarward reportyd; whiche reporte mouste enter in to ye earys of ye worthy prince whiche hathe made hym knyght, or of some odar, or ellys of some noble lady, for to take awaye ye lace frome ye shulder, sayenge thus: " Ryght dere lorde, I have herde so moche of yowr worshyppe and renowne that ye have done in dyvers partes unto ye grete worshype of knyghthode to yowr selffe and to hym that made yow knyght, that deserfe and ryght wyll that this lace be put and take awaye."   But aftar dynar ye worshipfull and worthy knyghts and esquiers shall come afore ye sayd newe knyght, and hym shall lede to ye kyngs presence, all tymes beynge before hym ye sayd esquirs, govornors. And when ye new knyght comythe in to ye presence of ye kynge he shall knele before ye kynge and shall say thus: " Moste drede and moste myghty prynce, of my lytyll powre of that that I may I thanke yow of all ye worshypes, curtesies, godenesse, whiche ye have done unto me; " and this sayde he shall take leve of ye kynge. And uppon that ye govowrnowrs shall goo and take theyr leve of thayre maysters, saynge thus : " Worshypfull Sir, by ye kyngs commaundement we have servyd yow, and that commaunde-ment fulfyllyd and parfwrmyd to owr powr, and what we have done in yowr service ayene yowr reverence we praye yow of yowr grace for to pardon us of owr neglygence. Fortharmore of ye custome of ye kyngs cowrt we aske and reqwere yow of robes and fees to the terme of owr lyffe covenable to ye kyngs esquiers, felowes to ye knyghtes of othar lands," &c.

Explicit.

[NOTE.—This article seems to have been transcribed by Stowe from the Cottonian MS. Nero C. ix. 168b., from which it has already been printed by Anstis in his *Observations Introductory*, Coll. No. 88, and by Nicolas in his *History of the Order of the Bath*, pp. 12-26. It is on the whole a very accurate transcript. The speech addressed to the esquire at p. 107 is, however, abbreviated, the passage stand-ing in the original as follows:—

seyenge secretly to the squyer thus :—" Right dere brother, grete worshipe be this ordre un to yow; and Almyghty God geve yow the praysynge of all knyghthod. Lo, this is the ordre. Be ye stronge in the feith of Holy Cherche, and wydows and maydones oppressed releve as right commaundith. Yeve ye to everych his owne with all thy mynde above all thynge. Love and drede God. And above all other erthly thinges love the Kynge thy soverayn lord, hym and his defende unto thy powere. And be fore all worldly thynges putte hym in worshipp and thynges that be not to be taken beware to begynne." In this wyse or better, &c. And when the *knyght* is thus counselled (&c. as above, Stowe having corrected the word "knyght" here into "esquire.")]

A memoriall of the Kyngs highnes wholl chardges sus-
teyned at Bolloigne from the xxvij of Septembar,
Anno xxxvj, to the ix of Octobar, Anno xxxvij.

The wages of tholle garison ther:

payde, lxxM.lxvjli. iijs.
wⁿpayde, xxviijM.vjc.li. xixs.⎬ iiij^{xx}xviijM.vijc.iiij^{xx}vjli. ijs.

The wages of artificers and laborars about y^e fortifications:

payd, xvijM.iiijc.iiij^{xx}viijli. vs. vj$d$. ob. ⎱ xxM.viijc.lxxvjli.
wⁿpayd, iijM.iijc.iiij^{xx}vijli. xixs. jd. ob. ⎰ ⅲjs. vⅲjd.

The wages of thofficers and ministars of y^e victualls:

payd, M.vjc.li. ⎱ MM.vjc.li.
unpayde, M.li. ⎰

Wasste and losse in the victualls, xjM.c.iiij^{xx}xvjli. xijs. vd. ob.

Forayne and necessarie payments over and besyds the provysyons
made and payd for in England vjc.iiij^{xx}xiiijli. xijs.

Out of the Kyngs Coffars, iiij^{xx}iijM.ccc.viijli. ijs.

In the price of victualls, vijM.iiij^{xx}xiiijli. xvjs. viij$d$.

For fryssys and matreses, c.xxxvli. viijs. ob.

Yet dewe for victalle, vM.iiijc.viijli. xs. xd.

In the hands of th'executors of S. John Jenyngs, vc xxli.

Sum of tholle chardges aforsayd, c.xxxiiijM.liijli. xjs. jd. ob.

The charges of the fortifycacions within y^e highe towne of bosse [a]
towne and the Yonge Man,[b] xM.viijc.xxxijli. vjs. vd. ob.

The charges of the fortyfications of tholde man,[b] vijM.vjc.lvli.
xixs. jd.

Md. Ther is dewe unto the garreson and werkemen of the forti-
fycations xxijM.vijc.vli. iiij$d$. ob.

Item. Ther remaynethe in victualls unspent the laste of Septembar, over and besyds xijM.viijc.li. vijs. vj$d$. ob. Reyceyvyd and
to be receyvyd for victualls, MM.CCC.li.

[a] "Of Bosse," qu. "and Basse," $i.$ $e.$ Haute and Basse Boulogne?
[b] The Old and Young Man were two fortresses at Boulogne.

Anno Domne 1561, y⁰ yere begynyng at New Yers daye.

The xxiiij daye February, which was Saynt Matheus daye, at vj aclocke at nyght, was sene at London as gret a flashe of lyghtnynge as lightly hath ben sene at any tyme, and a gret clape of thunder wher with fell a gret 'shure of haylle and rayne which sodenly turned to a gret snow, and all this was in on quarter of an owre. For y⁰ space of an owre after y⁰ ellemente semed westward as rede as fyre. It is to be notid that all this whylle y⁰ wynde was very bytter colde.

Anno Domini 1561.

The x daye of Apryll was one Wyllyam Jefferey, an heretyke, whyppyd at a carts arsse from the Marshallse in Sothewarke to Bethelem with out Byshoppys gatte of London, for that he belevyd one John More to be Crist, the Savyour of y⁰ worlde. He was very sore whypyte, and on his hed wer pynyd papars, and also abowt the cart wer hangyd the lyke papers, wher in was wrytyn as folowythe: " Wyllyam Gefferey, a moste blasfemous herytyke, denyenge Cryst our Savyowr in heven." And when he the sayd Wyllyam Geferey was brought to Bethlem gate there the Marshalls sarvaunts cawsyd the cart to staye and John More to be browght out of Bethlem, whiche John More dyd professe hym selffe to be Cryst the Savyowr of the worlde. And afftar examynacion and his aunswers, whiche wer very doubtfull, he wase lykewysse strypte and tyed at the carts ars and whypte a byrdbolt shute be yonde Bethlem and so bake a gayn, and sent into Bethelem prisoner ageyne. And Wylyam Geferay was sent agayn to the Marshallse. They had bene in the presons before namyd ny a yere and a halff before this tyme, the one for affyrmynge hym selff to be Crist, the othar affyrmynge hym selffe to be Seynt Petar the Apostyll of Crist.

The descrypcon of Troionovaunt.

Anno 1561, ye 4 day of June, betwen 4 and 5 of ye cloke [in] ye afftar nonne, beynge Wedynsday and Corpus Cristi eve, ye stepull of Powlles was fyeryd by lyghtnynge, ye whiche lytenynge dyd take ye stepulle, as it dyd seme to ye beholders, ye space of ij or iij yardes benethe ye crosse and so byrnt round abought in ye same place that ye toppe felle of with ye crosse wnperyshed (or wn byrnt) and ye crosse fell southe, and so the sphere byrnt downe ward lyke as a candil consumyng, to ye stone werke and ye bells, and so to ye rouffe of ye churche, and thorow ye rouffes of ye churche all fowre ways, east, west, northe, and sowthe. With in ye qwiers or chawnsylls was brynt no thyng but only ye communion table, and in ye rest of ye churche was brynt nothing but a sartayn tymber werke whiche stode at ye northe-west pyllar of ye stepull, which was fyeryd with ye tymber that fell in to ye churche owt of ye steple; whiche was a lamentable syghte and pytyfull remembraunce to all people that have ye feare of God before theyr eyes, consyderynge it was ye hous of owre Lord, erectyd to prays hym and pray to hym, ye beawty of ye syte of London, ye beawty of ye holle Reallme. A mynster of suche worthy, stronge, and costly buldynge, so large, so pleasant and delectable, it passyd all comparyson, not only of mynstyrs within thys realme but ells where as sure as travayll hathe taught ws in other realmes ethar Cristyn or hethyn. Wherfore feare we God that so sore hathe chatysyd us, and let ws well know that he whiche hathe not spayrd his owne hous wyll not spare owres, exsept we repent owr formor wykyd lyffe and serve hym in holynys and newenys of lyffe, with a parffyt faythe in God and parffyt charytye to owr neyghbour, ye whyche our Lorde for his byttar passyon grawnt. Amen.

That same day at Gylford was brynte a carsy hangynge on ye tayntars, which carse dyd contayne lx yards, and it was conswmyd to powdar and ye tayntar not hurt; allso v mylle beyend Gylford a woman was byrnt with ye same lyghtnyngc. That day was many great harmes done by lyghtynyng in England, as at Shafftesebury the steple with parte of y^c churche was brynt.

Anno 1561, the xxx and y^c last day of June in ye afftarnoone a cart ladyn with haye browght in to Sothewarke was set a fyre ————^{a} and clene brent, ye hey, ye carte, and y^c tylle horse to dethe, whiche was a thyng to be notyd, or rathar to be wonderyd at, that in suche a place, at that tyme of y^c day and in y^c syght of so many beholdars, it shuld so be consumyd with owt helpe.

The confessyon of Master Rychard Allington esquere, the xxij of Novembre, 1561, abowte viij of ye clocke at nyght, before Master Doctour Caldewalle, Master Doctor Good, Master Garthe, Master Jones, and Ser John of ye Rolles, &ct.

Maisters, seinge that I muste nedes die, whiche I assure yow I nevar thought wolde have cum to passe by this dessease, consyderinge it is but ye smalle pockes, I woulde therfore moste hertely desyre yow in ye reverence of God and for Christes passions sake to suffer me to speake untyll I be dede, that I may dyscharge my consiens, accuse myn adversary the devyll, and yelde my selffe holie to Almightie God, my Savior and Redemer, upon whose justice yf I loke and behold I am condemnede eternally, but one ye othar syde yf I loke apon his merci, then I trust he wyll shewe unto me as he will do to y^c worst sorte of men, amonge whome I assure yow I accompt my selffe to be one, for nevar man hathe had more especiall tokenes of Godes singuler grace at offten and sundery tymes shewyd unto hym then I have had, and so letyll regardyd them as I have done. And good masters, for Christs passions sake give good eare unto me, and pray continewally for me upon your knes, for I will tell yow of straunge thyngs, whiche I assure yow by that faithe I beare to God I speake

^{a} Blank in MS.

not of vaine glorie or prayse of myselfe or any other cawse, but only
thanke God for his greate marcys shewed dyverse and sondry wayes
by me, and also to accuse my adversarie yᵉ devyll.   Yt is so when
I was a childe I was brought up, thoughe I saye it, with a good
father and mother whom ye knewe, who daylye used us children
vertiouslie and kepte us for one hower or ij everie eveninge and
mornige to prayers, and then when prayers wer don to owr bokes.
Aftarwarde we wer wonte to go to playe into an orchard nere
adjoynynge to my fathers howse, where as offtyn tymes for yᵉ space
of iij yeres there apperyd to me in a thicke hedge a goodlye comfortable vision, I do well remember, from ten yers olde unto thirtene.
Ther apperid, I say, to me yᵉ very Image of our Saviour Jesus Christ
as he sufferyd his blisyd passion upon the crose; whiche Image
apperyd to me very lyvely and that verie often so lovyngly and
tenderly as evar any erthely man culde desyre and wishe, shewinge
suche speciall tokens of his great marcie and goodnes to me as I
thynke nevar mortall man coulde desyre or wyshe yᵉ lyke, whiche I
did evermore kepe verie secret to my selfe for my greate comforte
and consolacion.   Goode maisters, for Christys passyons sake, geve
good eare unto me and pray, styll pray, pray, pray.   Then longe
aftar I cam to London, and at laste I was maried, sythe whiche
tyme I assure yow I have offended my Lorde God and Savyowr
Christ so sore, many foldely comittinge of so abhominable userie,
that I am a frayd I shalbe condempned eternally, and indede one
greate occasion was becawse I nevar gave my selffe to prayer as I was
wont to do, but spent my tyme to muche in wordlynes, for yᵉ whiche
my conscience did oftymes accuse me.   I will tell yow more anon.
I beseche yow pray, pray, pray.   And thus my consciens storringe
with in my selffe brought me to mervelous trobles of mynde, so that
nevar man was in suche case as I was of a longe tyme.   And beinge
in this greate troble, at yᵉ last yᵉ selfe same vision appered to me
agayne even sence this laste terme, and put me in remembraunce
agayne even of Gods speciall grace before shewed to me, and allso
of many othar thyngs, willynge me to leve of yᵉ worlde and yᵉ

besynes therof, and not to troble my selffe to muche there withe,
sythen whiche tyme I assure yow I have gone abowte to leave of all
my trobles of y° law agayne, and so to have lyved more quietlie
with that owr Lord had sent me. Nowe, good mastars, pray styll for
me and I wyll shew yow verie straunge thyngs. The second nyght
aftar I felle secke, beinge in perfecte memorie lyenge in my bed
brode a wake, and, as I thowght, all my folkes beinge a slepe here in
my chamber, ther apperid unto me suche strange thyngs and ferefull
which greatly amased and put me in wonderfull feere. I can not
tell what I shall tearme theme or call them, and as I doe remember
they were lyke puppets, they came up and downe my chamber, and
at laste, beinge marvelous sore afrayde, they came unto me rounde
aboute my chamber, my bedde, and apon my bedd pulled and
tossed me, stearde me, and tarde me, and so vexed me as I was
never in all my lyffe so soore troubled and vexed, shewynge suche
terrable and fearefull sytes, so that I was all most broughte to utter
desperacyon, so farforthe that I coulde not tell what to doe; yet at
the laste remembrynge with my sellfe and callynge to my remembraunce the goodlye graces that my Lorde and Savior Jesus Christe
at dyverse and soundry tymes had shewed unto me, saydo unto
my sellfe, "O good Lorde what do these thinges meane, what shall
I doe?" With that ther appered unto me my vysion agayne, which
shewed unto me in wrytinge all ye usery that ever I had recceaved
in all my lyffe so playnly that I redd yt, and in dede the sommes
were true and named every man of whom I had resseyved yt,
namynge the persons and ye somes, as of one Mr. Wilkokes thus
muche, of my L. Scrope thus muche, of Mr. Fynes thus muche,
namynge every some, and he shewed me also what I had
resseyved of Spanyardes, of Frenchmen, of Italyans, and suche
lyke, which came to vj^{xx}li., shewinge so playnely I assure you
every thinge that I much marveled at yt, and at the last I made
answer unto my vision and saied, "O Lorde, all thes thinges are true
in dede, what shall I do to yt?" Then my vision made answere and
comforted me verye muche agayne, commaundynge me fyrste to

paye all ye userie money agayne to every man as he had shewed
me ye somes, which came to xviijc.*li.* Then he badd me pay
agayne the fyftie poundes which I gat for bienge of a house in
Holbarne, and for ye vj^{xx}*li.* which I hadd of straungers he wylled
me, because that I know not wher they dwell, to gyve yt to y^e
poore prisoners and goode men that be in prison.   And maisters,
I can not tell of what relygyon you be that be heare, nor I care not,
for I speake to tell you the truth and to accuse myne adversary the
dewelles, and in dede I have gyven them some thinge all redy and
wyll gyve them all ye rest, God willinge, and will paye all y^e
userye mony to every man as my vision commaunded me, and do
intende, God willinge, tomorrow to send for them yff I lyfe so
longe; yf not, I wyll desyre ye Master of ye Rolles, as my trust is in
hym, that he will se it dischargid and payed out of hand that my
soulle may beare no perill for yt.   And masters, then my vysion
comforted me more and more, and he sayd he would shew me ix
psalmes, which yf I dede saye every daye I shuld never synne
agayne mortallie, for I assure you I have not used my sellfe to
prayer as I was wont to doe, nor never wente to ye churche at any
tyme of comon prayer, bycaus I dyd condeme my conscyence for
sufferynge me to commite suche abominable usery and other most
detestable synnes agaynst my hevenly Father, who had so many
folde wayes and sondry tymes shewed me such lovinge kyndnes
and synguller graces.   And ye psalmes were thes: 1. *Meserere mei
Deus.* 2. *Beati omnes qui temet*^a *Dominum* (128). 3. *Ad Dominum
cum tribuler.* 4. *Levavi oculos meos [in] montes.* 5. *Nisi quia Do.*
6. *Qui confidunt in Do.* 7. *Judica me Deus.* 8. *Illumina oculos
meos.* 9. *Domini*^a *non est exultatum cor meum.*

Anso so my vision left me.   Sith which tyme I assure you I
have had as muche quyetnes as any man can wishe, and have sene
soch comfortable syghtes as nether harte can thyncke nor tonge
expresse, and this I had to shew you.   Now, good Sur John, say
ye vij psallmes, and *Domine Jesu Cristy* with *gloriosa passyo* he

^a So in MS.

sayd hymsellfe, and then he thought he shuld have died, but then
brothe beinge geven unto hym he revyved agayne and fell to prayer
and gave hym sellfe wholly to quyetnes, &c. ·

In the yeare of our Lord 1562, ye 8 day of Septembar, was a
pryste (whose name was Ser —— Havard) taken (by sertayn pro-
motars and my Lorde of Elies ^a men) for sayienge of masse in Fettar
lane at my Lady Cares ^b housse, whiche pryste was violently taken
and led (as ten tymes wors then a traytur) thwrowe Holburne,
Newgate markyt, and Chepsyd to the Cowntar at the stokes callyd
the Pultrie, whithe all his ornaments on hym as he was ravist to
mas, with his masse boke and his porttoys borne before hym, and y^e
chalice with the paxe and all othar thyngs, as myche as myght make
rewde poople to wondar apon hym. And the nombar of people
was exsedynge great that folowyd hym, mokynge, derydynge,
cursynge, and wyshynge evyll to hym, as some to have hym set on
ye pelory, some to have hym hangyd, som hangyd and qwarteryd,
some to have hym byrnt, sum to have hym torne in pesys and all
his favorars, with as myche violence as the devill collde invent, and
myche more then I can wryte, but well was he or she that cowld
get a plucke at hym or gyve hym a thumpe with theyr fyst or spyt
in his face, and to scorne hym with sange, *Ora pro nobis Sancta
Maria* becawse it was owr Lady day of hir nativite (but not kept holy),
and all so they sange *Dominus vobiscum* and suche lyke. My Lady
Care, with my Lady Sakefylde, and Mistres Perpoynt, and Sherewod
and his wyffe war taken for beynge at ye same masse, and browght
before ye Byshope of Elly, then lyenge in Holburn, and theyr housys
sherchte, theyr bokes were all brought to ye Byshope of Elly, who
afftar examynation of them and theyr bokes sent them to prison.
My Lady Care, and my Lady Sakefelde, Mistres Perpoynt to y^e
Fleete, and the othar iij to ye Cowntar, and with in iij days afftar
the prist was sent to ye Marshalse in Sothewarke. And on the

<hr/>

^a Richard Cox, Bishop of Ely.

^b I cannot find who this Lady Cary was; but as it is stated below that she was of
the Queen's blood she was certainly related to Henry Cary, Lord Hunsdon.

second day of Octobre my Lady Care (beinge of yᵉ Quens blode), Mistris Perpoynt, the prist, and Sherewode and his wyffe were all v parsons browght from yᵉ prysons above namyd to the Sessions howsse at Newgate, and were ther arraynyd amongeste theves and mowrderars, and by xij men condemnyd as gilty.   Yᵉ prist for preparinge hym selffe to say masse, the Lady Carie and Harv Sherwode and his wyffe for beynge wyllynge to here and se masse (for this is to be notyd, yᵉ prist did not say masse, but was redy ravist to masse and entered ther in, when he and they were taken).   The prist had judgement gyven to hym prisoner in Newegatte xij monythis, my Lady Care and Mistres Perpoynt to ly prisoners in yᵉ Flett iij monythes, and in the thre monythes to pay to the quenes use ethar of them one hunderithe marks, or ells ther bodyes to remayn prisoners to yᵉ quenes plesure.   And Henrie Sherwod and his wyffe, beynge a marchaunt taylor, wer adjudgyd syx monythes prisonment and to pay ethar of them an hundred marke, or ells there bodyes at yᵉ quenes plesure.

In yᵉ yere of owr Lord 1563 was suche scarsytie of victualls in London by the servyng Newhavne,ᵃ that in yᵉ Lent heryngis was sold for ij a penye when they was best cheape ethar whit or red, Essyxe chesse for vj *d.* ye *li.* baryll buttar for vij and viij *d.* ye *li.*, a bad stockefyshe for vj *d.* or viij *d.*, and so forthe of all othar victualls. On Estar evyne yᵉ Parliament brake upe and gave to yᵉ queue a subsedie, and that was of everie man beynge valewyd worth iij *li.* on goods, or lands, or otharwys, and so uppewarde, ij *s.* viij *d.* of yᵉ *li.*, besyds they gave her ij fyfftens.

The viij daye of Julii, anno 1563, in yᵉ mornynge was great lyghtnynge and thundar, in yᵉ whiche was slayne a woman mylkynge and iij kyne, with in yᵉ Covynt gardyn whiche some tyme belongyd to yᵉ Savoy be yond yᵉ Temple bare; and many othar placis it dyd myche harme, of whiche one wase yᵉ steple of Seynt Androw in Howlburne wase smyttyn, many men, wemen, and cattayll wer slayne.

ᵃ Havre de Grace, which was in possession of the English from September 1562 to July 1563.

Anno Domini 1563, ye 9 daye of Julii, being Frydaye, a commysyon was sent frome y^c quenc and counsell to London that everie houshowlder should at vij of y^c cloke y^c same nyght lay owt woodd and make bonfyers in y^c stretes and lanes to that intent they shuld therby consume ye corruptc ayers, whiche othar wyse myght infect y^c sitie with y^c plage, as it was at that tyme begon, and dyed sum weke more and some weke lesse, but y^c greatyst nombar that dyde there of any one weke in London and y^c sowbarbes of ye same was xvij on weke, xxv ye next weke, xxiij ye third weke, xliiij y^c last weke, before those boone fiars began; it wase commaundyd to contynew ye same iij tymes a weke, Monday, Wednesdaye, and Frydaye, and where anny had dyed of y^c plage to syt up a hedlesse cross over ye dores. Y^c next weke afftar, endynge ye x day of Julii, ther dyde of y^c plage in London lxiiij. Y^e next weke endynge ye xvij day of Julii dyde c.xxxj of ye plage. Y^c next weke endynge ye xxiij of July jc.lxxiiij of ye plage. The next weke endynge the xxx day of July dyed ijc.iiij^{xx}ix of ye plage. The next weke endynge the vj day of August dyed of ye plage ijc.iiij^{xx}xix. The next weke endynge the xiij day of August, dyed of ye plage vc.xlij. The next weke endynge y^c xx day of August, dyed of ye plage vjc.viij. The next weke endynge ye xxvij day of August, dyed of ye plage ixc.lxxvj. The next weke endynge ye iij day of Septembre, dyed of ye plage ixc.lxiij. The next weke endynge y^c x daye of September, dyed of ye plage xiiijc.liiij, and nevar a paryshe in London clere that weke. The next weke endynge the xvij daye of Septembre, dyed in London of y^c plage xvjc.xxvj, and one paryshe clere. The next weke endynge y^c xxiiij day of September, dyed of ye plage in London xiijc.lxxij, and iij paryshes clere. The next weke endynge ye fyrst day of October, dyed in London of y^c plage xviijc.xxviij, and one paryshe cleare. The next weke endynge ye viij day of Octobre, dyed in London of ye plage xijc.lxij, and iiij paryshes cleare. The next weke endynge ye xv of Octobre, dyed in London of ye plage viijc.xxix, and ix parishis cleare. The next weke endynge y^c xxij of Octobre, dyed in

London of yᵉ plage xc., and v parishis clere. The next weke endynge yᵉ **xxix** of Octobre, dyed in London of yᵉ plage ixc.v, and one paryshe clere. The next weke endynge the v of Novembre, dyed in London of yᵉ plage iijc.lxxx, and parishis clere xvj. The next weke endynge yᵉ xij of Novembar, dyed in London of yᵉ plage ijc.lxxxiij, and parishis clere xxvij. The next weke endynge yᵉ xix of Novembre, dyed in London of yᵉ plage vc.vj, and parishis clere xiiij. The next weke endynge yᵉ xxvj of Novembre, dyed in London of the plage ijc.lxxxj, and parishis clere xx. The next weke endynge yᵉ iij of Desembre, dyed of yᵉ plage in London jc.lxxviij, and parishis clere xxx. The next weke end-ynge yᵉ x of Desembre, dyed of yᵉ plage in yᵉ citie ijc.xlix, and parishis clere xxvj. The next weke endynge yᵉ xvij of Desembre, dyed of yᵉ plage in London ijc.xxxix, pariches clere xxviij. The next weke endynge yᵉ xxiiij of Desembre, dyed in London of yᵉ plage jc.xxxiiij, parychis clere lj. The next weke endynge yᵉ xxxj of Desembar, dyed in London of yᵉ plage jc.xxj, parychis clere lj. The next weke endynge yᵉ vij of Januarye, dyed in yᵉ citie and lybertys therof of yᵉ plage xlv, parichis clere lxj. The next weke endynge yᵉ xiiij of January, dyed in yᵉ citie and lybertys ther of of yᵉ plage xxvj. The next weke endynge yᵉ xxj of January, dyed in yᵉ citie and lybertys therof of yᵉ plage xiij. The next weke endynge yᵉ xxviij of January, dyed in yᵉ citie and libertis therof of yᵉ plage xj. The next weke endynge yᵉ iiij of February, dyed in yᵉ citie and lybertys therof of yᵉ plage x. The next weke endyng yᵉ xj of February, dyed in yᵉ citie and libertis of yᵉ plage xviij. The next weke endyng yᵉ xviij of February, dyed of yᵉ plage in yᵉ citie and lybertis ther of xxxv. The next weke endynge yᵉ xxv of Fe[b]ruarye, dyed of yᵉ plage in yᵉ citie xiij. The next weke endyng yᵉ iij of Marche, dyed in London of yᵉ plage ix. The next weke endynge yᵉ x of Marche, dyed of yᵉ plage in yᵉ citie vj. The next weke endynge yᵉ xvij of Marche, of yᵉ plage vj. The next weke endynge y xxiiij of Marche, of yᵉ plage iij. Yᵉ next weke endynge yᵉ xxxj of Marche, of yᵉ plage v. The next weke endynge yᵉ vij of

Aprill, of y⁰ plage iiij. The next weke endynge y⁰ xiiij Apryll, of
y⁰ plage v. The next weke endynge y⁰ xxj of Apryll, of y⁰ plage
iij. The next weke endynge y⁰ xxviij of Apryll, of y⁰ plage iij
The next weke endynge y⁰ v day of Maye, of y⁰ plage 4. The next
endynge y⁰ 12 of May, 3. The next endynge y⁰ 19 of May, 5.
The next endynge y⁰ 26 of Maye, of y⁰ plage 1. The next endynge
y⁰ 2 of June, of y⁰ plage 4. The next weke endynge y⁰ ix of June,
of y⁰ plage iij. The next weke endynge y⁰ xvj of June, of y⁰
plage ij. The nexte weke endynge y⁰ xxiij of June, of y⁰ plage j.
The ij next wekes dyed none of y⁰ plage in London.

Anno 1563, y⁰ xxx of July, beyng Fryday, was one ———
whipt on a sckaffold at y⁰ Stondard in Chepe, his neke, his hands,
and fett made faste to a stake a bove y⁰ sayd skafold with kolars of
iron by y⁰ bedeles of y⁰ begars; some tym one, som tyme ij,
some tym iij attonce whipte hym, and they strove who mowght
whype hym moste extremlye; it was for that he had betyn a boye
with a lethar gurdle havynge a buckle of yron, whiche buckle
smate in to y⁰ fleshe of y⁰ boye very sore.

Anno 1563, y⁰ 29 of Julii, was Newehaven delyveryd up to the
Frenche men.

The 8 of Awgust, Turnar, commonly cawlyd Turnar of Bullyn,
for that he had ben a prechar and ministar amongst the sowldiors
at Boloigne, and had remayned there so longe as Boloigne was
Englishe, so that he was called y⁰ parson of Bolen, prechid at
Pauls Crosse, wher he made ij solome pettyssyons to my Lorde
Mayre of London. The one was that the deade of y⁰ cittie shuld be
buryed owt of the citie in y⁰ fylde; the othar was that no bell shuld
be tollyd for them when they lay at y⁰ marcie of God departynge
owt of this present lyffe, affyrmynge that y⁰ ryngynge or tollynge of
y⁰ bell dyd y⁰ partye departynge no good, nethar affore theyr deathe
nor afftar.

Anno 1563, the 27 day of July, beynge Tuesdaye, Elys Hawll,
of Manchestar, was whipt at Bedlem by to mynysters or prechars,

Philpot,[a] parson of Sent Myhells in Cornhyll, and Yownge,[b] parson of Sent Bartylmews ye Lytyll, Fulckes ye comon cryar of London stondynge by.

In Anno 1564 (accoumptynge ye yere to begyn ye xxv of Marche), the xxv day of February, at xj of ye cloke in ye nyghte, deseasyd the abovesayd Eliseus Hawll, and was buryed on Shordche Churche-yarde on ye Twesday, and ye xxvij day of February, at xj of ye cloke before none.

Anno 1563, in Septembre, the old byshopes and dyver doctors wer removyd owt of ye Towre in to the newe byshopes howssys, ther to remayn prysonars undar theyr custody (the plage then beynge in ye citie was thowght to be ye caws), but theyr delyve-raunce (or rathar chaunge of prison) dyd so myche offend ye people that ye prechars at Poulls Crosse and on othar placis bothe of ye citie and cuntrie prechyd (as it was thowght of many wysse men) verie sedyssyowsly, as Baldwyn at Powlls Cros wyshyng a galows set up in Smythefyld and ye old byshops and othar papestis to be hangyd theron. Hym selfe died of ye plague the next weke aftar.

This yeare, 1563, was the tenauntis of the Chambre of London callyd before ye Chambreleyn of London, beynge cawlyd ———— Sturgyn, Ser Thomas Lodge beyng Mayre, theyr renttis wer raysyd duble and treble, and forsyd to take leasys and gyve fyns for the same, or ells to for go theyr howsys, and they to have them that wold gyve moste for them. That same Ser Thomas Lodge (to ye great slaundar of ye wholl city) in ye ende of his maioralitie pro-ffessyd to be banqerowpte.

This yeare 1563, in Septembre, the Quenes Majestie lyenge in hir castell of Wyndsore, ther was set up in ye markyt place of Wyndsore a new payre of gallows to hange up all suche as shuld

<hr />

[a] John Philpot. He was deprived of his benefice in 1567.

[b] His name does not occur in Newcourt's list of the incumbents. After Thomas Taylor, collated 29 Nov. 1558, Newcourt gives Adrian Redlegge, collated 13 Dec. 1569.

come ther from London, so that no parson or eny kynde of warrs mought come or be browght from London to or thrughe, netbar by Wyndsor, not so mycho as thrughe yᵉ ryver by Wyndsor to cary wood or othar stuffe to or from London upon payne of hangynge with owt eny judgement, and suche people as reseyvyd eny wares out of London in to Wyndsor were turnyd owt of theyr howsys and theyr howssys shut up.

Anno 1563, yᵉ 26 of June, was a mynyster,[a] parson of Sent Marie Abchurche, of Sent Martyns in Iarmongar Lane, and of one othar benefice in yᵉ cuntrie, takyn at Dystaffe Lane ussynge an othar mans wyffe as his owne, whiche was dawghtar to Ser Myles Partryge and wyffe to Wyllyam Stokebrege, grosar, and he beyng so takyn at yᵉ dede doynge (havynge a wyffe of his owne) was caryed to Brydwell thrughe all the stretes, his breche hangynge aboute his knes, his gowne and his (kyvar knave) hatt borne afftar hym with myche honor; but he lay not longe ther, but was delyveryd with owt punyshment and styll injoyed his beneffysis.[b] They were greatly blamed that aprehended hym and comitted hym.

Turnar, of Bullyn, prechinge at Powlls Crosse yᵉ xxiiij of Octobre, anno 1563.

Syr Thomas Lodge, beynge Mayr of London, ware a beard, and was yᵉ fyrst that (beynge Mayr of London) ever ware eny, yᵉ whiche was thowght to mayny people very straynge to leve yᵉ cumly aunsyent custom of shavynge theyr beards; nevartheles he ware yᵉ comly auncient bonet with iiij cornars as all othar his predysesowrs had done befcre hym. This Sir T. Lodge braky and professe to be banqwcrooute in his maioralitie to the grete slandar of yᵉ citie. But yᵉ next yere afftar Ser John Whit, beynge mayre, ware bothe a longe beard and allso a rownd cape that wayed not iiij ouncis,

---

[a] His name was George Barton.

[b] He was, however, deprived of both his London benefices some years later, viz. of St. Mary, Abchurch, in 1567, and of St. Martin's, Ironmonger Lane, in 1568. But before the occurrence mentioned in the text a George Barton is said to have been deprived of St. Swithin's rectory in London, in 1561.

whiche semyd to all men, in consyderation of ye auncient bonyt, to be very uncomly.

This yere of our Lord 1563 was great lytnynge and thundar in Desembre from ye fyrst day to ye xij lyghtly every evynnyng and nyght, spesyally on ye xij nyght, beyng Sonday, from viij of ye cloke tyll somewhat past ix, that gretar lyghtnyng hathe not bene lyghtly sene at eny tyme.

Poynts of Devinitie: Anno 1564 (by order of the Kalendar), ye yere to be accomptid from newe yers daye forward, on ye Wedyns-daye, beynge ye 26 of Januarie, wasse a solome sermon made at Powlls Crosse by Coale,[a] Archedecon of Essyxe, wherunto was warnyd ye Lord Mayre of London with ye Aldarmen and Shrives, with allso the crafftis of ye citie in theyr lyveries. Wher in ye prechar dyd move ye awdyence to rejoyce that ye plage wasse cleane sessyd, and that God had cleane takyn it awaye from us. He sayd ye cawsse ther of was ye superstysyows relygyon of Rome, whiche was (as he sayd) so myche favoryd of ye sytysyns. He gave ws warnynge to be ware therof, callynge it a fallee relygyon, worsse then ethar ye Turkis or ye devyles relygyon. Moreover he sayd it stode uppon iiij pilars which wer rotyn postis, that is to say, Imagis, Purgatory, ye Sacraffice of ye Masse, and Transubstansyation, agaynst ye which he dyd invaye, and sayd that yf we dyd not beware of falce relygyon, all thowght God had cleane takyn a way ye plage, he wold send a worse apon use, that is to say, fyre and sword, which shuld slee ye children at ther mothars brestes, ye wyffes shuld be slayn from theyr husbonds, ye husbonds from theyr wyffes, and one neyghbour shuld sleye an othar to have his goods. But to conclud with all, he perswadyd all states of ye citie to rejoyce for that ye plage was sesyd, for now, sayd he, shall yowr mayre ryde honorably acco[m]panyed with ye aldermen and othar ther assystence ye wor-shypffull of ye citie; now shulde ye lawyers be frequentyd and set a worke, now shall ye skolles be openyd, now shuld the marchantis have fre traffryke into all cuntries and nacions, wher as before all

[a] Thomas Cole, A.M.

nasyons dyd abhoro them, now shall yow artyffysers rejoyce, for ye shall now sell yowr wares aboundantly, and now shall ye be sett a worke even thorowly, wher as of longe tyme ye have had no worke but lyvyd in great penurye. Now, O ye artyfysers, shall ye take mony aboundantly. O ye prentysys rejoyce, for now shall ye have yowr bellys full of meate, whiche of longe tyme have bene starvyd thrughe your mastars skarsytie.

On Wedyndyns daye, beynge Sent Mathews eve, and ye xx day of Septembar, anno 1564, was suche hye tydes that all ye maryshys abought East Hame, and so to London, was ovar flowyd with watar, whiche dyd myche harme.

On the xxvj day of Septembar, in anno 1564, beynge Tweseday, ware arraynyd at ye Gyldhalle of London iiij personas and there caste, for ye stelynge and receyvynge of ye queens lypott,ᵃ combe, and lokynge glasse, with a bodkyn of gold to brayd hir heare, and suche othar small ware out of hir chambar in her progresse. And on Thursday next afftar, beynge Myhilmas even, and ye xxviij day of Septembar, ij of them whiche had bene servantis in Chepesyd, one of them with Master Bakehowse, dwellyng agaynst ye Standard, beyng a sylke man, were bothe hangyd before ye Cowrte gatte, upon ye gallows that stode on Haye Hyll, whiche was for that tyme removyd for that purpose to Saynt James, before ye wall, beynge at that tyme ye quee[n]s cowrte.

The xxix of Septembar, in Anno Domini 1564, was ye Lorde Robart Dudleye, mastar of ye queens horsse, creatyd Baron of Denbyghe and Erle of Lescestar at ye queens cowrtte, then beynge Saynt James, be sydes Charing crosse.

The second day of Octobar, beynge Mondaye, in anno 1564, was kepte at Paulls a sertayne kynde of evenynge prayer as an osequye or memoriall of ye deathe of Fardynando, latte Empcrowr of Germanye, where ye Lorde Hyghe Tresorar of England was ye cheffe mowrnar amongest dyvars othar, as ye Byshope of Cauntowrbery,

---

ᵃ Chamber pot.

yᵉ Byshopes of London and Rochestar, with yᵉ Deane of Powles, &ct. And on yᵉ morow, beynge yᵉ iij of October, was selebratyd a comunyon to yᵉ offatory and no farthar, and so yᵉ Byshope of London went to the pulpyt and prechyd a sermond, and yᵉ herce, whiche was very fayr, of clothe, velvyt, and sylke, with frynge of golde, and banars very many and fayre, but no lyghts of waxe or othar wyse, stode tyll Monday next folowynge, whiche was yᵉ ix dai of Octobar.

The vij day of Octobar, beynge Satowrdaye, anno 1564, at viij a cloke at nyghte, was sene comynge out of yᵉ northe easte very great lyghtes lyke great flames of fyre, whiche shott forthe as it [were] gonepowdar fyeryd and spred out in a longe frome yᵉ northe easte, northe, and northe west, in dyvars placis at once; and all mett in yᵉ mydes of yᵉ fyrmament, as it war ryght ovar London, and desendyd somewhat west warde, and all yᵉ flames beynge ther gatheryd grew in to a rednys, as it were a very sangwyn or blode cowlar, and this contynewyd tyll ix of yᵉ cloke; and all yᵉ same nyght was more lyghtar then yf yᵉ mowne had shone moste bryght, wheras no mone shone that nyght, for yt chaungyd but one day before, whiche was Fridaye.

Anno Domini 1564, Master Newalle, Deane of Powles, preachyd at Polles Chrose yᵉ 19 of Novembar, where he protestyd that ther was not one trew worde in Master Dormars boke latly browght ovar from beyonde yᵉ seas.

The 20 of Novembar, beynge Monday, in yᵉ mornynge, a bowt vj of yᵉ clocke, throghe neglygence of a mayden with a candell, yᵉ snoffe ther of fawlynge into an hundryd wayght of gonne pothar, thre howssys in Bucklersbury war sore shaken, and yᵉ backar partes of yᵉ same howsys wer all to blewne and shattard in pecis, and yᵉ afore sayde mayde was so byrnt that she dyede ther of with in ij dayes afftar; yf this powthar had bene in a sellar, as it was in a garret, it had donne myche more harme.

This yere 1564 was a sharpe froste, whiche began on Seynt Thomas daye before Cristmas, on yᵉ 21 daye of Desember, beynge

Thursdaye, and contynewyd tyll ye 3 day of Janewarie beynge
Wednysdaye; on ye whiche Wedynsedaye it thawyd bothe ye daye
and nyght folowynge, and ye morow beyng Thursdaye allso this
forst as before is sayde begynynge on Sent Thomas day before
Cristmas was so sharpe that on newyers even men went ovar y^e
Thams as saffe as on the dry land, not only betwyxt Westmystar
and Lambythe, but in all placis betwyxt Lambethe and the Olde
Swane, they wente bothe ovar y^c Thames and alonge ye same from
London to Westmystar and from Westmystar to London, comynge a
lande salffelly (thankis be to God) wher they wolde betwen Westmystar and ye Olde Swan, whiche is very nere unto ye brydge. And
y^c same newyers even, beynge Sondaye, people playd at ye footte ball
on ye Thams by great nombars. On newyers day beynge Monday,
and on Twesday and Wednyseday, dyvars jentyllmen and othars set
up pryckes on y^c Thams and shott at ye same, and great nombars of
people beholdynge ye same standynge at ye prykis as boldly (and
thankis be gyvyn to God a saffly) as it had bene on ye drye lande.
And I my selffe who write this notte wentte on ye Wedynsday before
namyd frome Lambythe to Westmystar and there dynyd with Master
Burre, who went thetar with me. And then we went agayne to y^e
comon stayrs of Westmystar, and so upon ye Thames to y^c Baynards
Castell, where we went a land (thankys be to God) as salffe as ever
I went in eny place in all my lyffe, where we sawe men shewte at
a payre of prykes set up agaynst ye qweens cowrte upon ye Thams,
and costardmongars playnge at ye dysse for aples, and ye people
went on y^c Thams in greatar nombars then in eny streat in London. The people went ovar ye Thams on ye Thursdaye at nyght,
and on ye morow, beynge Fridaye, was no yce on ye Thams to be
sene, but that all men myght rowe ovar and alonge ye same, it was
so sodaynly conssumyd.

Anno 1565, ye yere beginynge ye first of Januarie. The xxvj
day of Januarie, beynge Frydaye, at nyght was ij tydes at London
brydge; and on ye morow, beynge Satardaye, was ij tydes in y^e
mornynge and ij in the evenynge of ye same day, and ye morow,

beynge Sonday and yᵉ xxviij day of Januarie, was lyke wys ij in yᵉ mornynge and one in yᵉ evynynge.

The iij daye of Februarye yᵉ Lorde Darley departyd toward Scotland, who afftarward maried yᵉ Quene of Scotts, &ct.

The vij of Marche beynge Asshe Wedensday, in anno 1564, Master Newalle, Deane of Powls, prechid at Westmystar before yᵉ Queens Majestye, wher he so handelyd his mattar that the Quenes Majestie spake to hym owt at a wyndowe and bad hym goo to his texte, &ct.

The xxviij day of Aprylle in yᵉ afftar none, anno 1565, fell so great an haylle that yt lay on yᵉ grownd in many placys abowt London more then xxiiij owres and ther with was iij or iiij great clapps of thundar. The morow, beynge Lowe Sonday and yᵉ xxviiij day of Aprille, was Wylyam Man, of Soffolke in Sudbury, fownde hangyd with in Mistres Kyrtons palle in S. Andrews Wndarshafft paryshe in London; he honge hym selffe with his nyghte kercheffe on one of yᵉ pykes of yᵉ palle so that one of his fett towchyd yᵉ grownd. The morow, beynge Monday and yᵉ xxx day of Aprill, one mane rode on two staves borne on iiij mens showldars at S. Katheryns for that his next neybor sofferyd his wyffe to beat hym. There went with hym ny iijᶜ. men with handgunes and pikes well armyd in cowrslytts.

On Lowe Sonday an Eryshe byshope of Irlande, beyng prisonar in yᵉ Towr of London, went quietly frome thens, beynge sene and spokyn with at his so goynge, and yet not knowne, whiche was myche to be merveylyd at, but he cowld not be founde.

Anno 1565, yᵉ 20 dyay of June, at vij of yᵉ cloke at nyght, was yᵉ Lady Lynyt[a] sent prisonar unto yᵉ Towr of London.

Anno 1565, the 16 day of Julii, at nyghte, beyng Monday, was very tyrable lyghtnynge and thundar, that the lyke in many yers hathe not bene sene; yᵉ moste force therof was frome xij of yᵉ cloke at nyghte unto iij of yᵉ cloke in yᵉ mornyng; whiche dyd myche hurt in many placys of this realme.

[a] Lennox.

Anno 1565, ye 11 day of Septembar, beynge Tewsdaye, the K. of Swedons systar[a] cam to London, and lodgyd at ye Earle of Bedfords place at Yve brydge, and was ther delyveryd of male childe on ye Satarday at nyght next folowynge, or ye 15 day of Septembre.

Anno 1565, ye 8 day of Octobar, ye Mayre of London, beyng Ser Richard Malarie, ridynge toward the Towr Hyll thorow Towar Streate to take the mustar of sertayn horsmen, was mett by Ser Frauncis Jobson, Levetenaunte of the Towr (with a band of men dyd assalt),[b] who forsably wolde have taken the swerd from the swerdberar before ye mayre, in so myche that, the swerdberar holdynge the same very fast, the leffetenawnt so pulld therat that he pluckyd a way ye skabard, rentynge the same with stryffe of them and ye mayrs offysser, so that the mayre and his offysars had mycho wyrke to deffend and kepe the sayd swerd, in so myche that the lyfftenaunt callyd for more ayde and assystaunce out of ye Towr, and the offysars war myndyd to have rayssyd the Towre Streate, and so the holle citie with wepons, but the lord maior made proclaymacion that no man shuld draw eny wepon or stryke eny stroke, but every man to depart home, and all so the horssmen lyke wysse to depart tyll they were warnyd agayn, whiche on ye same daye sevennyght, beynge lykewys Monday and the 15 day of Octobar, they dyd ther mustar beffore the maior in that sam place on the Towr Hyll before apoyntyd, and ther the mayr bare his swerd peasably as it befor tyms had bene used.

A Noate of Divinitye.

Colle, Assedeacon of Essexe, prechinge at Powlls Crosse, anno 1565, the xj day of Novembar, lykenyd the pristes unto appes, for, saythe he, they be both balld alyke, but y^t the pristes be balld before, the appes behynd.

[a] Cicely, wife of Christopher, Margrave of Baden. See Stowe's Chronicle, 659.
[b] "(with—assalt)" This is an interlineation which spoils the grammar.

Anno 1565, yᵉ Lorde Ambros Dudley, Erle of Warwyke, yᵉ 11 day of Novembar, maryed yᵉ Earle of Bedfords dowghtar, named Lady Anne, at Westmynstar. For yᵉ space of iij wekes before, a chalenge was set on yᵉ cowrt gate at Westmyster, as folowythe:

> Yow that in warlike ways and dedes of arms delight,
> Yow that for cuntryes cawse or ells for ladyes love dare fyght
> Know yow foure knyghts ther be that come from foren land,
> Whos hawtye herts and corage great hathe movd to take in hand,
> With sword, with speare and shild, on fote, on horse backe, to,
> To try what yow by force of fyght, or otharwyse, can do.
> Prepare yowr selves ther fore this challenge to defend,
> That trompe of fame yowr prowes great abrod may sownd and send.
> And he that best can do, yᵉ same shall have the price.
> Yᵉ day, yᵉ place, and forme and fyght, loo here before yowr eys.

The day was apoyntyd yᵉ iiij of November, whiche was put of to yᵉ xj day of Novembar. At yᵉ tylt with eache one vj courses, at yᵉ torney xij strokes with yᵉ swerd. Thre pusshes with the pounchen staffe and xij blows with yᵉ swerd at barryars, or twenty yf any be so dysposed.

The same xj day at nyght, sertayne peales of chambars was shot of at yᵉ bank ovar agaynst Westmyster, and one of yᵉ chambars brekynge slew yᵉ quenes scheffe mastar goonnar of Engeland, which was Master Robart Thomas.

The xxiij day of Decembar, beynge Sondaye, at nyghte, in anno 1565, was a greate tempest of wynde where thrwghe many persons were drownyd on the Thams and othar placis, and the great gattes at the weste ende of S. Pawls churche in London, wher is the brasen pilar was blowne wyde open, the wynd beynge in yᵉ west was of suche force.

The xxij day of February, 1565, beynge Friday, the howsys nere to yᵉ Cunduite in Cornhylle, abowt yᵉ nombar of lx housholds, poore and ryche, were cryed by the bell man a bowte yᵉ citie of London to be solde to them that wowld gyve moaste for them, and remeve the same from thens, that in that place yᵉ marchaunts mowght buyld theyr bursse. Thos howsys were dyverse tymes so cryed and at y[c] last solde, and they beganc to pull downe y[c] same shortly aftar owr Lady day in Lent. In y[e] pullynge downe wherof dyverse persons were sore hurt and ij in great poryll of deathe; and by Whitsontyd next followynge in 1566 y[c] same howsys were all pullyd downe and y[e] grownd clearyd: all whiche chargis was borne by y[e] citizens of London, and then possessyon gyven by sertayn aldarmen to Syr Thomas Gressham, who layed y[e] fyrst stone (beynge bryke) of y[e] fowndacion on y[e] vij day of June, beynge Friday, in y[c] aftar none next aftar Whitson halydays, betwen 4 and 5 of y[e] cloke.

The xxvj day of Marche, in anno 1566, beyng Twesday, y[c] parsons and mynystars of y[e] churches in and abowght London were (by commaundyment) at Lambethe, before y[e] Archebyshoppe of Caunterbury [a] and othar of y[c] cownsell, wher charge was gyven to them to sarve theyr churchis and were theyr aparayll accordyng to y[e] quens injunctions, or ells to do no sarvyce. And that same weke or y[e] begynyng of y[e] next came forthe a boke in print subscribyd by y[e] Archebyshope of Cauntorbury,[a] y[c] Byshopps of London,[b] Wynchester,[c] Elii,[d] and dyvers othar, whiche apoyntyd y[e] sayd mynistars to were theyre gownes and clokes with standynge colars and corneryd capse, and at theyr servyce to were syrplysys, or els not to mynystar, &ct. Afftar this folowyd myche troble with y[e] mynystar of y[e] citie of London; for in moost paryshis y[e] sextyn of y[e] churche dyd all shuche servys as was done, and that in his coate or gowne as he comonly went about othar busynes. In sume placis y[e] mynystars themselvs dyd servyse in theyr gownes or clokes with turnyng colars and hatts as they wer wont to do, and prechid stowtly and agaynst y[e] ordar taken by y[e] queue and counsell and y[c] byshopps for consentynge ther unto. And on y[e] 23 [e] day of Apryll a beryeng beynge at S. Gylls with owt Criple gate, vj clarkes weryng

[a] Matthew Parker. [b] Edmund Grindall.
[c] Robert Horne. [d] Richard Cox.
[e] Originally written " 22." The second figure is corrected, but whether into a " 3 " or a " 1 " it is difficult to say.

syrplicys befor yᵉ corps, Crowley,ᵃ vickar of that churche, stode in
yᵉ churche dore and with stode them ther to entre, saynge the
churche was his, and yᵉ quene had gyvne yt hyme duryng his lyffe
and made hym vickar therof, wherfore he wold rule that place and
wold not soffer eny suche superstycius rages of Rome ther to entre;
wher uppon was lyke to have bene a great tumolte by the reson of
partyse takynge, but in yᵉ end yᵉ clarks and those who toke theyr
parte accordynge to yᵉ quenes prosedynge wer fayne to gyve ovar
and to tary with owt yᵉ churche dore.   Yᵉ 7 day of Aprell, beyng
Palme Sondaye, yᵉ paryshe of S. Marie Magdalyn in Mylkestret,
makynge labour to yᵉ byshope, had by hym a mynister apoyntyd to
serve them with communion that day.   And when yᵉ sayd mynystar
was at sarvyce in a syrplyce and came doune to rede yᵉ pistle and
ghospell, in yᵉ meane space one of yᵉ same paryshe cawsyd his
servant to convey yᵉ comunyon cupe and yᵉ bread frome yᵉ table,
wherby many persones that were determyned that day to have
reseyvyd wer dysapoyntyd, yᵉ which fact was aftar but made a
lawhyn game.

    The xxx day of Marche, 1566, beyng Satarday, in yᵉ aftar none
was a sore tempest of lyghtenynge and thundar with rayne very great.
The day before was yᵉ Prynce and Martgrave of Badyn ᵇ arestyd or
stayed at Rochestar, wher he was dysguysyd lyke an espye and so to
have stolne owt of yᵉ realme and his Lady Cisily his wyffe to have
stolne afftar hym, levynge a great nombre of creditowrs unpaid, as
theyr buttchar, bakar, bruar, mercer, taylowr, skynar, grocer,
habbardashar, and othar, and yet his creditors for yᵉ same stayeng
of hym were by yᵉ cowncell commaundyd, some to the Flett and
some to yᵉ Marshalsey.   The 26 or 28 of Aprell Ciscily Marquese
of Bawde was conveyed thrughe Kent towards Dovar and so to sayll
towar hir natyv cuntrye.

─────────

ᵃ Robert Crowley. See p. 139.   ᵇ See page 13⅟, note ⸗. 3/ ⸿/

Robart, Erle of Leccstar, 1566.

The 2 of Aprell y⁰ Erle of Leycester cam to London, beyng accompanyd with lords, knyghts, y° pencionars and a great nombar of gentylmen and othars with y⁰ quenes fottmen and his owne also, all in theyr riche cotes and to y⁰ nombar of 700. He came in at y⁰ Temple barre and so thrughe Ludgate, Powlls churchyard, Cheape, Cornhyll, Gracious Strete, and then turnyd downe Lombard Strete and downe S. Nicholas Lane, and so to London Stone to y⁰ Erle of Oxfords place in S. Swythyns churche yard, wher it was apoyntyd that the Quenes Majestye (who had come frome Grenewytche secretly in to Sothewarke, takynge a whiry with one payr of ors for her and two othar ladyes at S. Mary Overyes stayres, and so rowyd ovar to the Thre Crannes in y⁰ Vyntre, wher she entryd a cowche cyveryd with blewe and so rode to y⁰ same Oxforde place) to mett with y⁰ sayd Earle of Lescestar, who or her gracis comynge was retorned with his trayn thrughe Candelwyke Strete and Easte Cheape, and downe New Fyshe Strete, ovar y⁰ brydge, thrwghe Sothewarke, and so by S. Georgys churche toward Grene wytche. Not fer be yonde y⁰ sayd churche of S. George he stayde tyll y⁰ Quenes Majestie came frome y⁰ sayd Oxford Place before namyd the same way that she had passyd thethar tyll hym. She cam owt of hir coche in y⁰ highe way, and she imbrased y⁰ earle and kyssed hym thrise, and then they rode togythar to Grenewytche. The same day at nyght from vij of the cloke tyll ix was sene in y⁰ elyment as thowghe the same had openyd y⁰ bredghte of a great shete and shewyd a bryght flame of fyre and then closyd a gayne, and as it ware at every mynute of an howre to opyn and close agayne, y⁰ whiche I beyng at y⁰ Barrs with owt Allgate sawe playne easte as it war ovar the churche namyd Whitchappell. It is sayd y⁰ Erle of Leycester was retornyd frome London Stone be fore y⁰ Quenes Majestie came ther, for that she was not come when he came thethar.

Y^e same Palme Sonday in anno 1566, ye 7 of Aprill, a Scott (who prechid ij tymes every day at Sent Magnus, and mynysteryd every day to all comars of ye paryshe or eny othar in his gowne or cloke) prechid in ye afternone at Lytle Allhalows in Thams Stret. Y^e moaste part of his sermon was (as the othar of his sermons were and are) agaynst ye order takyn by ye quene and councell for ye aparayll of mynystars before namyd, with very byter and vehement words agaynst ye queue not here to be namyd, and allso agaynst mynystars as receyvyd ye same ordre.   The mynyster of ye churche for savgarde of his lyvynge had receyvyd ye cappe and syrplyce, where fore some tyme in ye sermon he smylyd at vehemente talke by ye prechar usyd to the contrary.   Wher upon aftar ye sermon sertayne of ye paryshe, namly, Wyllson, a dyar, and Dyckynson, a fyshemonger, resonyd with ye mynystar for his smyllyng at ye prechar, who resonably aunsweryd; but they toke ye matter so grevowsly that they fell from rwghe wordes at ye last to blowes with them who toke parte with ye mynystar.   The lyke dysquyet doyngs wer that daye in dyvars churches of ye citie, and allso ye lyke on Estar day or rathar worsse, so that in some paryshe churchis ye people in great nombar beynge redy to reseyve, suche quarylynge and contencion was betwen ye mynystars and parishoners that to quyat ye mattar ye churche dores wer fayn to be closyd, and ye paryschyns to departe unreseyvynge for that day.   And on Low Sonday, beynge ye xxj of Aprell, ye worshypffull of ye paryshe of Seynt Myldred in Bred strett, bryngynge a mynystar to serve the aftar none with a syrplyce, wer with stand by ye parson and his adherents, so that at ye last the cheffe of ye paryshe with ye aldar- mans deputy of ye warde were fayne to cawse ye mynystar to put on his syrplys and to do his servys, they standyng by on ethar syde to defynd hym tyll ye end of servyce.   Y^e mynistars and prechars that wer prehibytyd to preche or mynister dyd mayny of them nevartheles mynystar and preache as they before had don, yewsynge words of great vehemencie agaynst ye ordar before sayd set forthe, as also agaynst ye quene, counseyll, and byshops for settynge forthe y⁴ same. Yᵉ lyke sedycious lybells wer wryttyn and strewyd abowt in yᵉ strets, and ij sortis of sedycious bokes wer set forthe in prynt and gyven at theyr mornynge congratyngs; the one entytelyd "The Voyce of God," set owt by one Towrs yᵉ coole takar of the Towre, a smaterar in musyke, and hathe of longe tyme laboryd to serve in Powls churche, and ther dayly to were a syrplice wer it but for xli. the yere. Thothar by yᵉ wholl multytud of London mynystars, every one of them gyvynge theyr advyce in writynge unto Robart Crowley (somtym a boke sellar), now redar at Sent Antholyns, person of S. Petar yᵉ Powre, prebend of Pawlls, vickar of S. Gills with owt Criple gate, and deane of Harfford in Wales, who com-pilyd yᵉ same in to one booke, namynge yᵉ same "Yᵉ Unffoldynge of yᵉ Popyshe atyr;" agaynst yᵉ whiche boke an othar boke, beynge "A Playn Confutacion," was set forthe in print with yᵉ quens priveledge. It is to be notyd that yᵉ awcthors of thos two books before namyd were no ways punyshid for yᵉ same, but only yᵉ printars were kepte in yᵉ Contar nyghe a fortnyght, tyll they had openyd who war yᵉ awcthors, but they had frinds ynowe to have sete yᵉ whole realme togethar by the eares.

On the 3 day of June, beynge Whitson Monday, at nyght, yᵉ Scott (who before had ussyd to preche at S. Magnus and so sore to envey agaynst yᵉ capps, syrplisis, and suche lyke) dyd servys at S. Margaret Pattyns in Roode Lane, wher he ware a syrplice; and a sertayne nonbar of wyves threw stons at hym and pullyd hym forthe of yᵉ pulpyt, rentyng his syrplice and scrattyng his face, &ct.

On yᵉ 4 day of June, beynge Twewssdaye in Whison weke, Philpot, summe tyme a scrivoner, othar redar at Sent Antholyns, person of S. Mihells in Chornhyll, person of Stepnye and othar spirituall possesyons, and Gowghe, an othar scrivoner, the third redar of S. Antholyns, person of S. Petars in Cornhyll, for that they were the moaste ernyste withstondars of yᵉ lawes of this realme before namyd consernynge yᵉ ordar of mynystracions, and yᵉ greatyst animators of all yᵉ wholl citie to do the lyke, upon whom yᵉ greatest nombar of othar mynystar dyd depend, beynge apoyntyd by the byshops to go to Wynchestar to Robert Horne, ther byshope, withe hym to perswad or be perswadyd for ye space of xxj days, toke theyr jorney ovar London brydge thrughe Sothewarke and so forthe to ward Wynchestar, beynge accompanyed with a great nombar of wymen to ye nombar of ij or iij c. ladyn with baggs and bottells to bancket at theyr departynge, gyvynge them golde, sylvar, sugar, spice, or othar wyse suche as they had, anymatynge them moaste ernystly to stand fast in y^e same theyr doctryn whiche they had tawght touchynge syrplysis, caps, and suche lyke.   At Myhelmas next foloyng, Philpot subsribyng to them came to London agayn, wher beyng myche rebukyd of his brethern he sold up his movable goods and went to Rie, in Kent, wher he hathe xxx$li.$ a yer, and servythe with owt a syrplice, and kepithe all his othar promocions still as Stapney, Cornhill, &ct.

The 26 day of Januarie next folowynge, beynge Sonday, y^e Byshope of London comynge to Seinte Margarets in Olde Fishe Strete to preache in the fore none, the people (especially the wymen) that ware in ye sayde churche unreverently howtyd at hym with many oprobrious words, and cryed " Ware horns," for that he ware a corneryd capp.   For ye whiche on ye Satarday next, beynge the 1 day of February, one woman, beynge the wyfe of one ——^{a} Symsone, a tyukar, dwellynge in Sowthewarke, was sett uppon two laddars lyke a cuckengstole before the same churche, where she satt the space of one owre, greatly rejoysynge in that her lewde behavowr, and that she was punyshyd for the same, and lyke wyse the beholdars of ye same dyd myche rejoyce ther in and anymatyd the lewde woman to rejoyce and prayse the Lorde for that He had made hir worthy to soffer persecution for ryghtwysnes, and for the truths sake (as they said) and for crienge owt a gaynst supersticion as the termed it.

The 17 day off Februarie at nyght, beynge Monday, was a great watche in ye citie of London, so that ye Lord Maior, ye shrives, and dyvers aldarmen them selves were abrode in the strets all that

* Blank in MS.

nyght with great nombars of people; whiche great watche contynewyd all that weke. Whiche watche was for feare of an insurrection agaynst y⁰ strangars whiche wer in great nombar in and
abowt y⁰ eitle, as in all othar porte townes and havens of the whole
realme, and styll increasyd and do tyll this day, for y⁰ whiche we
ar bownd to pray to God that some ordar may be taken by owr
Prince for y⁰ contrarie. They have browght mayny howsys in y⁰
citie frome 40s. y⁰ yere to 20 nobles or 10li. with othar anoyauncis
to y⁰ comon welthe with out nombar. The occasyon of this watche
was thrwghe a portar who went about to dyvars prentises, tellynge
them that that nyght folowynge wowlde be y⁰ lyke stire agaynst
straungars as was at Evyll May Day,ᵃ &ct.; some of whiche pre[n]-
tesys gave knowledge ther of to theyr mastars and theyr mastars to
y⁰ lord maiore, &ct. The same portar was take, layd in y⁰ Countar,
and on Friday aftar stod in Cheape on a scaffold.

On Shrove Monday, beynge y⁰ 10 day of Februarie, in y⁰ mornynge, y⁰ Lorde Henrie Dernley, Kynge of the Scotts, was mourderyd
in Scotland. And on Fryday, beynge the 22 day of Februarie, in the
evenynge about 5 of y⁰ cloke, y⁰ Lady Lynioxe, mothar to y⁰ sayd
Kynge of Scotts, was delyveryd owt off the Towr of London and
loddgyd at Salysbury Courte, callyd Sakvyll Place, in y⁰ Flete
Strete.

1567.

The 4 day of Aprill, beynge Fryday, at nyght deseasyd Alderman Lambart, one of y⁰ shrives of London; and on y⁰ 5 day, beynge
Sattarday, was chosen shrive for hym Alderman Langleye.

On Twsdaye, y⁰ 15 day of Aprill, y⁰ Earle of Arondell aryvyd
at Dovar, and on Thursday in y⁰ aftarnone, whiche was y⁰ 17 day
of Aprell, he was honorably and with a great traync of horse men
conductyd thrughe y⁰ citie of London.

James, y⁰ bastard of Scotland,ᵇ with his brothar and othar
Scots, came to London on Wedyneseday y⁰ 16 of Aprell. The xxij

ᵃ In 1517.   ᵇ The Earl of Murray.

day of Aprill iiij^{xx} howses was brente, and xv in Oswestre, and xviij barens,^a it began byrynynge and contynuyd but vj owrs.

The 24 day of Aprell, beynge Thursday, the Sargaunts feaste was kepte at Greys In, nere to Holborne, and aftar dynnar the new sargaunts, beynge 7 in nombar, cam in theyr gowns, hodds, and coyves to Seynt Thomas of Ackars, nere to the great Conduite in Cheape, and from thens to Seynt Pawls, and in bothe placis observyd serimonys, and then went in the same order into Flete strete, and then departyd to theyr severall lodgyngs.

The 4 daye of Maye, beyng Sonday, in the mornynge was fownd sertayn bylls agaynst the Flemyngs that latly had fled owt of Flaundars, with galowsys, and as it wer hangynge of Flemyngs, drawne in the same papars, or bylls, fyxid on postes abowte the citie, for the whiche was aftarward very strayght watche kepte in London ye same nyght and longe afftar.

The 2 day of June, beynge Monday, in ye fornone, one ambasador from ye Emperowr and one othar from ye Lady Regent of Flaundars, landyd at ye Towr stayres, and wer ther receyvyd by ye Earle of Sussexe and by hym convayde to Mastar Dymoks place in Fanchurche Strete and ther lodgyd. On ye Thursday next folowynge they went to ye quens cowrte at Westmynster wher ye ambasador from ye Emperowr delyveryd to ye queue one boke and one lettar, beynge bothe seallyd. And the Sonday next folowynge ye Emperowrs ambasadowr, to the marvayll of many, went to ye Duche churche in London, and ther herd ye sarmond and servysse done by ye Calvenystys, and then went to ye cowrte. And on Fryday next in ye aftarnone they wer at ye Towr, and from thens to ye Mynorys, were Capitayn Pellam made them a banquit with bakon and powlderyd netts tonges, wher was suche eattynge and drynkynge that (by ye reporte of thos which made clean v^e hows) ye howse was mervelowsly by pyste and by spewyd to the great shame of thos banquettars; at which banquet was ye Dutches of Suffolke, and it was moste parte or all at hir cost. The same embasadors went

---

^a In margin—"iiij^{xx} & xv howsys & xv barns byrnt in Oswestrye."

to Richemount to ye Quenes Majestie of ye Sonday next folowynge, and agayn ye next Sonday, &ct. And on Wedenseday, beyng ye 25 day of June in ye mornynge, the Earle of Sussex with ye yonge Lord Northe went onward of his jurney as ymbasador to the Emperowr, and the same day in ye aftarnone ye embasadors of ye Emperowr and of ye Lady Regent of Flaundars departyd from London toward the sea to pase home warde.

The fyrst day of Julii to carts loden with haye, one betwen Eslendoune and Clerkenwell, ye othar beyonde Eslyndon and Holow-way at Ryuge Crosse, wer set affyre and byrnt, no man can tell how, excepte ye beate of ye axeltrie showld be ye cawse.

The ij day of Julii Syr Nycholas Throkemorton toke his jorneye towards Scotland (as it was sayd by comon reporte, to fetche ye yonge Prynce of Scotland); ye 10 of September he enteryd into London homeward agayne.

The xxix day of Julii ye yonge Prince of Scotland was crownyd Kynge of Scotland.

About that tyme were many congregations of the Anabaptysts in London, who cawlyd themselvs Puritans or Unspottyd Lambs of the Lord. They kept theyr churche in ye Mynorys with out Algate. Afterwards they assomblyd in a shype or lyghtar in Seynt Katheryns Poole, then in a chopers howse, ny Wolle Key in Thamse strete, wher only the goodman of the howse and the preachar, whose name was Brown (and his awditory wer cawlyd the Browyngs), were comyttyd to ward; then aftarward in Pudynge Lane in a mynisters hows in a blynd ally, and vij of them were committyd to ye Countar in ye Poultrye. Then aftar, on ye 29 of February, beyng Shrove Sonday, at Mountjoye Place, wher ye byshop, beyng warnyd by the constables, bad let then alone. Then at Westmystar, the 4 of Marche, and in a goldsmythis house nere to the Savoy, the 5 of Marche, wher beynge taken to the nombar of 60 and odd, only 3 were sent to the Gatehous. In many othar placis were and are the lyke. On Estar day at Hogston in my Lord of Londons mans house to ye nombar of 120, and on Lowe

Sonday in a carpentars hous in Aldarman bury.   It is to be noated that suche as were at eny tyme comitted for suche congregatynge were sone delyvered without punishemente.

Anno Domini 1564, from ye 7 of Julie of ye plage in London.

Unto ye 14 of Julie, 1.
Unto ye 21 of Julie, 1.
Unto ye 28 of Julie, 2.
Unto ye 4 of August, 3.
Unto y^c 11 of August, 2.
Unto ye 18 of August, 1.
Unto ye 25 of August, 1.
Unto ye 1 of Septembar, none.
Unto ye 8 of Septembar, 3.
Unto ye 15 of Septembar, 1.
Unto ye 22 of Septembar, none.
Unto ye 29 of Septembar, 6.
Unto ye 6 of Octobar, 1.
Unto ye 13 of Octobar, none.
Unto ye 20 of Octobar, none.
Unto ye 27 of Octobar, none.
Unto ye 3 of Novembar, 1.
Unto ye 10 of Novembar, none.
Unto ye 17 of Novembar, none.
Unto ye 24 of Novembar, none.
Unto ye 1 of Decembar, none.
Unto ye 8 of Decembar, none.
Unto ye 15 of Decembar, 2.
Unto ye 22 of Decembar, none.
Unto ye 29 of Decembar, none.
Unto ye 5 of Januarie, none.
Unto ye 12 of Januarie, none.
Unto ye 19 of Januarie, none.
Unto ye 26 of Januarie, none.

Unto ye 2 of Februari, none.
Unto y^c 9 of Februari, none.
Unto y^c 16 of Februarie, none.
Unto ye 23 of Februaryc, none.
Unto ye 2 of Marche, none.
Unto ye 9 of Marche, none.
Unto ye 16 of Marche, none.
Unto ye 23 of Marche, none.
Unto ye 30 of Marche, none.   1565.
Unto ye 6 of Aprill, one.
Unto ye 13 of Aprill, none.
Unto ye 20 of Aprille, none.
Unto ye 27 of Aprile, none.
Unto ye 4 of May, none.
Unto ye 11 of May, none.
Unto ye 18 of May, none.
Unto ye 25 of May, none.
Unto ye 1 of June, none.
Unto ye 8 of June, none.
Unto ye 15 of June, none.
Unto ye 22 of June, none.
Unto ye 29 of June, none.
Unto ye 6 of Julii, none.
Unto ye 13 of Julii, none.
Unto ye 20 of Julii, none.
Unto ye 27 of Julii, none.
Unto ye 3 of August, none.
Unto ye 10 of August, none.
Unto ye 17 of August, none.
Unto ye 24 of August, 1.
Unto ye last of August, none.
Unto ye 7 of Septem. none.
Unto ye 14 of Septem. none.
Unto ye 21 of Septem. none.

Unto ye 28 of Septem. none.
Unto ye 5 of October, none.
Unto ye 12 of October, none.
Unto ye 19 of October, none.
Unto ye 26 of October, none.
Unto ye 2 of November, none.
Unto ye 9 of November, none.
Unto ye 16 of November, none.
Unto ye 23 of November, none.
Unto ye 30 of November, none.
Unto ye 7 of December, none.
Unto ye 14 of December, none.
Unto ye 21 of December, none.
Unto ye 28 of December, none.
Unto ye 4 of January, one.
Unto ye 11 of January, none.
Unto ye 18 of January, none.
Unto ye 25 of January, none.
Unto ye 1 of February, one.
Unto ye 8 of February, none.
Unto ye 15 of February, none.
Unto ye 22 of February, none.
Unto ye 1 of Marche, none.
Unto ye 8 of Marche, none.
Unto ye 15 of Marche, none.
Unto ye 22 of Marche, none.

1566.   Unto ye 29 of Marche, none.

Unto ye 5 of Aprill, none.
Unto ye 12 of Aprill, none.
Unto ye 19 of Aprell, none.
Unto ye 26 of Aprell, none.
Unto ye 3 of Maye, none.
Unto ye 10 of May, none.
Unto ye 17 of May, none.

Unto ye 24 of May, one.
Unto ye last of May, one.
Unto ye 7 of June, none.
Unto ye 14 of June, none,
Unto ye 21 of June, one.
Unto ye 28 of June, none.
Unto ye 5 of Julii, none.
Unto ye 12 of Julii, one.
Unto ye 19 of Julii, none.
Unto ye 26 of Julii, none.

BRIEF NOTES

OF OCCURRENCES UNDER HENRY VI. AND EDWARD IV,

FROM MS. LAMBETH, 448.

1307. Coronacio Regis Edwardi Carnarvan apud Westmonasterium 14 Kal. Decembris, qui duxit Isabellam Regis Francie filiam.

[This is the first of a series of chronological notes of which almost all prior to Henry VI. are here omitted, being destitute of historical value.]

1390. Mulier apud Cok in Le Chepe erat combusta et ij pandoxatores sine reatu et immunes suspensi.

1409. Filii Regis verberati in Estchepe.

1411. The gold coyne alayed.

1412. Dominus Cobham arestatus et fracto carcere fugit.

1413. Coronacio Henrici V^{ti} Regis apud Westmonasterium ix die Aprilis, dominica in Passione Domini, in magno frigore et gelu, &c.   Et insurrectis Domını de Holdcastel domini de Cobham.

1422.   Henricus vj^{us} Rex qui incepit regnare primo die Septembris Anno Domini 1422, ille existens infra (?)[a] iij quarter' anni ætatis. Hic incepit Newgate edificari.

1423.   Dominus Johannes Mortemer suspensus.

1425.   Contentio inter London' et episcopum Wynton'.

1426.   Hic factus fuit episcopus Wynton' cardinalis.

1429.   Coronatio Henrici vj^{ti} Regis apud Westmonasterium.

1430.   Jak Scharp erat tractus et suspensus propter insurrexionem.

[a] "n^{l}," MS.

1431. Coronatio Regis nostri Angliæ apud Parisium.

1432. Concilium generale apud Basyle, et stella comata visa per xv dies.

1433. Gelu magnum et pestilentia magna.

1435. Dux Burgundie obsedebat Calisiam.

1436. Dux Burgundie fugit et ejus obsidium erat combustum.

1437. Pons lapideus London' fregit et cecidit in Tamisiam.

1441. Domina Elinora Cobham egit publicam penitentiam London', et quedam phitonissa et incantatrix combusta.

1444. Campanile de Waltam crematum est.

1445. Campanile Sancti Pauli, London', cremavit ab hora tercia post nonam usque ad horam novenam in vigilia Purificationis, et Coronacio Margarete Regine.

1446. Interfectio ducis Glowcestrie apud Bury, et quinque homines suspensi et tamen non mortui.

1449. Dux Suffolchie captus in mari et interfectus, et Normannia perdita.   Communitas Cancie insurrexit.

1450. Gasconia et Gyan perdite erant.

1452. Dux Eboracensis cepit campum in xl^{ma} añ (?) in Blakheth in Cancia contra ducem de Somershet.

1453. In festo Sancti Edwardi Regis, id est iij° idus Octobris, natus erat Edwardus princeps, filius Regis Henrici vj^{ti} et Margarete Regine, apud Westmonasterium.

1455. xj kl. Junii dux de Somersheth et plures alii interfecti sunt apud Sanctum Albanum.

1456. xiij° die mensis Novembris, dominus Egremond aufugit extra Nugate, Lond', qui incarceratus erat pro pace conservanda et obligatus per se et per alios erga certos dominos in xvij mill' marc.

Memorandum quod anno Domini M.cccc.xlvj vel xlvij, et anno regni Regis Henrici vj^{ti} xxv°, circa festum Purificationis Beate Marie, erat parliamentum apud Bury tentum, ubi Rex erat vigilatus et protectus qualibet nocte et die illuc veniens ubicumque jacuit, apud Royston, Cantebr', Novum Mercatum, et apud Sanctum Edmundum, quasi cum lx^{ta} milibus hominum et villanis, ad excita-

tionem et concilium domini Pole ducis tunc tempore Suffolchie,
pre timore domini Umfray ducis Glowcestrie Regis avunculi, qui,
nichil malum cogitans vel suspicans, venit a Wallia juxta præceptum
Regis ad parliamentum predictum ut haberet benevolentiam et
gratiam Regis pro domina Elienora uxore sua, ut dictum erat, in
Wallia inclusa et incarcerata.   Verumtamen ad presentiam Regis
venire minime potuit, nec cum eo loqui, sed clam missis a latere
Regis, ut dicitur, ad eundem ducem quibusdam dominis secreto in
camera ejus, ubi quid extitit ei dictum vel factum, diversi diversa
suspicantur et dicunt ; sed sine dubio post recessum dominorum
ab eo taliter infirmabatur quod nullo modo ultra iij dies vivere [a]
potuit, nulla tamen lesione corporali exterius apparente; quo mortuo
et apud Babwelle inter Fratres Minores ibidem sepulto, parliamentum statim dissolvebatur.   Ante cujus mortem vise erant a
diversis hominibus stelle mirabiles et cometa etc. ; unde postea plura
propterea contingebant inconvenientia &c.   Nam eo tempore erant
quinque homines suspensi et tamen non mortui.

1448.   Tempore quadragesimali visa est stella comata a pluribus
in Occidente, id est, ante Annunciationem Beate Marie.

1449.   Item in festo Sancti Georgii, feria iiij[a] contingenti, extitit
terremotus in mane parum ante horam quartam, que duravit quasi
per spacium unius *Ave Maria.*

1449.   Dominus Johannes Say erat tractus per quendam capitaneum de Kent qui insurrexit cum multis de Cancia et intravit
London' cum manu forti, nullo ei in primis resistente vel contra-
dicente; cui tradite erant claves civitatis London' per majorem et
vicecomites et aldermannos ; qui capitaneus decollavit predictum
dominum Johannem Say in medio in le Chepe et spoliavit quendam
divitem vocatum Mampace,[b] et pompose p . . . . .[c]   Set hoc con-

---

[a] After " vivere " the word " non " occurs in the text, but it is rather faint, as if
purposely obliterated.

[b] Philip Malpas.

[c] " et pompose p . . . ."   This is an addition to the original text, the word " et "
being inserted at the end of a line, and " pompose p . . . ." interlined below; but
the sentence has been left incomplete.

siderans Dominus Schalys, London' existens, timens ne destrueret
civitatem et plura et alia mala faceret, fortiter cum pluribus contra
eum pugnavit; et statim venerunt plures de curialibus et Fletestrete
architenentes, et de civitate sufficientes, pugnantes cum eodem
domino contra Cansientes,[a] qui fugarunt dictum capitaneum cum
exercitu suo ultra pontem Londonie cum magno conflictu ex utraque
parte quasi per magnam partem noctis ejusdem diei; qui capita[ne]us
et qui cum eo erant combusserunt pontem London', unde plures erant
submersi et interfecti ex utraque parte, inter quos quidam nobilis
Matheus Goo[b] interfectus erat et honorifice sepelitur apud Fratres
Carlemitarum[c] ibidem per capellam Beate Marie in choro et Allex-
ander Aysac'(?), &c.

1449. Hoc anno Dominus Willelmus Asku episcopus Salisberi-
ensis et Episcopus Cestrie[d] interfecti erant; Episcopus Wygornie,
Episcopus Lincolnie [et Episcopus Londonie][e] moriebantur; ac
etiam Dominus Thomas Langton Episcopus de Batho [Sc̃i David],[f]
cancellarius Cantebrigie et episcopus Carletensis, et duo notabiles
et famosi doctores, magister Gylbertus, et magister Cote, doctor,
mortui sunt.

[g]Anno Domini M°cccc.liiij° apud Royston, ut fide digni dixerunt
et audierunt quod necessitate cogente propter inopiam[h] pecuniarum
quidam agricultor firmarius vendidit x quarteria frumenti pro
xx s., hoc est j cumb pro xij d. et j quarterium brasii pro xvij d.

1455. Hoc anno, feria quinta ante festum Pentecostes, id est,
xxij° die mensis Maij, venit Dominus Ricardus Dux Eboracensis cum
filio suo comite de Marche, Domino de Cromwell et alij plures cum
magno exercitu, ac etiam Dux Northfolchiæ et Dominus Bowcer

---

[a] "contra Cansientes." These two words are added in margin.
[b] Matthew Gough.   [c] So in MS.
[d] Should be " Cicestrie."   [e] Crossed through in original.
[f] Interlined as a correction, but the words "de Batho" in the text are not struck
out.
[g] This note, which is repeated elsewhere out of place, has been inserted here at
the bottom of a page.
[h] Interlined in place of *carenciam* in the text.

comes de Hyu cum eo et unanimi concensu, ad fortificandum predictum Ducem Eboracensem contra Ducem de Somershed, eorum
capitalem adversarium, ad concilium domini Regis versus Leycester.
Set omnes isti irruerunt super predictum Ducem de Somershed cum
manu magna armata tunc cum rege apud Sanctum Albanum existentem; et ibi in magno conflictu interfecti fuerunt antedictus Dux de
Somershed et comes Northhumbrorum, Percy nomine, et Dominus
de Clyfford, Willelmus Cotton, armiger, et Dux de Bokyngham
Iesus et plures alij de chevelria quasi xl^a ibi graviter erant vulnerati.
Et episcopus de Carlhyll, filius dicti comitis de Northhumbyrland,
erat spoliatus omnibus bonis suis, tam in equis, jocalibus, familia sua
et etiam a capa sua relictus erat solus tantum in rocheto fugiens
pedester usque ad Islam, &c.

1456.   Stella comata visa erat in occidente quasi per quindenam
ante festum S̃ci Johannis Baptiste et post, que extendebat radium
globosum sursum in ayerem usque firmamentum ad longitudinem
unius lancee quo ad visum, &c.

1456.   Feria secunda in vigilia Sancti Thome Apostoli in mense
Decembris per quarterium unius hore ante horam tertiam post mediam
noctem erat terre-motus magnus ex quo plures audientes et sensientes [a] erant exterriti; qui duravit per spacium dimidii unius *Ave
Maria.*

1457.   Quinto kalendas Septembris, die Dominica super B contingente, circa horam quartam in mane venerunt Francigene et
pirate et inimici cum magna multitudine, quasi xv. milia hominum,
cum navibus, et applicuerunt ad villam de Sandwych, a Cantuaria vij
miliariis distantem, quorum vij milia exierunt per ij vel tria miliaria
in patriam ibi custodientes et defendentes predictam villam quousque
alii socii eorum, magna multitudo, intraverunt villam de Sandwych
et interfecerunt ballivos [b] et ministros sive rectores ville et plures
alios divites in patria, et spoliaverunt totam villam omnibus jocalibus

---

[a] So in MS.

[b] The word *majorem* was first written before *ballivos*, but was afterwards struck
out.

et bonis inibi inventis per totam illam diem dominicam usque ad noctem, cariando cum bigis et *waynis* ad naves suas in mare; et abduxerunt secum plures divites et uxores atque mulieres alias; et fugerunt, relicta predicta villa in magna paupertate et miseria. Et eodem tempore ceperunt duas galeas diversis mercimoniis onustas qui (*sic*) proposuerunt venisse ad Londonias et ad nundinas de Stebrigge, sed omnibus gubernantibus illas interfectis et in mare projectis, illas galleas secum asportaverunt.

Anno Domini M.cccc.lix° et anno regni Regis Henrici vj[ti] xxxviij°, mense Julii, venerunt comes de Warwyk, comes de March et comes de Salisbery, quia cum prius venissent ad Northampton et andito quod Rex erat presens clam fugierunt a[d] mare quousque &c. et tunc venerunt a Calissia de ultra mare ad Sandwych in Canciam, cum magno exercitu in London', et honorifice erant ibidem recepti, tam a domino Archiepiscopo Cantuariensi, episcopis Eliensi et Excestrensi, et aliis pluribus; unde in adventu eorum dominus Schal' et alii existentes in Turri London' sagittabant fundibila (*sic*) extra Turrim ad eos, sed nemini nocuerunt. Et predictus comes de Warwyk assignavit quemdam armigerum validum cum sufficienti adjutorio ad custodiam predicti (*sic*) Turris ne inclusi exirent; sed cum predictus armiger navigaret sub muris Turris statim erat captus ab eis et membratim confractus &c. Unde, predictis dominis in itinere suo ad Regem tunc apud Northamton existentem progredientibus, cum ij legatis qui excommunicarunt certos dominos, contigit quod omnes venerunt ad exercitum Regis x°. dies mensis Julii ejusdem anni, et Eboracensis dux cum alio magno exercitu ibidem erat, ut creditur, fere c.m[l]; et in conflictu facto die Mercurii ab hora iiij[a] usque ad horam vj[am] interfecti erant dominus Umfridus dux Bokyngham et dominus Beemond, dominus Scherwysbery et plures alii. Dominus Egrimond et episcopus Hertfordensis decapitatus (*sic*); et postea dominus Scal' exiens extra Turrim Londoniarum captus erat in Tamysia et interfectus, et plures alii ibidem incarcerati.

Anno Domini M°.cccc[mo].lx, iij die et iiij[to] ante festum Sancte

Katerine, tanta inundancia aquarum effluxit in comitatibus Hunt
yndon et Cantebr' et Northefolchie et in Insula Eliensi atque
Sanctum Neotem quod quasi nunquam talis visa erat per prius;
nam prostravit pontem cum magna parte hospicii et Fratrum[a] apud
Thetford in Northfolch et pontes apud Cantebrigiam, currendo ultra
et super rotas molendinorum aquaticorum ibidem, destruendo plures
domos, intrando per fenestras earundem, apud Cantebrigiam,
Cleyhethe, et Upwere et alibi, in tantum quod potuerunt navigare
homines supra omnia calceta de Stunteney et Soham; et in Caucia
et quasi per totum regnum Anglie.[b]

Item, eodem anno, die Martis post festum Natalis Domini venit
dominus de Somershet filius . . . . .[c] ad dominum ducem Eboracensem existentem apud castrum de Powmfr' prope Sothwerke,[d] capta
prius et concessa treuga usque feriam quintam post festum Epiphanie proximo sequentem; sed predictus dominus de Somershet,
fracto federe pacis, repente et fraudulenter cum exercitu ibi prope in
silva vel nemore abscondito, irruit super prefatum dominum ducem
Eboracensem, et eum interfecerunt, et comitem de Salysbery et
comitem de Roteland, capitaneum de Kent, et quendam fratrem
ductorem belli, et alii (sic) quasi ix. milia hominum ex utraque parte,
in loco vocato Wakfeld grene, et Sandynforde, et capita prædictorum
dominorum suspensa erant super muros castri de Pownfray, et
caput ducis erat coronatum cum [*Added in another hand:* etc., ut
dicitur].

Item, anno Domini M[l]cccc.lx, xvj[e] die mensis Februarii venit
Regina a boriali cum duce juveni (?)[f] de Somershed, principe
————————[g] et cum Andrea Trollop, magno capitaneo et quasi

---

[a] So in MS. Apparently a word omitted.

[b] The last clause is imperfect, and appears to have been added afterwards, as it is
in a different ink. In the margin also the scribe has written, "et in Denschire et
quasi per totam Angliam."

[c] A short illegible word, perhaps intended for "juvenis."

[d] So in MS.   [e] Indistinct: may be xj., xij., or xvj.

[f] The same word apparently as before, but the reading is very doubtful.

[g] Half a line left blank in MS.

ductore belli, qui cum magno exercitu Scotorum, Wallensium, et
aliorum alienigenarum et Northenmen, destruendo villas de Grantom,
Stamford, Peterborw, Huntyngdon, Royston, Melleborn, et fere
omnes villas per viam usque ad Sanctum Albanum, et ibidem prope
villam Sancti Albani apud Luton quasi per unum miliare et dimidium
a Sancto Albano, Nomannyslond vocat', Rex cum duce de Norfolk
et comite de Warwyk et aliis, cum magno exercitu, tam de Caucia,
Excessia et de Norfolch et Suffolch et al' quasi cc.m^l., et ibidem xix ^{vc} Burgundia.
die predicti mensis bellum attemptatum, ex casu infortunato omnes
ex parte Regis et populi australis vieti redierunt retrorsum et fugerunt
[quia ventus erat eis contrarius]^a; eo quod quum Burgundenses
sagittabant fundabilia sua ventus retorquebat ignem in proprias facies,
et combusti et interfecti sunt ex illis xviij persone et alii ex utraque
parte, quasi vij milia et v.c.   Et predictus Andreas Trollop captus
per viam et lesus est; Dominus Bonvyle et Thomas Curiel miles
interfecti sunt.   Et eo tempore dominus comes de March cepit
dominum comitem de Pencebroch [et dominum de Wylschire]^b in
quadam obsidione juxta Notyngham.   Et dominus Willelmus
Gray episcopus Eliensis eodem tempore misit pro hominibus omnium
villarum snarum in Essex, Norfolch et Suff., et comitatu Cantebrigie, et cum xxxv. de Burgundiensibus cum fundibilibus et
crosbowys ad custodiendum insulam Eliensem et castrum de Wysbech
in manu forti et armata (per aquam, quia omnes marisci circa insulam
erant submersi per magnam aquam), pre timore Northynmen, quia
spoliabant plures villas, monasteria et ecclesias per viam, et aliorum
auferendo equos, jocalia, utensilia, pannos, linthiamina, cocliaria,
ollas et patellas eneas et de plectro, et destruentes victualia per
totam viam, ut predictum est ultra, et salvi ad North redierunt,
ducentes secum Henricum Regem.

1460.   Item, Edwardus comes de March filius ducis Eboraci erat
ordinatus et constitutus in Regem London' quarto die mensis Marcii,
Anno Domini M^o.cccc.lx^o, Henrico Sexto predicto ablato per,
dominam Reginam et alios dominos in partes Boriales usque Trent,

---

^a Crossed out.   ^b Crossed out.

etc. Item, eodem tempore comes de Warwyk interfecit apud Coventriam dominum Excestre, bastardum filium ducis de Bokyngham. Et j quarter' brasii vendebatur London' pro xiiij s. ut dicebatur.

Anno Domini M°.cccc.lxij°, quinto die mensis Novembris, videbatur stella comata in Australi parte circa horam quintam in mane, que extendebat radium sursum et seorsum ad modum gladii, et[a] alios radios habuit mirabiliter extensos, &c.

Eodem anno in mense Novembris Rex Henricus, Regina Margareta, dux de Somershed et dux Excestrie, et plures alii ab Anglia expulsi et fugati, conduxerunt plures alienigenas, Gallicos, Scotos et alios, ad ingrediendum partes Anglicanas contra Regem Edwardum iiij[tum]; et Regina Margareta predicta cepit castrum de Anwyk et obsessa erat in castro de Banburw. Et cum cc. Anglici intrassent quandam parvam insulam in illis partibus ad succurrendum se si necesse fuisset, ipsis nescientibus, advenerunt cccc. de Francigenis ad eos includendos et capiendos, et subito in Anglicos irruerunt; sed capti et interfecti erant ex Francigenis cc. et plures, et alii fugierunt ut dicitur.

[b]Anno Domini M.cccc.liiij° apud Royston ut fide digni viderunt et dixerunt quod necessitate cogente propter carentiam pecuniarum quidam firmarius vendidit x. quarteria frumenti pro xx s., hoc est j quarterium pro xij d., j quarterium brasium (sic) pro xvij d.

1464. Thes tythynges hath my lord of Lyncolne, and the same be come to Stamford, and now be al þe contre, that on Wednesday, id est, on Seynt Markes day,[c] a feld was takyn be twyn my lord Mountynghew on Kyng Edwardys party, and the lord Hungyrford, and many odyr on Kyng Herrys party. And þer is slayn þe lord Hungyrford, Sir Raf Percy, Sir Raff Gray, the duk of Somershed, the lord Roos takyn and Taylboos the erl of Kym and many odyr gentylys and comons slayn on that party. How many be slayn on Kyng Edward party is not spok of as yt.

---

[a] "et" repeated in MS.
[b] See p. 151, note [g].
[c] April 25. The battle referred to is that of Hedgley Moor.

Thes be the namys of dewkes, erlys, barons, and knytes beyng with owre soveryn lord Kyng Edward in hys jorny in to Scottlong at the fest of Scynt Andrew in þe month of Decembyr, Anno Domini M°.cccc.lxij°.

The Duke of Northfok, the duk of Suffolk.   ij.

Erlys.

The erl of Warwyk, the erl of Arundel, erl of Schrewisbury,   vij.
erl Wysertyr, erl of Kent, the erl of Westhumbyrlond, þe erl of Esex.

Barons.

The lord Grey Ruffyn, lord Hastynges, lord Grey Cottenor, lord   xxxj.
Grey Wylton, lord Antony Scalys, lord Latemer, lord Herberd,
lord Ferreys Charteley, lord Stanle, lord Wenlok, lord Greystoke,
lord Oxyll,[a] lord Lomney, lord Glýnton, lord Sowtwyk, lord Revers,
lord Dakere of the Sowthle, lord Dakere of the North, lord Say,
lord Cromwell, lord Cobham, lord Benerforth, lord Herry Bokyngham, lord Mowntener, lord Fyhew, lord De la Ware, lord Powes,
Scrop of Bolton, lord Dodley, lord Storton, lord Burgeyny.

Milites.

Ser Per Ale, Ser Wyliam Stanley, Ser William · Norys, Ser
Thomas Mongorye, Ser Jon Fooge, John Howard, John Aschley,
Ser Jamys Stannyewyssche, John Scot, John Conyas, Raf Pygot,
John Colvyle, John Hevyngham, Ser George Seynt Gorge, John
Wyngfeld, Leonard Hastynges, John Savey, Thomas Mownforth,
John Constabyl, William Reyner, Ser Raf Grey, William Everyng-
ham, William Haryngton, William Bothe, William Hastynges,
Ewrard of Bedoun, Thomas Fyndern, Roger Danby, John Grakyng-   lix.
thorp, John Boteler, John Acheton, Moreys of Berkley, Herry of
Osey, John Stanley, John Grysseley, Thomas Nocston, Ser Pers
Glyfton, John Hodyliston, Thomas Lampole, William Ale, William
Marcham Dale, Ser Rychard Dokette, Thomas Crowen, Crystofer
of Carowen, Thomas Garard, Thomas Acheton, Henry of Bolde,
Peers Padolyse, Jaffery Gate, John Apylton, Thomas Malery,
Thomas Feryr, John Swan, Peers of Grethorn, Roger Coneres,

---

[a] *Sic, qu.* Ogyll, or Ogle?

Crystofer Coneres, John Gryffon, Robert Harecourte, and Ser Robert Constabyl.

Ad Conceptionem Beatæ Marye, Anno Domini M⁰.cccc.lx . . .ᵃ

Blyssyt be God, diverse of owre adversaryes be owre throwyn, and we undyrstond the privyte and fals ymaginacions of the French party. Also there is oon callit Jon Worby, of Mortlond, a spye, in the county of Herteford, servuant to Ser John Russel, in the county of Wysceter, takyn be the lord Suthwell, and the seyd aspye ther takyn hath confessyt the Kyng Herry, late Kyng of Inglond in dede but not in ryth, and sche that was queyn Margarete hys wyf, and Edward hyr son, the duk of Brytayn, Edward the duk of Burgoyn, Syr Wylliam Taylbos, the lord Roos, Sir Richard Tunstall, Thomas Ormond, Ser W. Catisby, Thomas Fykeharry. Þes lordes and knytes be in Scotlond with the Scottes. The duk of Exceter, erl of Penbrok, the baron of Burford, Jon Ayne. Thes schal lond at Bumeryes be þe appoyment of Robert Gold, capten of the duk of Burgoyn. Duk Herry of Calaber, the lord Hungyrford, the lord Morton, the duk of Somersete with lx Mˡ of men of Spayn. Þes schal londyn in the coost of Norfolk and Suffolk. Þe lord Lewys, the duk of Spayne, Herry the dolfyn of Franch, Ser Jon Foskew, Ser Jon Russel of Wyceter, Ser Thomas Burtayn, the erlys brother of Denschyr, Ser Thomas Cornwaylys. Thes lordes and knytes schal londyn at Sandwych by Þer appoyment. Than com- yng after thes lordes and knytes byfore wryten to a siste them with al the powre possibill they may make; the Kyng of Fraunce wyth a c.Mˡ, the Kyng of Denmark with xx Mˡ, the Kyng of Aragon l Mˡ, the Kyng of Navern with xx Mˡ, the Kyng of Cesyl with xxv Mˡ, the Kyng of Portyngale with x Mˡ; the wych be appoyntyt to enter the reme of Inglond.

The Wednesday by fore Cristmasse, Anno Domini M⁰.cccc.lxij⁰.

ᵇ In Castello de Banburw sunt dux de Somerset, comes de Pen brok, dominus de Roos et Radulfus Percy, cum ccc. hominibus.

ᵃ Margin mutilated.

ᵇ The whole of this part about the sieges in Northumberland is bracketed in the margin, and the words " Non scribuntur " written opposite.

At the seege of Hem sunt comes de Wyceter, comes de Arundel, dominus de Ogyl et dominus de Muntegew cum x M¹.

In castello de Anwyk sunt iij stat.(?) quorum nomina adhuc ignorantur, cum ccc. hominibus.

Istos obsident dominus Comes de Warwyk, comes de Kent, dominus de Powys, baro de Greystuk, dominus de Cromwell, cum x.M¹ hominibus.

In castello de Dunstalborw sunt dominus Ricardus Dunstal, dominus Thomas Fyndern, doctor Murton, ballivus de Kam cum vj^xx hominibus.

Istos obsident dominus de Wenlok, dominus de Hastynges cum ij aliis dominis, cum x m¹ hominibus.

Rex tenet Natale suum apud Dorham.

1462.   Thes been the tydynges sent owt of Scotland that the Erl Dowglas hath done now late in the begynnyng of March, anno Domini M°.cccc.lxij°.

The worthy Erle Dowglas hath takyn of the Scottys the Erle of Creyforth, the Lord Lyle of Crayle, Lord Maxon', wardeyn of the West Merchen, Lord Wakeup, Lord Correy, Charlys Murrey, John Styward, Dolgotys brother, Lord Domelyn, Autrys hys brother of Hemyldon, Lord Cragge, Syr Robert Homyldon, Lord Preston, Lord [Charlys of Murrey],ᵃ William Welles, knyght, Lord Crakkes brother and [Lord Currey],ᵃ numbyr of xvij lordes.

And besyd Þes ben takyn and slayn un to the numbyr of cccc at the Esthyl in Scotland, &c.

Anno Domini M.cccc.lxiij vendebatur quarterium frumenti pro ij s., quarterium brasii xxij d., et quarterium pisarum pro iij s. iiij d., et quarterium ordei pro xiiij d.

Eodem anno, ut dicebatur, vendebatur j quarterium de sigulo in Norfolch pro xij d.; et in aliqua patria, ut dicitur, j quarterium frumenti pro xx d., j quarterium brasii xx d. et quarterium ordei xij d.

1461.   Nomina eorum qui erant interfecti in die Palmarum et

ᵃ Erased.

die Lune sequenti apud Seeton et Charoncros que distant ab Eboraco citra quasi per viij miliaria, Anno Domini M⁰.cccc.lxj, scilicet:

Domina Regina cum principe filio suo.
Edwardus dux de Excestre.
Dux de Somersheth.
Comes de Northumbyrlond et Westhumbirlond.[a]
Comes de Schrewysbery.
Comes de Denschyre.
Dominus de Clyfford.
Dominus de Nevell.
Dominus de Welle.
Dominus de Sealys.
Dominus de Dakerys.
Dominus de Fyhu.[b]
Dominus de Mullens'.
Dominus Henricus de Bokyngham.
Dominus de Bewmond.
Dominus Wilby.
Dominus Roos.
Dominus Gray Cotyner.[c]

Nomina militum.

Duo filii ducis de Excestre bastardi.
Dominus R. de Percy.
[Dominus Radulphus de Gray.][d]
Dominus Johannes Heyron.
Dominus Gerwys Clyfton.
Dominus Edmundus Hammys.
Dominus Thomas Crakynthorpe.

[a] "et Westhumbirlond" (*sic*) is an interlineation, and is altogether an error. The Earl of Westmoreland was not slain at Towton, but lived for more than twenty years after.

[b] Fitzhugh.   [c] Cottnere in the cancelled list noticed below.

[d] Struck out.

Dominus Johannes Crakynthorp.

Dominus Willelmus Harylle.

Dominus Johannes Ormund.

Andreas Trollope.

Summa nominum omnium interfectorum dominorum, militum et aliorum per estimationem xxxvм¹.iiijˣˣ et xj, ut dicebatur.

1461. [Nomina dominorum existentium ex parte domini Henrici vjᵘ nuper Regis Angliæ apud prelium de Seton, ut supra dicitur.]ᵃ (Here follows a list which is crossed out, pretty much the same as the preceding.)

Ex parte domini Edwardi Regis, Humfridus dux Nortfolch, dominus Edwardus Comes de Warwyk, dominus Fywater, Joh' Stafford, Henricus Raclyf de Framysden, et Rogerus Wolferston.

1461. In prelio ibidem interfecti sunt comes de Northumbyrlond, Comes de Denschire, Comes de Schrewysbery, dominus Nevel, dominus Clyfford, dominus Fyhew, dominus Wellys, dominus Dakerys, dominus Syvas (?), dominus Fytzhyth, dominus Malley, dominus Schalys, dominus Rogerus Mellyn miles, dominus Radulphus Piggate miles, dominus Henricus Norbochewe miles, Andreas Trollop, Davy Trollop et domina de Dytton, et multi alii milites armigeri et alii quorum nomina ignorantur, in numero quasi xxxiij milia et plures, scilicet:—

[Item, ex parte Regis interfecti sunt]ᵃ Dominus Johannes Hotham, dominus W. Nerwell, duo bastardi de Exceter, dominus Ed' Hammys miles, dominus Johannes Crakynthorp, Johannes Burton, capitaueus Eboraci, dominus Thomas Krakyngthorp miles.

[Ex parte Regis Edwardi, dominus Fywater, Johannes Stafford, Henricus Raclyff de Framysden, et Rogerus Wolferston.]ᵇ

Item, ut dicitur, Comes de Wylschir, doctor Mackerell, doctor Morton, et dominus Will' Plomtun adducti erant ad Comitem de Warwyk. Et decapitati sunt Comes de Denschire, Comes de Kyme, dominus Will' Hyll. cognatus Trollop, quorum capita suspenduntur supra portas Eboraci. Et nota quod istud bellum incepit apud

---

ᵃ Struck out. ᵇ These words are crossed out.

Wentbrygge, et sic usque ad Ferybrygge, et campus in quo pugnabant vocatur Duntyngdale, juxta locum vocatum Charyngcross prope villelam vocatam Seton, &c.

Anno Domini M.cccc^{mo}.lxj°, xxviij° die mensis Junii, scilicet iiij^{to} kl. Julii, contingente in die Dominica, Coronacio Regis Edwardi quarti Comitis de Marche, filii Ricardi ducis Eboraci apud West-monasterium a duobus Archiepiscopis cum magna sollempnitate. Nam ibi erant plures Episcopi, dux Norfolch, Marischallus Anglie, Dux Suffolch, Seueschallus Anglie, dominus Georgius frater Regis, dux Clarencie, dominus Ricardus frater ejus, &c.

1461. Item, eodem anno, xxiiij° die Julii, id est in vigilia Sancti Jacobi, contingente in die Veneris, pluit sanguis apud Pokrych' et apud Ware, ut dicebatur.

Item, anno Domini M°.cccc°lxj°, in mense Novembris in festo Sancti Leonardi, obiit dominus Umfrydus Moubry dux Norfolchie.

Item, eodem anno, in mense Februarii, arestati erant et adducti ad Regem et concilium suum London', abbas de Bury cum iij monachis ejusdem loci, dominus Thomas Tuddenham, Heydon, Harslston,^a et dominus T. Porter de Norfolch cum aliis; et eodem tempore circa festum Sancti Valentini dominus Ambry (Aubrey) filius comitis Oxonie erat suspensus et tractus London'. Et eodem tempore, ut dicitur, insurrexit quidam capitaneus qui cum iiij^{or} milibus vel pluribus regnavit in Schirwode. Circa festum Cathedre Sancti Petri decapitatus erat comes Oxonie, Will' Terell, ex eo quod clam nitebantur insidias facere cum populo contra Regem Edwardum; nam quidam nuncius missus erat per illos et alios ad Henricum nuper Regem et Reginam et alios dominos in Scotia existentes cum literis proditorie, scilicet ut sequerentur Regem Edwardum equitantem in partem Borialem cum exercitu suo quasi pugnarent cum eo, et in bello essent contra eum, tam a dextris quam a sinistris, et post tergum ejus, ut sic eum Edwardum insidiose interficerent eum (sic). Contigit enim ut prefatus nuncius venisset in itinere suo ad quandam ecclesiam circa Northampton audire

* So in MS.

missam, semper occurrit ad mentem suam ut rediret ad Regem
Edwardum, nesciens veraciter quid ejus negocium proficeret, aut
pro se vel contra se. Sic sepius die ac nocte hoc in suo pectore
revolvens, domum ad se reversus, credens se magis Deo placere et
animam suam salvare, omisso negocii sui itinere, cum nimia festina-
cione ad Regem Edwardum cum omnibus literis in suo kascat
existentibus rediit, gratiam et misericordiam ab illo petens, qua a
Rege concessa, totum processum Regi intimavit ac omnes literas ei
demonstravit. Hoc omni comperto et cognito, Rex accepit copias
omnium illarum literarum et remisit nuncium prædictum in itinere
suo ut prius proposuit, precipiens ei, ut juratus erat, ut esset fidelis
sibi, et post negocium, si posset, rediret ad Regem, &c. Quo recesso
Rex statim misit pro dominis et aliis qui proditorie eum decipere
nitebantur, in quos judices Regis executiones impleverunt ut supra.

Anno Domini M.cccc.lxij post Pascha contigit quendam puerulum
quasi xj annorum etate in crepusculo ire in stratam circa novum
collegium Cantebrig'[a] et Clare Halle vel aulam Sancte Trinitatis
ibidem; ubi obviam habuit quendam senem, ut sibi videbatur, cum
prolixa barba et debili vestura; quo viso puerulus, nimio terrore
territus voluit aufugere nec potuit leviter. Cui senex dixit, " Veni
istuc proxima nocte isto tempore noctis et dicam tibi aliqua nova,"
et recesserunt ab invicem. Secunda nocte similiter obviaverunt ut
prius, sed puer valde erat timidus in ejus aspectu. Tertia nocte, ut
videbatur sibi, non potuit eligere, sed potins coactus rediit ad
eundem locum. Cui senex dixit " Vade jam et dic cuicumque quod
infra istos duos annos erit tanta pestilencia et famis ac interfectio
hominum quanta nullus vivens vidit perantea;" et hoc dicto recessit.
Spiritus ut credebatur, nam puerulus postea examinatus et interro-
gatus per Magistrum W. Mylcton, Theologie doctorem, et alios,
dixit quod non vidit nec audivit illum senem super terram ambu-
lautem, &c.

[a] King's College.

A BRIEF LATIN CHRONICLE

BEING THE CONCLUDING PORTION OF A WORK ENTITLED

"COMPILATIO DE GESTIS BRITONUM ET ANGLORUM."

[From MS. Arundel 5, College of Arms.]

Henricus vj^{cus} filius predicti regis Henrici apud Windeleshore in festo Sancti Nicholai episcopi et confessoris natus, in etate ix mensium et xv dierum, regnare cepit supra dicto ultimo die Augusti. Et in dominica die in festo Sancti Leonardi Abbatis, Anno Domini Millesimo cccc°.xxix°. et anno regni sui viij° apud Westmonasterium coronatur, Domino Henrico Wintoniensi episcopo tunc cardinali tituli Sancti Eusebii ibidem presente. Et anno regni sui decimo idem rex apud civitatem Parisiensem ix° die Decembris etiam coronatur, presente ibidem cardinale supradicto. Anno autem ——[a] hujus regis fuit prelium apud Vernoll in Perche inter Johannem ducem Bedfordie regentem Francie et Francos ac Scottos. Ubi cum dicto duce fuerunt Comes Sarum, Comes Southfok, dominus Wylughby, dominus Scales, dominus Ponynges, Willelmus Oldale cum retinencia ducis Exonie tunc infirmi. Et in dicto bello ex parte Francorum captus est dux de Launson; occisi vero sunt ibidem bastardus de Launson, Comes de Navern et Comes de Marrebon̄. Ex parte autem Scottorum perempti sunt Archibaldus Comes de Douglasse, Comes de Boghan, Comes de Marre, Comes de Murrey, Jacobus Douglas filius dicti comitis, Alexander Lyndesey miles; Willelmus Douglas de Danlanryk,[b] Matheus Pork, Hugo Orth, milites, et alii quam plures, tam de Francis quam de Scottis in ipso

---

[a] Blank in MS. [b] Drumlanrig.

bello et fuga ad numerum vij M¹ et ultra. Postea vero in foveis dicte ville inventa sunt, ut dicitur, iiij M¹ submersa.ᵃ Et super his omnibus semper Deo gratias.

Anno xiiij° hujus regis Henrici Philippus dux Burgundie, contra fidelitatem suam, villam Calisie obsidiavit cum magno apparatu et multitudine populi copiosa; fuerunt enim ibi, secundum estimacionem, plus quam c. milia virorum. In tentoriis et pavilionibus x M¹, in magnis gunnis xxviij, in cressetes ardentibus in nocte vij M¹, in gall.ᵇ vij M¹, in parvis gunnis vocatis ribaldis vij M¹, in crosbowcs x M¹, in carectis xij M¹.

Pro qua quidem obsidione dissolvenda transfretavit Dominus Humfridus, dux Gloucestrie, cum quam pluribus magnatibus et proceribus ac multitudine populi ad numerum lx M¹, Calisiam usque properans. Sed ante ipsius adventum, Comes de Morten et Dominus de Cammysh cum suis ad numerum ij M¹ di. dictam villam Calisie tutissime conservantes illam obsidionem infra dies paucos viriliter confregerunt et plurimos ibidem occiderunt. Qui quidem dux Burgundie cum suis, cognito quod dux Gloucestrie cum tanta potestate Anglorum in proximo adventaret, veritus et confusus, celerrime capit fugam. Postea vero quam predictus dux Gloucestrie Caliam ᵃ venisset, exinde in Picardiam et Flandiam per dies xj procedendo villas combussit. Ubi etiam Comes Huntingdon et sui villam de Popering cremaverunt ac plurimos peremerunt, et circiter festum Sancti Bartholomei Apostoli proximo sequens Dux Gloucestrie memoratus ac magnates cum proceribus et populo suo in Angliam prospere remearunt.

Anno eodem, infra mensem proximo sequentem quo prefatus dux Burgundie villam Calisie taliter obsedisset et inde gratia Dei profugatus fuisset, Jacobus rex Scottorum perjurus Castro de Rokesburgh in Northumbria cum suo exercitu, ut fertur, ad numerum c M¹ et ultra, obsidionem opposuit; ubi nichil profecit. Nam prenobilis ille miles Radulphus Greye, cum lxxx viris strenuis, dictum castrum fortiter custodivit et dicto regi Scottorum et exercitui suo

---

ᵃ So in MS.   ᵇ " Gally-gun, a kind of culverin."—Halliwell.

viriliter restitit. Andito autem quod Archiepiscopus Eboracensis,
episcopus Dunelmensis ac Comes Northumbrie cum maxima potestate
borealium eisdem obviare infra breve proponebant, rex prefatus et
suus exercitus territi et confusi protinus aufugerunt. Et circiter
mensem Martii extunc proximo sequentem idem rex, iniqua suasione
ac consilio Comitis de Athel, avunculi sui, et aliorum sibi in hoc
favencium, per quemdam Scottum, Willelmum Grame vulgariter
nominatum, et quosdam alios, nocte quadam, dum se rex ad lectum
disponebat, camisia et braccis solummodo indutus, improvise territus
et in cloacam proprie camere fugatus, cum spatis crudeliter et
inhumane est occisus. Fertur enim ipsum circa xxx vulnera in
corpore habuisse, quorum vij letalia videbantur. In evidenciam
cujus rei quidam legatus apostolicus in Scotia tunc existens dictam
camisiam postmodo Domino Pape, ut dicitur, deferebat. Benedictus
sit Dominus Deus qui tam sepius servulos suos eripuit de manibus
querencium eis mala, perjurosque et pacem turbantes confudit et
evertit !

    Anno Domini millessimo cccc°.xlv., xxx die mensis Maii coro-
natur Margareta filia regis Cecilie in reginam Anglie apud Vest-
monasterium. Sed advertendum est quod infra breve post con
tractum factum cum dicta Margareta in partibus transmarinis per
Willelmum ducem Suthfolk, amissa est Cenomannia cum Ande-
gavia. Deinde paulatim (quorum prodicione aut ignavia novit
Deus) amissa est tota Normannia cum civitate Parisius, &c. Deinde
similiter amissa est Burdegalia cum tota Vasconia, &c. Ad cujus
recuperacionem missus est nobilis ille belliger Comes Salopie cum
filio suo, domino de Lyel, et aliis, qui viriliter eam recuperaverunt.
Sed, quod dolenter refero, incaute seu capitose se dantes cuidam
conflictui cum Francigenis, ibi interfecti sunt, et readquisierunt
Francigene omnia que illic erant, et sic adhuc pacifice detinent.

    Anno Domini millesimo cccc°.lvij°. spoliata est villa de Fowe
in Cornubia per piratas; et eodem anno in mense Augusti spoliata
est villa de Sandwiche per piratas, et naves et pene omnia bona
mobilia in utrisque villis abducta sunt.

Anno Domini millesimo cccc°.lvij°. et lviij extitit quidam nomine Raginaldus Pokok, nacione Wallicus, sacre theologie doctor, et Cicestrensis episcopus, ingenio quidem et scientia satis clarus, et in primeva etate reputatus boni regiminis, et honeste fame; hic tamen posterius, instigante Diabolo, proprio nimis innitens ingenio, proprie salutis et aliorum factus quasi immemor, postposita, imo quasi fere rejecta, priori innocencia, et in multis fide spreta catholica, sanctorum doctorum et patrum sanctiones et dicta, imo scripture sacre supereminentem veritatem quasi pro vili habens, dictamen rationis humane in multis extulit super hec omnia. Unde sic, velut secundus Lucifer supra ceteros estimans se et extollens, veteres quasdam pestiferas hereses damnatas renovavit, novasque satis noxias superadjecit, quarum multas, tum propter earum enormitatem, tum propter aliorum infirmorum scandalum, silencio committendas esse sacius estimo quam dicendas. De Eukaristia divinissima protervissime sensit, et Sanctum Dionisium pro se allegavit, qui tamen Dionisius plane in contra scripsit. Ecclesiastica divina officia per sanctos patres disposita, et a multis sanctis probateque vite viris a diu in ecclesiis usitata ad Dei landem et fidelium salutem, vilipendit; quattuor articulos simboli sacro-sancti omisit, &c.[a]

Has et quam plures alias asserciones frivolas et hereticas in ejus libris sparsim inventas, et publice apud Lambyth coram Domino Cantuariensi Archiepiscopo, episcopis, doctoribus et clero inibi assistentibus prelatas et sibi objectas, non negavit se dictus Raginaldus dictasse, tenuisse, ac per se et suos precones propalasse, et alios quam plurimos eisdem infecisse. Examinate igitur diligenter et mature ibidem dicte hereses, et alie quam plurime, per Dominum Thomam Cantuariensem archiepiscopum, episcopos, doctores, et reliquum clerum damnate sunt, et multi de libris ejus hereticis publice combusti sunt; quidam Oxon. in proccssione generali, quidam autem in cimiterio ecclesie Cathedralis Sancti Pauli, London. Ubi et idem Raginaldus dominico die tempore sermonis omnia hujusmodi dogmata perversa et heretica publice in scriptis abjuravit, anathema-

[a] Here three lines are left blank in MS.

tizavit, abrenunciavit, canoniceque correccioni se subjecit. Unde et
episcopatu Cicestrensi privatus, vite private seu solitarie adjudicatus est.
Multi tamen ejus doctrina pestifera infecti, permanserunt in errore.

Circiter istud tempus Jacobus rex Scocie populum suum nobiliter
rexit, fures et oppressores cohibens, agriculturam amplians, sanctam (?)
justiciam servans.   Hic anno Domini 1460, cum suo exercitu obsedit
castrum Rokisburgh et per propriam gunnam suam diruptam, cui
astitit, interfectus est.   Exercitus tamen ejus idem castrum prostravit
et recessit.

Anno Domini millesimo cccc°.lvij., sacro tempore quadragesimali, London' facta est concordia inter Dominum Ricardum ducem
Eboracensem, Comitem de Warwyc, et comitem Sarum, cum suis,
ex parte una, et ducem Somersetie, et Comitem Northumbrie et
dominum Clifford, cum suis, ex parte altera, per illustrem regem
Henricum et alios dominos regni spirituales et temporales; gravis
enim, et periculosa dissensio orta fuerat inter predictos dominos
super interfeccione quorundam dominorum apud villam Sancti
Albani; quorum interfeccio inquietans et accendens corda multorum, satisfactione quadam facta, prestante Altissimo, partim sopita
est.   Sed non diu permansit.   Nam anno Domini millesimo
cccc°.lix°, insurrexerunt iterum predicti domini, scilicet Ricardus,
dux Eboracensis, comes Merchie, filius ejusdem ducis, comes Sarum,
comes Warwyc, cum grandi comitatu, et juxta Ludlaw circiter festum
Sancti Edwardi Confessoris, ad bellum campestre se parabant.   An
sic convenerant ad reformandum mala regni, aut sui ipsorum salvam
custodiam, vel quavis alia causa, novit Deus.   Contra quos rex ipse
cum proceribus regni et copioso exercitu in bellum properavit;
mora autem ibi facta, recesserunt multi a duce et comitibus et regi
se submittentes ad graciam ejus recepti sunt.   Dux autem Eboracensis cum predictis dominis et paucis de suis, relicto in nocte campo,
celerem fugam inierunt.   Dux namque Eboracensis cum paucis
Hyberniam adiit; tres reliqui comites cum paucissimis usque Calisiam
navigio pervenerunt.   Confiscantur interim eorum predia, diripiun-
tur alia bona.   Interim inter ducem Somersetie, capitaneum castri

de Geynes, cum suis, et Calisienses, facti sunt interdum conflictus, et multi corruerunt.

Eodem anno, circiter festum Sancti Edmundi Regis et Martiris, convocato parliamento apud Coventre, indictati sunt ibidem dicti Dux et tres Comites cum aliis multis militibus et magnatibus super grandi prodicione et declarati pro *ateyntid traytowrs* per dominos illius parliamenti; et ea que per dictos ducem et dominos de insur-reccione sua apud villam Sancti Abani in priori parliamento appro-bata sunt, in isto penitus sunt cassata. Et in festo Sancte Agnetis proximo sequente, dicti Dux et domini in civitate London. publice proclamati sunt pro *ateyntid traytours*, et sic manserunt usque cir-citer festum Sancti Johannis Baptiste proximo sequens.

Anno Domini millesimo cccc°.lx°, circiter festum Nativitatis Sancti Johannis Baptiste, redierunt predicti tres comites in Angliam cum comitatu mediocri, et multi, audito eorum adventu, adheserunt eis. Civitatem London. infra octavas Apostolorum Petri et Pauli pacifice ingressi sunt, et, quibusdam ob scelera sua in Chepa decapi-tatis, duo comites iter versus regem arripuerunt. Et in festo Sanc-torum Septem Fratrum, facto congressu juxta Northamptone, favore cujusdam domini ex parte regis regale tentorium ingressi sunt et victoriam obtinuerunt. Ubi interfecti sunt, ex parte regis, dux de Bokyngham, comes Salopie, dominus Beaumount, dominus Egre-mund, cum aliis, et multi ex ea parte fugientes submersi sunt. Rex vero cum comitibus Merchie et Warwic, London. honorifice redue-tus, in pallacio episcopi Londoniensis hospitatus est.

Interim, domino Scales cum multis aliis Turrim London. servante, factis jacturis gunnorum in extra existentes obsessores Turris et nautas in Tamesi, multi interfecti sunt. Tandem, reddita Turre pre-dicta Johanni Wenloc militi obsidenti eam, dominus Scales in nocte Sancte Margarete volens in cimba evadere ab insidiantibus sibi, captus et interfectus est. Et infra breve Thomas Browne miles cum aliis quinque qui super extorcione rapinis et prodicione damnati sunt apud Tyburne decapitati sunt.

Hoc etiam anno, circiter festum Nativitatis Beate Marie, dux

Eboracensis cum suis de Hibernia in Angliam rediit; et parliamentum apud Westmonasterium circiter festum Sancti Dionisii
inchoatum erat.   In Crastino Sancti Dionisii idem dux ad Vest-
monasterium veniens ense erecto palacium regale ingressus ibi
hospitari elegit. Adductis evidenciis quibusdam, se verum heredem
corone et regni. Anglie asserebat; cujus evidencie in illo parliamento
palam ostense in summa tenor talis erat:—

Edward þe Þrid, riȝth Kyng of Englond, had eschew, scilicet,
Prince Edward (j filius),[a] William Hatefeld (2),[a] Lyonell (3),[a] Jon of
Gawnte (4),[a] &c.   Prince Edward had Richard ij, wich died with
owte ysew. William Hatefeld died with owte ysew. Lyonell duke of
Clarence had ysew lawfully begete, Philipp hys only dowȝter and eyre,
þe wich was lawfully coupled to Edmund Mortimer, erle of Marche,
and had ysew lawfully begete, Roger Mortimer erle of Marche and
eyre; wich Roger had ysew Edmunde (j filius),[a] erle of Marche,
Roger (2),[a] Anne and Alynor; wich Rogere, Edmund and Alynore
died with owte ysew.   And þe seyd Anne, by þe sacramente of matrimony cowpled unto Richard erle of Chambryg, þe sone of Edmund
of Langeley, had ysew and lawfully bare Richard Plantagenet now
Duke of ȝork.   Jon of Gaunt gate Harry wich unryȝthfully entretid
Kyng Richard, þen beyng olywe, Edmund Mortimer, erle of Marche
son of. þe seid Philipp dowȝter to Lyonell.   To þe wich Richard
Duke of. ȝork and sone to Anne dowȝter to Roger Mortimer, erle
of Marche, sone and eyre to þe seyd Philipp dowȝter and eyre to þe
seyd Lyonell þe þrid sone of Kyng Edward iij. þe ryȝth and dignite
of þe corone apertenyt and belongitt afore any ysew of þe seyd Jon
of Gaunt.   Notwithstondyng þe seyd titull of dignite of þe seyd
Richard of York, þe seyd Richard, desiryng þe wele, reste and
prosperite of Englond, agreit and consentitt Þat þe Kyng Harry vj
be had and takyn Kyng of Englond duryng hys naturell liffe fro
þis tyme with owte hyrte of his titull, &c.

Where fore þe Kyng, understondyng þe seyd titull of þe seyd
duke, juste, lawfull, and trew and sufficiente, be þe awise and assent

            [a] Interlined in another hand.

of hys lordys spirituell and temporele and þe comyns in þe apparle-
ment and by þe autorite of þe same parlement, declarith, approwithe
ratifieȝt, confermitt, and acceptit þe seyd titull just, good, lawfull and
trew, and Þere wuto gifeȝt hys assent and agrement of hys free will
and liberte. And over þᵗ, be þe seyd awyse and autorite, declariȝt,
calliȝt, stabiliȝt, affirmiȝt and reputiȝt þe seyd Richard of York very
trew and riȝtfull eyre to þe corons of Englond and France. And
þᵗ all oþer statutes and actes made by any of þe Harrys late contrary
to þˢ awise be anulled, repelled, damned, canceld, woyd and of no
forse or effecte, &c. The Kyng agreitt and consentitt þᵗ þe seyd
Duke & hys eyres shall after hys naturell liffe rejoise þe corons,
&c. Also þᵗ all seynges and doynges aȝens þe Duke of York shall be
hye treson, and all actes of parlementes contrarye to þis principall
acte be woyde and of none effecte, &c.

Cassata et anullata sunt in hoc parliamento ea omnia que contra
dictum ducem Eboracensem, comites, et alios eis adherentes in parliamento priori apud Coventre edita sunt aut decreta, et restituti
sunt dicti domini dux et comites, cum sibi adherentibus, terris suis,
prediis et juribus prehabitis. Cassata sunt insuper et anullata in
hoc parliamento omnia que statuta seu decreta sunt per Henricum
iiij in suis parliamentis quo ad successionem sue sobolis in regnum et
coronam Anglie, cum ipse intrusor esset, et jus hereditarium corone et
regni Anglie pertineret ad Philippam filiam Leonelli filii tercii Edwardi iij, et per eam ad comitem Marchie et heredes suos ut supra. ⁄

Prorogato parliamento, iste dux Eboracensis (cum filio suo Edwardo),ᵃ et comes Sarum (cum filio suo Thoma),ᵃ cum decenti apparatu
iter ceperunt versus partes boreales ad sedandas turbulencias ibidem
et malefactores castigandos; unde ad villam de Wakefeld venientes
in sancta ebdomada Nativitatis Dominice, in crastino Sancti Thome
Martiris ad pugnam se parabant. Sed declinante jam die, sive
incuria et negligencia sua, sive fraude et fuga magne partis sui
exercitus, cum proceribus et valettis plurimis interfecti sunt per
ducem de Somersett, dominum Clifford, dominum Newyle, &c., qui
cum ferocibus belligeris in illos crudeliter irruerunt; quorum domi-

ᵃ Interlined in another hand.

norum interfectorum capita, ut dicitur, super muios civitatis Ebora·
censis obprobiose et dissone (?) nimis sunt exposita.   Hoc tempore
commissa est custodia Turris London. certis Aldermannis et civibus
ejusdem civitatis.

Quibus ita patratis rex Henricus cum duce de Northfolk, Comite
de Warwic et aliis dominis et magno exercitu versus boream pro-
perabat.   Vento autem ad villam Sancti Albani, occurrerunt eis
dux Somersetie, dominus Clifford, &c. cum suo exercitu; et conserto
gravi prelio xiij° kl. Marcii, sc. in die Carneprivii, multi inde et
hinc interfecti sunt.

Et fugientibus plurimis ex parte regis, fugam etiam inierunt dux
Northfolk, Comes Warwic, Comes Arundell, dominus Boughsher,
dominus de la Ware, cum multis aliis.   Regem Henricum sic in
campo derelictum accedens dux Somersete cum ceteris dominis, &c.
recepit in suam, ut ita dicam, tutelam seu custodiam.   Dominus
autem Bonwyle et Dominus Kyre,[a] cum viderent hujuscemodi
casum et fugam suorum, attoniti regi se submiserunt.   Quos et ipse
libenter suscepit in graciam; attamen, omni equitate seposita,
nequicia quorundam decapitati sunt.

Facti sunt tunc insultus et inclamationes satis superbe per boreales
belligeros adversus cives Londonienses, quibus illi viriliter resistentes,
quosdam eorum occiderunt; reliquos in fuge latebras compulerunt,
auxiliante Altissimo, cui sit laus perpes et humillima graciarum
accio.   Hac tempestate sevissima Borealium latronum prevalente,
multe domus religiosorum, multe ecclesie, multi burgi et ville per
eos nequiter spoliate sunt; nec impune, ut infra patebit.   Decreve-
rant etenim Boreales illi predicti, promittentibus hoc eis dominis suis,
ut nominatissimam illam civitatem Londoniarum cum provinciis
adjacentibus spoliarent, vastarent et subverterent; quod et ex veri-
simili perpetrassent, si non singularis gracia Christi Jesu servulis
suis celerius consolatorem et laude dignum destinasset defensorem.

Tercio namque kalendas Marcii illustrisimus ille princeps Edwardus, pro tunc Comes Merchie dictus, auditis prius his civitatis
London. et vicinarum provinciarum periculis, post victoriam inimi

* Kyriell.

corum snorum in partibus celitus Wallie adeptam, adjuncto sibi
Comite Warwic, cum grandi comitatu pacifice London. est ingressus.
Secessit interim rex Henricus cum ducibus, comitibus et belligeris
Borealibus versus Boream et Eboracum usque pervenit.

Edwardus autem predictus ij° die Marcii proclamari fecit London.
articulos concernentes jus suum ad coronam regni Anglie; et sequenti die, convocatis dominis spiritualibus et temporalibus illic
presentibus, expressi sunt predicti articuli coram eis et approbati.
Quarto autem die ejusdem mensis post processionem generalem
London. solenniter factam, episcopus Excestrensis ad crucem Sancti
Pauli sermonem fecit satis laudabilem, titulumque dicti Edwardi
ad regnum Anglie multiplici evidencia patefecit; objeccionibus que
in ejus oppositum fieri possent patulo respondit, et eas excussit.
Completo sermone isto eximio, dominus Edwardus cum dominis
spiritualibus et temporalibus et magna populi frequencia eodem die
ad Westmonasterium equitavit; ubi in Westmonaster hall sedis
regalis possessionem suscepit. A monachis quoque ibi cum pro-
cessione sibi occurrentibus honorifice receptus est. Commendato
eidem per eosdem sceptro regali, possessionem in regis palacio
obtinuit. Nec dum tamen inunctus est aut regio diademate insignitus; sed his decentissime peractis, ad locum suum London., con-
gaudentibus populis, remeavit.

Facta interim sagaci provisione pro magna pecuniarum levanda
copia, dictus Edwardus cum duce Northfolk, comite Warwic, domino
Fawconbrigge, in copioso exercitu septentrionales oras petierunt.
Cum autem pertransita Trenta prope Ferebrigge, advenissent, quo-
niam exercitus regis Henrici non longe a dicta villa aderat, ad pugnam
se protinus preparabant. Die igitur sacratissime Dominice Palmarum,
post meridiem, inter Ferebrigge et Tadcaster, accedentibus aciebus
utriusque exercitus ut mutuos ictus confligendo ingererent, plurimi
equestres armaciores ex parte regis Edwardi terga vertentes et dicti
Edwardi cariagium et annonam hostiliter auferentes effugerunt. Sed
rex Edwardus virili animo suos animavit ad certamen; dux quoque
Northfolke, Comes Warwic, dominus Fauconbrigge, cum suis turmis

audacter in adversarios irruentes, plurimos prostraverunt, et horren-
dam stragem eis intulerunt, multis ex parte sua occisis. Cumque
post diutinam pugnam belligeri Boreales, cernentes se imbecilliores,
fuge presidio se commississent, insecuti sunt eos viri acriores ex
parte regis Edwardi et magnam cedem eis intulerunt; plurimi quoque ipsorum Borealium per aquas evadere querentes submersi sunt.
Numerum interfectorum ibi solus veraciter cum suis civibus novit
Deus; secundum tamen estimacionem plurium numerus eorum ex-
cedebat [xxvij M¹].ᵃ Domini multi et milites multo plures cum
plebanis ibi pariter corruerunt.

Fugientes duces Somersete et Exetrie cum reliquis, insecutus
est dominus Edwardus cum suis dominis et exercitu, et Eboracum
usque pervenit; eos tamen minime comprehendit, quia Rex Henricus
et ipsi domini prius fugerant ab Eboraco ut alibi locum presidii
sibi obtinerent. His ita Dei gracia peractis, dominus Edwardus,
relicto in Borea domino Fawconbrigge cum militibus et armata
manu ad tutelam illius patrie, per Coventriam London' reversus est,
apud Lambythe hospicium eligens. /Interim Scotti in Berwicum
admissi sunt a rege Henrico. Deinde dominus Edwardus a Lambythe
usque ad Turrim London. veniens, creatis ibi militibus de Balneis,
die sabbati proximo sequenti a Turre London. cum dominis et
militibus per Chepam equitans Westmonasterium usque pervenit,
ubi in die dominica, scilicet in vigilia Apostolorum Petri et Pauli,
in regem Anglie eo honore quo congruit et ordine decentissimo
coronatus est. Qui etiam, gloriam glorie volens superaddere, in festo
Commemoracionis Sancti Pauli, in ecclesia cathedrali ejusdem London.
processioni et misse coram magna populi frequentia cum dominis
suis spiritualibus et temporalibus, corona insignitus regali satis
interfuit apparatu. Deinde rex Edwardus Cantuariam peregre
profectus partes meridionales pertransiit,ᵇ ubi Willelmum episcopum
Wintoniensem de manibus querentium animam ejus eripuit, in-
sectatores suos graviter redarguit et eorum capitaneos carcerali

---

ᵃ A pen has been run through these figures.
ᵇ pertinusiit, MS.

custodie mancipavit. Bristollie approperans, a civibus ejus cum maximo gaudio honoratissime receptus est. Et in breve ad Westmonasterium veniens, ibidem anno Domini millesimo cccc^{mo}.lxi. ij nonas Novembris solenniter parleamentum suum inchoavit, ubi indictati et atteyntati sunt Henricus vocatus nuper rex Anglie cum Margareta consorte suo ; duces etiam Somerset et Exetre, cum aliis militibus et nobilibus, ad numerum quasi centum personarum. Eodem anno, circiter festum Purificationis beatissime semper Virginis Marie, facta est conspiratio contra dictum dominum regem Edwardum per Comitem Oxon. et filium ejus, Tudnam, Terell, Mowgomere, cum aliis, ut in parte Esexie introducerent ducem Somersetie per navigium cum hostili exercitu ad eversionem regis Edwardi et snorum. Sed succurrente Altissimo, priusquam propositum suum perficerent, deprehensi sunt, et, cassatis frivolis machinacionibus suis, Comes ille cum filio suo et aliis Londoñ decapitati sunt. His diebus Henricus cum Margareta et filio suo Edwardo in Scotia commorati sunt, et villa de Berwyke sub dicione Scottorum erat longo tempore. Circiter festum Sancti Mathie dominus rex Edwardus, versus Boream· iturus, festum Pasche solenniter celebravit Leycestrie, et pretextu resistendi adversariis grandes pecuniarum summas per sua privata sigilla a viris spiritualibus et temporalibus, clericis et servientibus levari fecit.

Anno Domini millesimo cccc°,lxij° sexto die mensis Maii solutum est predictum parleamentum; et eodem anno circiter festum Nativitatis Sancti Johannis Baptiste capte sunt treuge ad tempus modicum inter Anglos et Scottos, fraudulenter ex parte Scottorum, prout palam postea patuit.

Hoc quoque tempore emissi sunt multi belligeri cum domino Fau conbrigge ad maria scrutanda et servanda, qui parum proficientes in breve remearunt. Rex Edwardus pro materia cujusdam vidue rapte discucienda in propria persona in bancho suo regali Westmonasterii, assistentibus sibi cancellario et justiciariis, &c. proprium locum tenuit.

Eodem anno, circiter festum Omnium Sanctorum, percurrente rumore de adventu regine Margarete cum copiosa multitudine Francigenorum, Scottorum, et Anglorum sibi adherentium, precessit festine prenobilis ille belliger Comes de Warwik cum suis, et subsecutus est rex Edwardus ut eam cum complicibus suis effugarent. Que fuga inita tuciora quesivit presidii loca.

Rege Edwardo in partibus illis residente, obsessa sunt per nostrates castra illa de Bamburghe, Alniwyke et Dunstanburgh; quorum duo reddita sunt in manus comitis Warwic circiter festum Natalis Domini; subjeceruntque se Dux Somersetie et dominus Radulphus Percy, cum suis, domino regi, et in graciam recepti sunt.

In aurora Ephiphanie venerunt Scotti cum Francigenis aciebus densatis ad tercium castrum, scilicet Alniwyke, nostris non audentibus eis resistere, et secum tulerunt multos illic inclusos de consociis suis; et sic in breve redditum est illud castrum in manus nostrorum, Francigenis remanentibus gratis abire permissis. His peractis recessit dominus rex Edwardus, relicto ibidem ad tutelam patrie comite Warwic, &c.

Et in hac tam longa mora tocius pene milicie Anglicane illic adversus adversarios nostros congregate, quid, queso, memorabile, quid laude dignum actum est, nisi quod predicta tria castra capta sunt? Et comes Warwic cum paucis campum tenens curiose viriliterque Scottos cum suis excuciens, protegente eum gratissima, ut solito,[a] Dei dextra, illesus permansit. Qui et infra breve cum aliis dominis, Boream relinquens, ad dominum regem Edwardum London. venit; epulantibusque illis London., et nescio quid agentibus, invaserunt Scotti cum Francigenis castrum de Bamburgh, et ipsum occupaverunt, cum aliis duobus castris.

Anno Domini millesimo cccc°.lxiij, xxix die mensis Aprilis inchoatum est parleamentum apud Westmonasterium; et interim dominus Radulphus Percy et Dominus Radulphus Greye, cum suis, fracto suo juramento, relicto rege Edwardo, ad partem Henrici redierunt.

Mense Junii, die xviij°, prorogatum est parleamentum usque ad ——————[b] et que mala ibi repressa aut reformata, vel quid boni ibi adauctum nescio.

Hoc anno, post Pentecosten, prenobilis ille comes Warwic ad

---

[a] *Sic* in MS.   [b] Blank in MS.

Boream, rediens 'dominos et milites cum reliquis belligeris colligens, ᚎ
partem regis Henrici cum Scottis, Francigenis, &c. infestare disposuit. Qui cognito celeri ᵃ ejus adventu, campum linquentes, tergaque
vertentes, vecorditer aufugerunt.

Hoc tempore convocatus clerus provincie Cantuariensis concessit
ut quilibet sacerdos stipendiarius dicte provincie capiens pro annuali
stipendio x marcas conferret ad subsidium regis Edwardi xɪɪj s. ɪɪɪj d.;
unde plurimi gravati murmurabant, tum quia pauperes erant, tum
quia pecunie taliter a sacerdotibus extorte raro vel nusquam ad
aliquem felicem effectum proveniunt, quin potins ad confusionem et
dedecus eis utentium. Nam et post festum Nativitatis beatissime
Marie semper Virginis rex Edwardus grandem exercitum advocavit,
adversarios suos terra marique subjugare disposuit. Nescio tamen
quid in illo viagio profecerit. Et comes de Worcester cum suo
navigio et marinariis litoribus maris et portubus quasi latitantes,
annonasque suas consumentes, infecto negocio vacui cum dedecore
remearunt. O infelix successus, opprobrium et confusio!

Circiter hec tempora quarterium frumenti vendebatur Oxon. et
[in] ᵇ patria illa pro ij solidis; unde et ruricole super precio parvulo
iterato murmurabant.

Dux Somersetie, in conversacione sua et promissis instabilis, relicto
rege Edwardo cum paucis ad regem Henricum confugit, &c. Rex
Edwardus, consiliariis accitis, minuit pondus nummismatis argentei,
et auxit valorem aurei, adeo ut unum nobile aureum valeret viijs. iiijd.

Hic etiam rex Edwardus redditus et proventus collegiorum eorum
nobilium, scilicet Beatissime Marie semper Virginis de Eton et beati
Nicholai Cantibrigie, per bone memorie Henricum Sextum funda-
torum et nobiliter ditatorum, etc. in suas manus suscepit. Partem
tamen aliquantulam eis restituens, unde pauperiorem quam solite
ducerent vitam, vasa argentea ᶜ multa et summam magnam pecunie ab
eis exegit et cepit. Bullis papalibus obtentis, collegium illud celebre
de Eton. cassare proposuit; quod tamen, ut estimo, beatissima Virgo
Maria nondum ad effectum deduci permisit.

ᵃ *celebri*, MS.   ᵇ Om. in MS.   ᶜ *argenta*, MS.

Anno Domini millesimo cccc°.lxiiij°, epulante rege Edwardo
cum dominis suis London., per belligeros regis Henrici capta sunt
castra de Norham et Shipton in Crawyn; et in breve processit rex
Edwardus versus Boream ut amissa recuperet et habita defendat.
Quid tamen utile ibi gesserit nescio.   Cumque tempora multa sic
vacua lucris et tediosa, inaniter vexatis legiis regis, sibi paulatim suc-
cederent, prenobilis dominus, dominus Georgius, pro tunc Exe-
terrensis episcopus et Anglie Cancellarius, condolens tantos labores
et sumptus inani dispendio et damnoso esse consumptos, assumptis
viribus, maturo consilio super his infortuniis reformandis prehabito,
divine gracie se et regni negocia commendans, ad consolandum et
animandum fratrem suum, dominum Johannem de Mowntagw, iter
versus partes Boreales fiducialiter arripuit.   Et in breve, Domino
de Mowntagw cum suis belligeris arma potentibus resumente, cepit
paulatim pars Henrici succumbere.   Secundo namque die mensis
Maii dominus de Mowntagw cum suis comitibus conflictum iniit
cum duce de Somersett, domino Roos, domino Hungarford, domino
Radulpho Percy, domino Radulpho Greye, domino Ricardo Tunstall, domino Thoma Findern, cum aliis capitaneis exercitus regis
Henrici et vulgo multo; et, interfecto illio domino Radulpho Percy
cum aliis quibusdam, reliqui fuge presidio evaserunt.

Quintodecimo insuper die ejusdem mensis Maii Dux Somersett,
dominus Hungarford, dominus Roos, armiger ille Treilboz[a] cum
suis complicibus, graviter ferentes suam repulsam et propositi
prioris frustracionem ad bellum campestre juxta Exham, iterum
spe fruende victorie ccnvenerunt.   Quos dominus de Mowntagw
cum suis, quasi subito insiliens, dictum ducem et dominum Thomam
Findern, dominum Egremound, bastard Waynsford, etc. cepit et
tutele arte[b] commisit.   Die Mercurii proximo sequenti capti sunt
per dictum dominum Mowntagw cum suis dominus Edmundus
Fysh, miles, nuper scissor Eboraci, Bernardus de la Mare, dominus
Roos, dominus Hungarford, dominus Phillippus Wentworth, Willelmus Penyngton, Husy miles; qui omnes decapitati sunt.

---

[a] *Sic*, pro Tailbois.   [b] *i.e.* arctæ.

Deliberata sunt in breve domino de Mowntagw castra de Langeley
þᵉ Tawne turris de Exham, castrum etiam de Bywell. In quo
quidem castro inventum est le helmet regis Henrici cum corona et
gladio et faleris dicti Henrici. Et quomodo aut quo ipse evasit,
novit Deus, in cujus manu corda sunt regum.

Deliberatum est etiam regi Edwardo castrum de Shipton in
Crawen.

Quintodecimo decimo ᵃ die mensis Maii apud Exham decapitati
sunt dux Somersett, Edmundus Fizthu miles, Bradshaw, Wauter
Hunt, Blac Jakis.

Decimo septimo die mensis Maii apud Novum Castrum decapitati
sunt dominus de Hungarford, dominus Roos, dominus Thomas
Fynderne, Edwardus de la Mare, Nicholaus Massam.

Apud Medelham xviij die mensis Maii decapitati sunt dominus
Philippus Wentworth, Willelmus Penyngton, Warde de Topcliff,
Oliverus Wentworth, Willelmus Spilar, Thomas Hunt, le foteman
regis Henrici.

Apud Eboracum xxv° die mensis Maii decapitati sunt dominus
Thomas Husye, Thomas Gosse, Robertus Merfyn, Johannes Buttlere,
Rogerus Water, janitor regis Henrici, Thomas Fenwyke, Robertus
Cocfeld, Willelmus Bryte, Willelmus Dawson, Johannes Chapman.

Apud Eboracum xxviij die mensis Maii decapitati sunt Johannes
Elderbek, Ricardus Cawerne, Johannes Rosell, Robertus Con-
querore. Interim etiam captus est ille armiger Treilboz et decapitatus.

Quibus peractis, dominus de Mowntagw factus est Comes de
Northumberland. Capta sunt tunc castra de Bamburgh et Dunstanburgh cum ceteris et redacta in possessionem Regis Edwardi; et
dominus Radulphus Greye cum ceteris illic inventis capitalem
accepit sentenciam, capite ejus pontem Londoniarum adornante in
vertice quasi lancee.

Et sic invalescente brachio regis Edwardi et principatum per
regnum obtinente pene cassata est fortitudo et milicia regis Henrici.

ᵃ *Sic.*

Regina Margareta has procellas precavens, incola elegit fieri trans-
marina. Adhuc villa de Berwyk remanet sub Scottorum dominio.

Anno Domini millesimo CCCC.m°lxiiij° estas fervida valde et
diuretica faciem terre adustam a gramine, herbis et ordeo, etc. fecit
pene sterilem. Et subsecuta est eodem anno frigiditas horrida in
yeme, homines molestans et pecora.

Hoc anno in insula de Ely estate torrida exorte sunt musce
grandes, venenose, cornute, cum aculeis que, pecora percucientes et
homines quosdam, ut asserebatur, eos protinus perimebant. Hoc
insuper anno, circiter festum Sancti Michaelis, quidam frater Car-
melita [a] Christi Jesu supereminentissime dominacionis et sue proprie salutis immemor, spiritu ductus elacionis et protervie, ad crucem
Sancti Pauli London. predicavit et publice proclamavit, dominum
Jesum Christum celi et terre Creatorem et Dominum in propria
venientem misere mendicasse.   Cujus errori devio favit provincialis [b]
ejusdem ordinis, lectura et sermone publice ejus dicta maledica con-
firmando cum ceteris doctoribus et fratribus ejusdem, quibus et
Jacobite quidam procaciter adherebant.   Quibus quoque multi
theologi seculares cum Catholicis juristis, spiritu veritatis edocti et
ducti, unanimiter, et predicando et lecturis publicis restiterunt, et
sic hec materia, fratribus ultra pro tunc prosequi cessantibus, silencio
commendatur.

Hoc etiam anno in festo Apostolorum Philippi et Jacobi duxit
rex Edwardus in uxorem Elizabetham filiam domini de Rivaye (?)[c]
et ducisse Bedfordie.

Anno Domini millesimo CCCC[mo].lxv°, xxvj° die mensis Maii,
scilicet in festo Sancti Augustini, Anglorum Apostoli, apud Westmonasterium, supradicta Elizabeth coronata est in reginam Anglie.
Et creati sunt tunc multi milites de balneo, inter quos quidam mer-
catores civitatis London. milicie dignitate insigniti sunt.

Hoc etiam anno, circiter festum Petri et Pauli, captus est Henricus

---

[a] Friar Harry Parker.   See Gregory's Chronicle, in Coll. of a Lond. Citizen, 228.

[b] This must be Dr. Thomas Halden. See Gregory, *ib.*

[c] Rivers, of course, is the name, but the spelling in the MS. is doubtful.

Sextus, nuper rex Anglie dictus, et publice per Chepam London. cum aliis secum captis, ductus usque ad Turrim London. ibique honorifice commendatus custodie mansit.

Hac insuper estate orta lite inter regem Francie et fratrem ejus commota sunt bella, et Dei gracia infra breve sedata.

Hoc quoque anno circiter festum Assumpcionis beatissime Marie semper Virginis misit dominus Papa, Paulus Secundus, bullam suam in Angliam, insinuans prelatis Anglie heresim illam pestifere asserentem quod Christus publice mendicavit esse antiquitus a Romanis pontificibus cum suis consiliis damnatam et eam pro damnata universe (?)[a] declarandam et conculcandam.

Hoc etiam anno multitudo latronum in variis Anglie partibus debachans multas ecclesias et alios legios regis spoliavit. Francigene quoque cum aliis adversariis regni Anglie per mare prevalentes, Angligenis damna multimoda intulerunt.

Isto quoque anno, circiter festum Sancte Scolastice Virginis peperit regina Elizabeth Regi Edwardo filiam, vocatam Elizabeth.

Anno Domini 1467, in ebdomada Pentecostes venit in Angliam bastardus Burgundie dimicaturus certamine singulari cum domino Antonio, domino de Scales; factisque in Smythfeld, London, barris et tentoriis, &c., in festo Sancti Barnabe, ingressi locum dictum quasi Indentes congressi cito cessaverunt. Et alii quidam post eos inibi congressi immunes a plaga recesserunt.

Hoc anno pax per treugas facta est inter Anglos ex parte una et Gallos, Britannos atque Scottos ex parte altera. Abundabant tunc in Anglia furta, homicidia et mala multa. Hoc etiam anno peperit Regina Elizabeth Regi Edwardo secundam filiam. Hoc quoque anno circiter festum Sancti Michaelis, et diu post, facta est gravis valde inundacio pluviarum impediens agricolas, itinerantes magnis periculis aggravans, &c. Venti etiam tunc horrendi acciderunt, submergentes naves, arbores et domos evertentes.

In principio quadragesime istius anni solute sunt treuge inter nos et Francigenas.

[a] " vn3," MS.

Anno Domini 1468 concessit parleamentum domino Regi duas quintasdecimas, et convocatus clerus concessit unam decimam, et etiam nobilia[a] sacerdotum, que raro aut nunquam ad felicem pertingunt effectum.   Hoc anno etiam Thomas Coke, mercator et miles, captus est, pretensa prodicione contra eum, et graviter multatus, receptus est in graciam.   Thomas Plummer etiam, mercator et miles, accusatus de prodicione, satisfactione prehabita, ad graciam regis rediit.

Hoc anno, circiter festum Sancti Johannis Baptiste, transfretavit Margareta soror Regis Edwardi et uxor ducis Burgundie effecta est.

Hoc etiam anno Comes de Wircester multa laude digna peregit in Hibernia, et castrum forte[b] in Wallia per dominum Harbard[c] captum est, et dominus Ricardus Tunstall cum ceteris ibi inventis captus est et in Turri London. clausus, qui tamen in breve graciam a rege consecutus est.   Duo nobiles ex illic captis decollati sunt.

Hoc anno dominus Antonius Scales, dominus Walterus Blownt, tunc dictus dominus de Mowtjoye, circiter festum Translacionis Sancti Edwardi Confessoris, cum multis milibus armatorum, naves ingressi et tempestatibus magnis turbati, nichil proficientes, in Angliam cum dedecore redierunt.

Hoc insuper anno circiter octavas Epiphanie ————[d] Cowrteneye Comes Devonie et dominus de Moleners sive de Hungerford convicti super prodicione decollati sunt.

Hoc quoque anno peperit Regina Elizabeth Regi Edwardo terciam filiam.

Anno Domini 1469, circiter festum Sancte Trinitatis, surrexit quidam, nomine Robin of Redisdale cui associati sunt multi, quasi peticionarii petentes multa corrigi in regno.   Contra hos circiter festum Translacionis Sancti Thome Martiris collegit paulatim rex Edwardus exercitum, volens eis occurrere.

---

[a] So in MS., apparently for *mobilia*, though the same error occurs in a marginal note.   [b] Harlech.
[c] William lord Herbert.   [d] Blank in MS.

Et cito post cum surrexit alter, nomine Robin of Holdernes, cum complicibus suis, petens Comitatum Northumbrie restitui legitimo heredi; quem captum fecit comes pro tunc Northumbrie decollari, et disparsi sunt congregati sui.

Hoc etiam anno in vigilia Sancti Jacobi Apostoli, facto conflictu militum et belligerorum borealium contra dominum Harberd cum suis Wallensibus, ceciderunt hine et inde multi; et dominus Harberd cum duobus fratribus suis captus est, et infra breve apud Northampton decapitatus est. Hic W. Harberd, gravissimus et oppressor et spoliator ecclesiasticorum et aliorum multorum per annos multos, hanc tandem justi Dei judicio pro suis sceleribus et nequiciis recepit mercedem. Die Sabbati proximo ante Assumptionem beatissime semper Virginis Marie captus est Dominus de Rywans cum domino Johanne filio suo, et juxta castrum de Kelingworth pariter decollati sunt.

Anno Domini millesimo lxx°, circiter festum Nativitatis Beate Marie regressi sunt in Angliam dux Clarencie, comes de Warwic, cum multis aliis, qui paulo ante per regem Edwardum in Franciam propter suas rebelliones effugati fuerant, et in Devonia applicantes exercitum colligerunt. Edwardus autem, videns eorum audaciam, fugit cum paucis in Flandriam, ubi a duce Burgundie honorifice est susceptus. Et in festo Sancte Fidis Virginis dux Clarencie, frater Regis Edwardi, et comes de Warwic, cum ceteris dominis, regem Henricum de Turri London educentes, regali apparatu indutum per Chepam usque ad palacium episcopi London. perduxerunt. Hoc anno Cantigene consueta nequicia agitati insurgunt et multos in Sowthwerk, London. spoliant, et infra breve recesserunt.

His diebus captus est ille trux carnifex et hominum decollator horridus, comes de Wiccester, et in Turri London. incarceratus, et in breve prope dictam turrim decapitatus, et apud Fratres Predicatores juxta Ludgate obscure sepultus. Interim, circiter festum Sancti Edwardi Martiris, in quadragesima, rediit in Angliam rex Edwardus, et in breve, recepto duce Clarencie ad graciam, circumivit et congregavit multos; et in Cena Domini London. pacifice cum duobus fratribus suis et magno comitatu ingressus est. Tunc fama volante quod comes de Warwic cum suo exercitu adventaret, rex Edwardus cum suo exercitu contra eum in Sabbato Sancto Pasche properavit, et in aurora Sanctissime diei Pasche (heu et proh dolor!) inito certamine juxta villam Barnett, ceciderunt hine et inde multi; et comes de Warwic, cum fratre suo, et multis aliis dominis et nobilibus cum plebanis, ibi interfectus est; et corpora dicti comitis et fratris sui perducta London., in ecclesia Sancti Pauli nuda jacuerunt publice aliquandiu, et postea sepulture comendata sunt.

Anno Domini 1471°, circiter festum Sancti Georgii, [Rex],[a] audito quod Regina Margareta cum Edwardo filio suo et aliis dominis et proceribus multis in partibus occiduis Anglorum applicuisset, et quod multi ad eam confluerent, cum suo exercitu etiam adversus eos festinavit, et juxta Tewkisberi acriter in eos insiliens multos truci davit, et quosdam nobiles ibi captos decollavit. Nomina preci puorum ibi interfectorum sunt hec:—Edwardus filius Regine Margarete, comes Devonie, dominus Johannes de Somersete, dominus Johannes Wenloc, Henricus recorder de Bristow, cum multis aliis. Nomina decollatorum ibidem sunt hec: dux de Somersete, prior domus Sancti Johannis in Smythfeld, London., dominus Hunfredus Awdelaye, cum multis aliis.

Margareta olim Regina ibi capta, cum uxore filii sui, et London. in curru deducta et in custodiam tradita est. Creati sunt statim post istud bellum plures quam xl[a] milites; et Henricus nuper Rex reponitur in Turim London., et in Vigilia Ascensionis Dominice, ibidem feliciter moriens, per Tamisiam navicula usque ad abbathiam de Cheltesye deductus, ibi sepultus est.

Cancigene cum bastardo Fawcunbrigge et nautis ejus insurgentes, insultus iterum fecerunt in Londonienses graviores quam solito et walvas porte nove super pontem London. cum domibus quibusdam adjacentibus combusserunt, et similiter alias juxta Algate succenderunt. Sed per dominum Antonium de Scales et dominum Duraste cum civibus London. viriliter eos aggredientibus plurimi eorum inter-

[a] This word is evidently omitted.

fecti sunt, et quidam capti et reliqui in fugam versi sunt; et bastardus predictus cum suis predonibus et piratis et navibus recessit. Et Rex Edwardus feria tercia Rogacionum London. adveniens cum potenti exercitu, extra civitatem aldermannos multos in milites creavit; et in die Assensionis Domini ad vesperam Rex Edwardus cum suo exercitu ad Cancigenas corrigendos iter arripuit; et videntes se insufficientes ad resistendum ei, subdiderunt se ei. Et eos Rex et bastardum predictum cum multis aliis recepit in graciam; alios autem maleficos convictos capitali damnavit sentencia. Et ad Westmonasterium reversus ibi festum Pentecostes celebravit.

NOTES.

I.—*The Earthquake of* 1382, *page* 49.

As to the meaning of the enigmatical lines " A post Dunstanum," &c. see Dr. Simpson's *Documents illustrating the History of St. Paul's Cathedral*, p. 59, note, and Appendix, pp. 219-221.

II.—*Christopher Margrave of Baden, pp.* 133, 136.

With regard to this person and his wife Cecily, Dr. von Weech of Carlsruhe has favoured me with the following particulars :—

Margrave Christopher II., of Baden, son of Margrave Bernard III., was born after his father's death, on the 26th Feb. 1537. In the division of territory with his brother, Margrave Philibert, in 1556, he received the lands of Baden in the duchy of Luxembourg, and became the founder of the separate line of Baden at Rodemachern. He took part with the army of Philip II. of Spain in the war with France, and fought at the battle of St. Quentin. In 1561 he made a journey to Sweden, and there was betrothed to Cecilia, daughter of Gustavus Wasa, and sister of King Eric XIV. Hereupon in the service of Sweden he took part in the war with Denmark in 1563, in command of a body of German horse. In November 1564 his marriage with the Princess Cecilia took place at Stockholm, with whom he thereupon departed to his possessions in the Netherlands, and took up his abode at Rodemachern. In the year 1565 he and his bride paid a visit to Queen Elizabeth in England ; but he himself remained at her court only a short time, leaving his bride behind him alone in straitened circumstances. The latter, on the 17th Sept. 1565, gave birth to Prince Edward Fortunatus. To enable her to continue her expensive abode at the English Court, the Queen, on the 22nd Nov. 1565, granted the Margrave a pension of 2,000 French crowns of the sun, which was paid to him every year in quarterly payments out of the Treasury at Westminster. But this contribution was not sufficient for the Margravine's expenditure at Court. She contracted serious debts, and the Margrave accordingly came again to London in 1566 to take her away. The creditors, however, took notice of his object, and detained him as a prisoner. Only when the Queen gave security for him did he venture to depart.

Margrave Christopher died at Rodemachern on the 2nd August, 1575. Margravine Cecilia did not die till 1627.

INDEX.

ERRATA.

P. 159, l. 1, for " Hem " read " hem."

P. 177, l 1, omit comma after " Boream " and supply it after " rediens."

P. 136, footnote [b]   The reference should be " See page 133, note [a] "

P. 170, l 21, insert comma after " Richard " and omit comma after " olywe."

85

art of

Lymeoster— 66

: St Thomas's watering. 68

Fire at St. Pauls — 116   & Shaftesbury 117

Clearance   in London on the   days, 13

London Bond c fails 149

Steeples burnt at Waltham & London.

Sandwich spoiled 152 — 166

Bridge & part of the convent at Thetford destroyed by